# Broom Closet

— to —

# Park Avenue

A Legacy of Vision, Determination, and
Entrepreneurial Success

## KEITH BYRD

with Jane Mackay

Publishing support provided by
Ignite Press
5070 N. Sixth St. #189
Fresno, CA 93710
www.IgnitePress.us

ISBN: 979-8-9885759-0-0
ISBN: 979-8-9885759-1-7 (Hardcover)
ISBN: 979-8-9885759-2-4 (E-book)

Library of Congress Control Number: 2023912042

Cover design by Shena Honey L. Pulido
Edited by Jane Mackay
Interior design by Eswari Kamireddy

**FIRST EDITION**

*For my grandchildren, so they will know*

# ACKNOWLEDGMENTS

I am deeply grateful to everyone who willingly and gladly helped out with this book. At the start of the project I reached out to people from every part of my life to ask if they would tell their version of our shared experiences, because I wanted this book to not just have my version of things. Your memories sparked further memories for me, and in that way made this account more detailed and complete. I also want to thank Jane Mackay for bringing an intuitive understanding to me and my story, absorbing a huge amount of information from scores of interviews, and, with careful attention to detail, crafting a story that captures the truth.

Along with grateful thanks to everyone who generously contributed their memories to this book, Jane Mackay offers gratitude and appreciation to Keith Byrd for his openness, understanding, trust, and patience.

# CONTENTS

# FOREWORD

I first met Keith Byrd to present his company, Transportation Impact, with the Governor's Award for Excellence in Workforce Development as an Outstanding Employer at their office in Emerald Isle, NC.

Prior to making my official visit, I did my homework. I read about an innovative high-tech company that had developed a process to save businesses money on delivery of packages by companies like UPS and FedEx.

Upon arriving at their office, I was expecting to be greeted by the typical preppy-looking, smooth-talking MBA types that are the profile of many tech entrepreneurs. But when my security team opened the door of my SUV, I heard a Southern accent say, "How you doing, Guv? Honored to have you here!" Shaking hands with Keith Byrd and Travis Burt was a pleasant surprise, and the beginning of a great relationship and never-ending friendship.

What was to be a brief in-and-out photo op on a busy scheduled day became a welcomed political break, as I learned about their detailed business plans from an incredible and brilliant team of entrepreneurs. After two hours of interaction about how the company started and their vision and strategic plans for the future, my bias of Keith's Southern twang and good ole boy attitude was gone. I knew I had met a brilliant leader and his team, who could run circles around any MBA graduate.

The amazing story that Keith Byrd tells the reader of this book

about his family, work, military experiences, friends, business partners, work ethic, and entrepreneurial success should be a required
case study at Harvard Business School.

*Broom Closet to Park Avenue* reads like a novel about the dramatic
ups and downs in life, which ultimately concludes with the hero of
the story, Keith Byrd, achieving the American dream, while never losing focus on where he started. It is not only a great story of
business success starting from the bottom, but also a story of never
giving up and of maintaining relationships with those who helped
him along the way. The book would make a great movie, but I am
not sure there are actors good enough to play the part of my good
friends Keith Byrd and Travis Burt. They are one of a kind. They
make North Carolina proud.

Keith, I am so proud of you for putting this amazing American
story on paper for people with similar dreams to be inspired!

Pat McCrory
Governor of North Carolina, 2013–2017

# AUTHOR'S NOTE

This is a story of hard work, timing, relationships, and vision. This is my story, but it is far from the story of just one person, because it is also the story of Transportation Impact and everyone who believed in the company and contributed to its great success. This book contains the voices of many people: my family; friends from early and later life; peers and mentors from the Marines and Highway Patrol; peers, team members, and bosses at UPS; my business partner, Travis, and the A Team leadership of TI; early employees; our loyal sales contractors; customers who believed in us and helped us grow; partners of TI; my wife, best friend, and true partner, Ginger. At times in these pages, these people speak for themselves, in their own words.

# 1

## THE BEGINNING

"If you want to accept Jesus into your heart, come on down! Come and get saved!" the preacher cried.

It was 1972 and I was nine years old. Side by side in the pew with my young aunts, I was filled with the emotions of the past hour. My grandma standing at the front of the church with her two friends in the Ambassador Trio, her beautiful alto voice soaring in praise of God. Preacher Herron's boisterous sermons about the consequences of right and wrong. Cries of "Amen!" ringing in the air. Lifted by the energy of the moment, I stood up, shuffled past my aunts' knees to the end of the pew, and walked down the aisle.

At the altar I knelt. Around me gathered the leaders of the church, among them my Mamaw Wiley, my beloved grandmother. I felt the strong warmth of their hands on my body as they raised their other hands and prayed aloud.

Shouts of "Hallelujah!" filled the church as I stood up, crying with happiness, cleansed and rejoiceful. Mamaw's arms wrapped around me.

Mamaw was my mom's mother, Lucille Wiley. Single-handedly she raised my mom and my three aunts after her husband left when the girls were very young. In those very poor times she would go to the grocery store and buy hot dogs or macaroni and cheese and then prepare it so it seemed a feast. She was a mighty fierce woman, strong-willed, with great character, work ethic, and stability. She was my biggest advocate, always believing in me and praying for me when things weren't going the way they should.

My mom, Donna Wiley Byrd, was the oldest of the four girls. When she was fifteen years old she got a job in a shoe store, where my father, Fred Raymond Byrd, Jr., was also working. Two years later, they married. When I was born on June 20, 1963, my mom was only seventeen, so my aunts, Teresa, Cathy, and Diane, were not a lot older than me and were still living with Mamaw. She worked for the High Point Housing Authority, and they lived in a Housing Authority complex called Clara Cox. It was basically the slums of High Point, North Carolina, a low-income, mixed-race, rough neighborhood that taught you to grow up quick. On Sundays when I stayed with them, they dressed me up in shirt, trousers, and tie, Mamaw put on a smart pants suit, and we went together to East Green Drive Church of God. The daughter of a preacher, Mamaw was deeply religious and very respected. It was an honor to go to church with her. I felt proud of her because she was raising those girls by herself. To know what little she had and to see her go in there and praise it and be happy and content and thankful to Jesus made a deep impression on me.

I was inspired to respond to altar call and be saved a couple of times, but those surges of intense emotion were short-lasting. What lasted was the impact of Preacher Herron's sermons. He was a good storyteller and demanded your attention. His sermons forced me to think about the consequences of doing the wrong thing—not in a scary way, but in a positive way. Those lessons have stuck with me all my life. Sometimes the devil on my left shoulder has won, but the early years in that church have always been the angel on my right shoulder.

am in my heavenly fathers garden now

*Mamaw Wiley was my mom's mother, Lucille Wiley, a mighty fierce woman, strong-willed, with great character, work ethic, and stability. She was my biggest advocate, always believing in me and praying for me when things weren't going the way they should.*

My real-life angel was my mom. Only seventeen years older than me, she was beautiful, with long, dark hair, a great sense of style, and very fit. All my school friends would tell me how good-looking my mom was. Both she and my dad were entrepreneurial. In her late twenties, my mom started her own company called Data Preparation, doing key-punch data entry, and landed the large Swiss pharmaceutical firm Ciba-Geigy as a client. She was a hard worker and really successful in that business.

My parents' entrepreneurial spirit and sales skills showed up in me in third grade, when I had the idea to soak toothpicks in cinnamon and then take them to school and sell them. I also sold candy, but the toothpicks were the big deal, because they were so inexpensive and a kid could suck on that cinnamon-flavored toothpick all day. I sold them for a couple of pennies to a nickel each. By fourth grade, I had people selling them for me. When I wasn't selling, I was gambling, meeting with my friends in the bathroom to pitch quarters. I just loved the game of chance, the entrepreneurial way to try to get ahead.

*First or second grade. I am at bottom row, center. My parents' entrepreneurial spirit and sales skills began showing up in me soon after this.*

In those early years I began to understand that relationships are necessary to get to where you want to go and to feel good and positive about yourself. It's always better to have people on your side. Two of anything's better than one. Not just relationships, but love. Not being scared to display affection, so people see that you're loyal and for real. Having people you can count on and talk to, people you can open up to and be honest with—all that is a healthy part of success in anything. My mom was the living example of that for me. We had a special bond. We could read each other and always had the other's back. My mom had deep faith in God and deep loyalty to her family. I saw how she always placed other people first, always sacrificed while providing for others. Integrity was a cornerstone of her character.

Up until I got my driver's license, I spent at least one or two nights a week either with Mamaw Wiley or at my Papaw Byrd's. Fred Raymond Byrd, Sr., was my dad's father and my hero. He never smoked, never drank, and I never heard a cuss word out of him. He was the perfect example of what a grandpa should be. Always worried if I was hungry, taking me fishing, enjoying mowing the yard and working in the garden together. On one particular day every May we would get really excited, because he said that the first full moon in May was when the fish started biting. At five a.m. he and I would get out of bed, careful not to wake Mamaw Elgie Byrd, and head to Herman Dunbar's pond to get our lines in the water right before the sun came up.

The core values that are important to me now and that I brought to Transportation Impact were life lessons that came from Papaw. Always behave with integrity. Always do the right thing by people, even when no one's looking. Do what you say you're going to do. And work ethic. In fifty years at Amos Hosiery Mill, Papaw Byrd missed only one day, and that was because of snow.

*Papaw Byrd, Fred Raymond Byrd, Sr., was my dad's father and my hero. He was the perfect example of what a grandpa should be.*

*I got my driver's license the day I turned sixteen. In high school, I had long hair!*

In my early teen years we lived in a little house on Highway 311, and right across the street was a small pool hall called Harvell's. That place taught me a lot. I got in a lot of trouble there. I also got really good at playing pool and earned enough from hustling to buy my first car: a '64 Chevy Nova that I paid seven hundred dollars for. I had just turned fifteen. I never did drive that car. I ended up selling it right before I turned sixteen and with the seven hundred dollars plus profit bought myself a '69 Camaro Z/28.

About a year later I sold that and bought a '68 Camaro. I had just put new tires on it when my friend Kent Cecil and I were out one night going too fast around a corner and hit a driveway culvert, went airborne, and came down and flattened out all four of those brand new tires.

But that wasn't my worst wreck. When I was sixteen I borrowed my dad's GMC Jimmy to go visit my girlfriend during a snowstorm. Coming home, I ran off a bridge, overturned, and went into the water. There was about a six-inch air gap. My whole body was in the water. At first it was icy cold and I was shivering, but after a while I stopped shivering and even started to feel a little warm. I knew that eventually the air would run out. I learned later that my dad came upon the accident scene. There were lights and people everywhere. They told him a car had gone off the bridge and into the water, and then someone said, "It was Keith Byrd." My dad ran down, but I was already in the ambulance. If they hadn't found me, I would have drowned.

I was particular about my cars and kept them in pristine condition. At the end of my last high school year, I had a Mazda RX-7. Out in it one day, my best friend Dennis Rebert took a bunch of Quaaludes, kept falling asleep, and burned seven cigarette holes in the passenger seat. I still haven't forgiven him for that.

You had to have a car so you could cruise Main Street on Friday and Saturday nights. That's all everybody did, drive up and down from McDonald's to the bowling alley, and sometimes you'd get out and talk to people.

One Saturday night Rebert and I were cruising with a couple of friends in Kent's green '72 Cutlass. I'd just had an argument with my girlfriend, and Rebert was depressed about something too.

"Are you ready?" I said.

"For what?"

"Going to Myrtle Beach."

"Hell, yeah. Let's go."

Myrtle Beach was two hundred miles away and we were both broke and carless, so we went back to his place. It was midnight, and the house was dark and silent. Parked in the driveway was his mother's '75 Buick. Dennis disappeared inside the house and emerged with the keys. Putting the car in neutral, we rolled it silently down the driveway and then started it and drove away. The fuel gauge showed less than half a tank. Around Rockingham, we stopped and bummed a couple of dollars off some guy and put two dollars' more of gas in. That got us about another twenty miles before the engine sputtered and died.

Abandoning the car on the side of the road, we started thumbing. Seven rides later, the last driver deposited us at Holden Beach, where Rebert's parents had a trailer. Inside were two bicycles that we planned to steal and ride the rest of the way. We broke in, found a bottle of vodka too, and strapped it to one of the bicycles, with the plan to take it to Myrtle and sell it to some teenagers like us to get us a little bit of money. But we hadn't gone far when suddenly there was a loud crash. Swerving to avoid the glass, I watched our revenue stream pour down the hill. We dropped the bicycles and started thumbing again. A guy in a yellow Rabbit picked us up and took us the last fifty miles to Myrtle Beach. He was going to stay with us if we wanted him to, but we weren't going that way.

I had a nickel and two pennies, and Rebert had nothing. We had nowhere to stay, no food. We were young and stupid, and we had left without thinking it through. Walking into the nearest hotel, we asked for rooms and promised to pay. No go. We tried another two hotels, but nobody would give two sixteen-year-old boys a room on credit.

In one hotel lobby there was a candy machine and a drink machine that you could put your arm up inside and pull down a can. Bunked under the hotel's outside stairs, for the next two days we shook the shit out of the candy machine and survived on that and Pepsi Mountain Dew. Eventually I broke down and called my dad to come and get us.

When he pulled up, I saw my mom was with him, thank God.

It was not a pleasant ride home.

That time I didn't succeed in having the vision of how to be three steps ahead of everybody else. My friends were used to hearing me say, "We're going to do this, and we're going to get in trouble. Let's be prepared for these consequences." I didn't make a lot of the best decisions at times, but I always tried to have vision, to know where I wanted to go and how I was going to get there, not only right now, but also looking ahead in my life.

# 2

## LEARNING DISCIPLINE AND LEADERSHIP

My father was wounded with shrapnel in Chu Lai, Vietnam, in 1966. I was three years old. I didn't understand a lot, but I knew that my dad was a Marine and that was something very special, something to be proud of. My uncle—my aunt Cathy's husband—was also a Marine, and that was all I ever heard about growing up. Up until I was about sixteen I would often pull out my dad's Marine Corps annuals and study them. I loved the beautiful uniforms, and I got educated on the infantry. They were always the first to go in, the ground pounders.

In June of 1981 I graduated high school as number fifty-eight out of two hundred and fifty in the senior graduating class. My mom really wanted me to go to college, so I applied to High Point College and got accepted. It's now called High Point University and it's very expensive, but when I went it was a small school. I worked and paid for that semester myself. It was eighteen hundred dollars. But college was not for me. I wasn't motivated. I didn't see where it was going to go. So at the end of the semester I decided to join the

Marines. I wasn't headed down the right road and needed to get out of High Point. I needed the structure and discipline.

Two of my buddies were supposed to go into the Corps with me, but one got in trouble with the law and the other one backed out, so on November 12, 1981, I went by myself to enlist. On the ASVAB entry test, I scored high enough that my recruiter asked me what I wanted to do. "I want to be in the infantry," I said.

He looked at me with disbelief. "You're kidding. Usually that's where they put people that score low. You've scored high. You can choose your occupation."

"No. I want to be in the infantry."

I was gung ho. I had that fighting spirit. I thought claiming the title of U.S. Marine was really cool. And if I was going to be a Marine, I wanted to be a *Marine*, not an admin or electrician. I could do all that outside of those walls. The recruiter joked that he had never had anyone insist on being put in the infantry, but he guaranteed in writing that I would be MOS 0300, which is the military occupational specialty code for the infantry.

Then I told my mom and dad. My mom didn't like it, but she said she would support me, as she always did.

There were a bunch of us on the bus from the airport to Parris Island. Everybody had long hair and we were all joking around and laughing. The moment we pulled up to the infamous yellow footprints, the bus door opened and two drill instructors jumped on and started going nuts, screaming at us and pulling us out. In one instant we went from joking around to scared shitless. They herded us onto the yellow footprints, and then started chewing us out. As soon as you put your feet on those footprints, your world changes. That's where it starts. The discipline, being told what to do, instant obedience. I thought it was crazy. Why were they doing this? These were maniacs.

And it wasn't only the instructors. The first couple of nights, we had to sleep on our back with our thumbs along where the seams of our trousers would be. As the weeks went on, some of the more confident recruits picked on some of the weaker ones who were bringing down the platoon, beating them in the middle of night. But that didn't happen a lot. It was for certain recruits who were holding everybody else back.

The daily routine was rigid. At night before lights out we had minutes to shit, shower, and shave. I learned really fast how to plan ahead for maximum efficiency. Everything you did had to have a purpose. As the time approached I was already planning how I was going to wash my body, how I was going to shave. Was I going to shave while I was taking a shower? When was I going to use the bathroom? Was I going to do it first? You had to plan everything because you only had minutes. They were teaching you to plan to work as a team, with a routine. But hygiene was also very important in the Marine Corps.

After that, we stood beside our lockers and they inspected us. The drill instructor had a scribe following him taking notes. They'd come up to you and he'd say, "Hairs protruding from the nose," or "Foul breath," or "Fingernails too long." Sometimes they would just jerk you by your neck. If your ears weren't clean, they would stick stuff in them. Everything they did was so you remembered the discrepancy that you were called out on. Everything always had a purpose and a consequence.

There was probably a really practical reason for the focus on hygiene. The Marines Corps had us living so closely together—the first couple of weeks, at times they even commanded us to all get in a pile—that if anyone had any disease, it would soon spread to everyone. But the discipline could get absurd.

When we got there, a few of the recruits were scratching themselves. Two or three weeks in, a third of the platoon was itching, and everybody was scared. Finally, one night, a recruit named Yacobic couldn't take it any more. He got out of his rack and went to the drill instructor's hut. On the wall beside the door was a handprint. He smacked that handprint three times and said, "Recruit Yacobic re-questing to speak to Senior Drill Instructor Staff Sergeant Wilson."

The door jerked open. Standing there in his skivvies, T-shirt, and campaign cover, the drill instructor glared at Yacobic. "What the fuck are you waking me up for?"

"Sir. Some of the recruits in the platoon have the crabs, sir."

The drill instructor reached into his hut and then shoved a piece of blank white notebook paper at Yacobic. "Go in that head and pull off a crab and show me."

A minute later Yacobic came back, holding out the piece of white paper with a tiny crab on it. The drill instructor went crazy.

"You have murdered a Marine Corps–issued crab!" he yelled. "They have to eat, too!"

He screamed at us all to get up and put on our uniforms. Sleepy and feeling like the shit was getting ready to hit the fan, we marched outside, lined up, and sang the Marine Corps hymn as we ceremo-niously buried the crab.

The next day, the infected recruits got treatment.

Our days started with PT, physical training. Every day we learned to march. Marching was a big art form they took a lot of pride in. We learned how to take apart an M16 rifle and put it back together, blindfolded. Doing that just became part of life. I got to be an Expert, which is the highest you could get on the rifle range. We had self-defense training, obstacle courses, very severe swimming qualifications in a pool. We would swim and swim. We'd put our hands on the side of the pool—it's human nature to try to get out—and they would smash our fingers with their boots so we got back in that water. They wanted to push us to a point right before where we couldn't take it anymore. The obstacle courses, the swimming qualifications, the rifle trainings, the correct nomenclature for ev-erything—it was constant head games. They were trying to break us to where we lost our shit. If you couldn't take it, then they got rid of you. They sent you back home.

If someone was overweight, they called them a "fat-body Marine" and put them on a strict diet of Jell-O and salad. By the end of the three months they looked like a million bucks. It was impressive how the Marines had it down as far as training.

At the very beginning they called me "shitbird," which is a word they use throughout the Marine Corps. The definition of a shitbird is somebody who is not squared away—in the military that means you've got the best look, your uniform's the best, everything's perfect—but they called me that because of my last name. One time I was standing with my rifle at port arms. That's when you hold it across your body and your elbows are supposed to be in. The drill instructor came up behind me and whispered, "Shitbird, I can see air in between your elbow and your chest." He come around, took my rifle, and smashed the handguard portion of the rifle into my head. I dropped to my knees but got right back up and reassumed port arms with my elbows jammed against my sides. Blood was trickling down my face. I didn't twitch. When you're at port arms, you can't move.

Some of the ones who came down on the bus with me didn't make it. I had the advantage that I'd heard my dad's and uncle's stories, so I knew what to expect. But there were still a lot of moments that I didn't expect. It seemed kind of excessive. The Marine Corps got cleaned up a lot in the mid-1990s because some recruits died during boot camp. But back in the early 1980s it was still pretty harsh.

At the beginning you're thinking, *What the hell is going on?* But as you get further along you learn that everything they do has a reason. It is about the definition of discipline: instant willingness, obedience to orders, respect for authority, and self-reliance. It is about teamwork, trust in your fellow Marine. It is about training you how to survive, whatever situation you find yourself in. And it is about leadership. The Marines has an acronym to help you learn the fourteen key leadership traits: JJ DID TIE BUCKLE. It stands for justice, judgement, dependability, integrity, decisiveness, tact, initiative, endurance, bearing, unselfishness, courage, knowledge, loyalty, enthusiasm. If you displayed all of those traits, you should have a successful Marine Corps career. We studied each of them individually so we understood exactly what they meant and how we should live them. We absorbed them and believed them. What I didn't know then is how they would help me later on in life, through life lessons, through business lessons, through dealing with people, through leadership.

At the end of the thirteen weeks, those of us who had made it through boot camp at Parris Island reached our graduation day. My mom and dad came. My platoon—platoon number 3097, Third Battalion, India Company—lined up in formation. My dad was very proud to see me standing there, knowing that I had earned the right to wear the Marines uniform. Even though my mom didn't like it at first, when I graduated, she was also proud. I had two weeks' leave after graduation, and my dad took me and some of my friends out to celebrate his son becoming a Marine like him.

For me, it was a magnificent feeling, knowing I could claim the title of U.S. Marine. It was the proudest day of my life to that point. I had gone in at 145 pounds and I came out at 160, just toned to death. It was a great experience. I wouldn't give anything back. I loved it.

After my two weeks' leave, they sent me all the way across the country to infantry training school at San Onofre in Camp Pendleton, a long, sandy stretch of California coast just sixty miles north of San Diego. There I was assigned to MOS 0351 infantry assault Marine. In those intense four weeks, I learned to use a light anti-tank weapon (LAW) to blow up tanks. At the end I was chosen for sea duty, which was a prestigious duty within the infantry to be chosen for because you got to travel. So after graduation I went down to San Diego for another six weeks of training at Sea School.

Sea School is for the elite of the elite out of the infantry, and it trains you for a very special duty as part of a detachment of about sixty Marines among five thousand Navy sailors on an aircraft carrier. As my reward for graduating near the top, I got to pick the aircraft carrier I wanted to be assigned to. At the school they had a board with a list of all the carriers that had opening billets. My strategy was to pick the one that had the most Marines getting off. All of them had six, four, three, two billets opening up—all except the *USS America*. It had twelve spots. I reasoned that if twelve new Sea School graduates were going to that one ship, I had a better chance of being promoted because twelve out of sixty were at my own level. So I chose the *USS America*.

As Marines on board an aircraft carrier, we had two areas of responsibility. For one, we were the showpiece of the Marine Corps. Some countries, all they see is the United States military, and so to be chosen for sea duty you have to be really squared away. When the ship hit a port we got in our dress blue uniforms and threw the rifle and did all kinds of honors for dignitaries overseas representing the United States. In our off time on board ship, we practiced twirling the rifles and marching in cadence, so that when we performed on-shore, we would show the greatness of America to the country that we were visiting.

But our main responsibility was to guard the nuclear weapons of the ship. Only they didn't call them nuclear weapons. We referred to them as "special weapons." If some other country ambushed our ship and took over the special weapons, they could do a lot of damage in the world. It was our duty as Marines to prevent that happening. We had to memorize the whole ship, every access point, all the halls, the portholes, the doors, the latches—basically the whole blueprint of the ship—so that if ever there was a security breach, we knew how to secure the whole vessel. Fast.

From San Diego I flew to Norfolk, Virginia, where the *USS America* was in port. I wanted to make a good impression as soon as

I got there, so I hand-carried my dress greens onto the plane. I was meticulous about not getting anything wrinkled. When we arrived on the ship, we went down into the quarters of the Marine detachment, where we reported to First Sergeant Taylor. Sure enough, he ordered us to get into our dress greens and report back in twenty minutes. The Marines quarters are very small and there was no time to iron anything, so we just had to get changed, tidy up the best we could, and hurry back. All twelve of us stood there while First Sergeant Taylor went down the line looking at each one of us and asking us questions. My uniform was neatly pressed. Everybody else's was wrinkled.

I was assigned to the section of Sergeant Darrell Brown. Darrell became my inspiration. The moment I saw him, I thought, *Wow. Who is this guy?* His boots always shined, his camouflage uniform was always pressed; his demeanor, the way he demanded respect from his peers—he was a really squared-away dark green Marine. That's what we called Black Marines. We were all green, but you were either light green or dark green, and Darrell was dark green. We took a liking to each other, and over the next months he taught me a lot, especially about leadership. The way he led our section turned us from a group of trained infantrymen into a tightly knit team that strove for perfection in everything we did. He was my hero.

Every morning in the guard mount, Darrell inspected us and made sure we were all squared away and in line on everything we did together, our knowledge of the job, the security on board the ship. And then our section spent every day basically joined at the hip. For our duty as the first reaction team, it was critical for us to always be on the same sheet of music, as Darrell put it. So we did everything together, from breaking bread—that's what he called our meal times—to learning how to press our cammies perfectly, to spit-shining our boots with a baby diaper. I thought I knew how to shine boots until I met Darrell Brown. He taught me his technique, and then after he left I had the best-shined boots. Darrell trained us all together so we knew what he was doing, and he knew what we were doing. There was no room for miscommunication. We got to where we almost knew what each other was thinking.

He and I became good friends. Some days after lunch we would sit down and write letters together. That was good, quality time. I wrote to my girlfriend, and he wrote to his. Syndie and I had been together since high school, but we kept breaking up. When I came on board we were broken up, but we wrote to each other and ended up getting back together. One time when the ship was in Kenya, I'd had some drinks on leave and I wanted to call her. To make a call in those days you had to get an operator through Nairobi. It was two or three in the morning back in North Carolina and Syndie's dad answered. I had several funny phone moments like that, because there weren't many opportunities to call anybody. At some point during that two-year tour, I decided for certain that I wanted to spend the rest of my life with her, and I proposed. She accepted, and we agreed to have the wedding the next time I was home on leave.

*At the end of the thirteen weeks, those of us who had made it through boot camp at Parris Island reached our graduation day. It was a magnificent feeling, knowing I could claim the title of U.S. Marine.*

*On board the USS America, of our group of twelve, nine of us got promoted to Lance Corporal at the same time. I am at bottom right.*

*As a U.S. Marine, in my neatly pressed dress blues. Ready to proudly represent the United States.*

*As a U.S. Marine, in cammies. Ready at all times to defend the special weapons on board the USS America.*

With the Marines, usually you sign up for four years, but I happened to enlist at a time when you could join for three, and it was my goal to make corporal before I left the ship. It normally takes three years, but I was determined to do it in less than that. To help you earn the rank of corporal, you could take extra courses called MCIs, so I crammed in something like fourteen of them. I overloaded, because knowledge was power. It was very competitive to make corporal within two years, and I tried to outwork everybody. Thanks to that extra work and to Darrell taking me under his wing and grooming me, when he left the ship about eight months after I arrived, I was made sergeant of the guard and put in charge of the whole detachment of sixty Marines as section leader. I got promoted to lance corporal, which is pay grade E3, and then on November 1, 1983, I was made corporal, pay grade E4. I made it in less than two years. Among us peers, we celebrated with a small ceremony. I was now the leader among the peers. The gunnery sergeant was over me, then there were the executive officer and the commanding officer. I was the leader of the day-to-day stuff, and I was actually doing the work of a sergeant while holding the rank of corporal and getting a corporal's pay. I was very proud because I knew that my thought process and my vision of having a better chance of being promoted by choosing the *USS America* had come to fruition.

As sergeant of the guard I was in charge of what they called the sitting SAT—the special reaction team. When the siren and flashing light of a security alert went off in our area, the first two people to go in response was the sitting SAT: they were called the SAT1 and the SAT2. For guard duty of the special weapons we had the two-man rule—there's always somebody else watching you. If we ran into any sort of threat at that alarm area, then we were armed with our weapons and ammunition to deal with it. After we secured the area, I would call back to the guard house to tell them to reset the alarm. False alarms were quite common. Sometimes sailors would unsecure the special ammunition storage space so they could work in there, and then once they were inside they wouldn't secure it properly, which would trigger an alarm. I never encountered a situation of a real threat, but you always had to respond like it was a real threat. You couldn't let down your guard or get complacent, ever.

Not long after I was promoted, a new group of Marines flew on board to join our detachment. As I walked down the line inspecting them, the same way Darrell had inspected us when my group came on board, one Marine caught my eye. He was more squared away and stood above and beyond the new guys around him. "That guy, he's going to be something," I said and pulled him aside. His name was Tim Fletcher, and from that moment on I started grooming him to take over from me when I left the ship, the way Darrell had groomed me.

But my strategy didn't go quite as planned. A couple of months after Tim arrived, the post of captain's orderly came open, and I nominated Tim for it. This was an important position. The captain's orderly is the admiral's bodyguard—the captain of an aircraft carrier is an admiral—and basically never leaves his side. Tim was chosen for the position and left my section, but we still stayed friends. I ate better too, because he would sometimes sneak me a steak from the captain's table.

As Marines on an aircraft carrier, we got to travel all over the world. In only two years I did two Mediterranean cruises, one Indian Ocean cruise, and one North Atlantic cruise, in addition to stays in our home ports of Norfolk and Portsmouth, Virginia. I got to see Scotland, Greece, Kenya, the U.S. Virgin Islands, the Bahamas, Sri Lanka, England, Venezuela—and Spain three times. It was amazing getting that opportunity to visit a lot of different places that I normally wouldn't go. The ship would stay out at sea for thirty or forty days, and then we would visit a port for two or three days. There we would often put on our show for the dignitaries, representing the Marine Corps worldwide.

On board ship, we didn't have anything to spend our pay on except gambling. We played a lot of acey deucey. That's the old Marine Corps gambling game. It's high risk with high rewards. Back in shore life, I introduced it to all my friends, including my current ones, and I still play it today. When we had shore leave, most guys would blow their pay in the bars, but Tim and I saved ours to buy nice clothes and other things that had value. In Spain we bought some really nice shoes. When we did go out on the town on leave back in North Carolina we dressed to the nines.

Some of the nightclubs in the ports where we stopped were in unexpected places. In Mombasa, we found our way down to a beach where loud music enticed us from a cave. Walking in, we found the cave strung with lights and full of twenty-one- and twenty-two-year-olds dancing to music that was really cool. One of the kids told us the artist was a guy called Eddy Grant. We fell in love with his song "Electric Avenue," but we couldn't find it in the States. Finally we got hold of a cassette tape, and whenever we were home on leave we would play it. Tim likes to joke that we brought Eddy Grant to the U.S. and he owes us royalties.

As we steamed around the world taking part in exercises with the military from other countries, performing peacekeeping duties and other operations, we would periodically return to the shipyard at Norfolk, Virginia. In spring 1984 we had a month in Norfolk preparing for our next deployment, so I flew home to marry Syndie, taking four or five Marines with me. Tim was in the wedding.

A couple of months later, my two years on the ship were up. Now it was time for our group of twelve Marines to leave. When you're on sea duty, after two years it doesn't matter where that carrier is, the Marine Corps gets you off. We took a helicopter from the boat to Rota, a U.S. naval base in Spain. It had been a great adventure. The first time in my life that I really became a leader was on that ship, and I was very proud of it, because I was one of the youngest ones. My strategy worked out because, sure enough, the math tells you that with twelve out of sixty, you've got a better chance.

For the final six months of my three years, I was sent to Quantico, Virginia. Syndie and I got an apartment at a place called Spanish Gardens Apartments right outside of Quantico, in Woodbridge, Virginia. Before I got out they offered me the Marine barracks in Hawaii. They really wanted me to stay in. But I knew I didn't want to stay in. Being a Marine was like a bucket list item. I wanted to get it checked off. I knew from the beginning that in the Marine Corps, there is no in between. Either you get out or you stay twenty years. I was ready to go on to my next adventure. I had always admired people that served, and my dad going to Vietnam played a big part in my wanting to serve my country. I loved my time in the Marine Corps and was proud of it. It taught me how to be self-reliant. To not depend on anybody else. Complete self-reliance, complete discipline. It was really challenging, and there was a big sense of self-satisfaction in accomplishing it. And I knew I would use the fourteen

*My DD214, showing my dates of service and my classification. It lists only some of the extra courses I took – there were too many to fit them all on the form!*

leadership traits of JJ DID TIE BUCKLE throughout the rest of my life and my work. My three years in the U.S. Marines Corps shaped me from being an immature punk into a disciplined, independent individual laser-focused on setting and achieving goals.

*After I was discharged, Syndie and I moved from Quantico into a mobile home*
*that used to be my Mamaw's, in Sophia, North Carolina, near where I grew up.*

After I was discharged, Syndie and I moved from Quantico
into a mobile home that used to be my Mamaw's, in Sophia, North
Carolina, near where I grew up. A few months later, on March 11,
1985, Syndie gave birth to a baby boy that we named after me:
Brian Keith Byrd II, but unlike me, we would call him by his first
name, Brian. After the nurse handed him to me, I ran up and down
the halls of the hospital. I couldn't have been prouder when I saw his
beautiful face. It was breathtaking. The proudest moment in my life.

We struggled as a young family living in that trailer, with me
in between jobs. At one point, I sold my dress blues for seventy-five
dollars to pay rent. I still kick my rear end for that, and I wish I
could retrieve them. Syndie and I were very frugal. When we lived
in Quantico, Pizza Hut had just come out with a deal that if you
ordered a pan pizza at lunch and didn't get it in a certain period of
time, it was free. Syndie and I would purposely go to Pizza Hut when

it was crowded at lunch, and most of the time we got our pizzas free. Living in the mobile home, Syndie used to buy a lot of cheap, filling foods like macaroni and cheese, pinto beans, and spam.

I never lost confidence, though. I knew better things were coming. I knew that I would make them happen.

Before I went into the Marines, all through high school I had worked with my dad plumbing. He was now working for someone else, but when I got out, he told me that if I came on with him, he'd go independent again. So I did, and when we needed extra help Syndie's cousin, Jeff Earnhardt, joined us.

One day Jeff and I were replacing the kitchen sink in a woman's house, when her phone rang. It was my dad. "Keith, you need to come to the office. I got into a fight last night. The guy's calling the secretary and threatening to come up here and blow up the place. Come on back." My mom and dad were divorced by this time, and Dad had converted the front of the house he was living in into an office.

It turned out that the night before, Dad had been out at a bar and got into a fight with a guy he used to run around with and beat him over the head with a barstool. Now the guy wanted retribution. The office phone rang. Dad grabbed it from the secretary and managed to talk the guy—his name was Greg—into not coming onto the property and instead meeting us at a church parking lot, of all places.

I was driving Syndie's old car, an orange Datsun B210. My dad sat up front, and Jeff was in the back. Dad's strategy was to meet Greg and try to just talk to him, to defer him from taking this any further and bringing it to the office. We got to the parking lot and sat there waiting, but Greg didn't show up. "Dad, let's get out of here," I said, starting the car.

Suddenly a truck came rolling into the lot. The guy slammed it in park and got out, holding a shotgun. "He's got a gun. Let's go!" Dad said. My Marine Corps training told me: Don't turn your back on the gun. My dad and Jeff got out and ran across the street, while I stayed there with the car. Greg pointed the shotgun at my dad across the street and they started having words back and forth. Greg's face was black where my dad had beat him with a barstool. He was upset.

I was forty to sixty feet from him, crouching behind the driver's door. "Greg, calm down," I said. I didn't even know him. Every time I said something he took that shotgun and pointed it at me to get me to shut up because his concentration was on arguing back and forth with my dad. I thought quickly and decided to try to get him off subject. I said some derogatory things trying to get him to focus on me so I could talk him into putting the gun down.

Well, he didn't like what I said and started shooting all around Syndie's car. I ran, trying to use the car as a shield. Every time he blew that shotgun a hundred pellets came firing at me. Syndie's car was all shot up. I didn't notice at the time, but I took four or five of those pellets in my leg. I worked my way around to the trunk, where I had a .22 rifle because I had been squirrel hunting with it the weekend before. When Greg paused to reload I took the rifle and pointed it at him just to scare him. From across the street I heard Daddy saying, "Keith, don't shoot him. Don't shoot him."

At that moment, when Greg was reloading and I was pointing a weapon at him, a railroad detective arrived on scene. Somebody had called the law because they heard all the gunshots, and the church was right by the railroad so he was the closest law enforcement officer. He tackled Greg. I was so amped up after being shot at that I went over and started beating Greg, then my dad came running across and joined in. Wrestling with me to get me off Greg, the railroad detective hit me in the head with his walkie-talkie. I ended up in hospital with a shot-up leg and a cracked-open head, and of course there was a police report on the whole thing.

When I was recovered enough I went back to work with my dad. That continued okay for a while, then we had a tiff. I don't even remember what it was about, but I decided I was going out on my own. Back then where we lived, everybody was hooking up to city sewer. For doing the connection, you could get six dollars a running foot. So if it was a hundred feet from the house to the street where you connected, at six dollars a foot that was six hundred dollars. I didn't have any equipment, but I found a guy that would dig my ditches for one dollar a foot, and my Papaw had a truck he let me use. To fit the 20-foot-long pipes in the truck, I cut them in half. I was a pretty good salesman, so I would go to a neighborhood and start knocking on doors and get commitments from multiple people. That way, when I hired the guy with the Ditch Witch, it would be more profitable for me to hire him to dig six people's ditches than coming out to do just one.

My best friend Dennis Rebert's father-in-law also hired me to connect the building where he had his mattress shop to the city sewer. That was a great opportunity because it was a commercial job. I was digging the ditch by hand, and with one stroke I sliced through the water line. But I fixed it and got the job done.

Adapt and overcome. That was what I was doing. I was running sewer lines everywhere and didn't have any equipment or assets, and I was making good money with a nearly seventy percent profit margin. The problem was I was doing it under my dad's plumbing license.

One day the inspector came out and told me, "You can't do this anymore. Your dad doesn't want you doing it under his license." So I decided to go get my plumbing license. I thought it would be an easy task because I knew about plumbing. I'd been doing it since I was fourteen. I took the exam twice and failed it both times. If you passed, they wouldn't tell you your score. If you failed, they would. You had to have a 70, and I got a 68.25. After the second time of failing, I decided it was time for a new line of work.

In the Marine Corps, we were the security of the ship, and apart from plumbing, that was the only thing I knew. I had always liked the highway patrol—the uniforms and how squared away they were—and I had always respected it as a law enforcement agency. I decided to try it out and went to the local Highway Patrol office to apply. I found out fast that you just don't walk in and say, "I want to be a highway patrolman." Back then it was very prestigious, and you had to have the political backing of somebody to get in. But I walked in, and they actually let me apply.

The highway patrol always did a thorough background check on you. Really thorough. They called members of my family, friends, even distant people who knew me, asking in-depth questions and trying to dig up any kind of trouble I'd ever been in. So of course they saw all the documentation of that incident with Greg and the shotgun. They drilled me on that. I had to tell the whole story and convince them that I had just been in the wrong place at the wrong time. I hadn't been charged with anything. It was just another sales job to sell myself on being allowed to apply. Then after all that I took the test and didn't make it.

At five o'clock one morning, Syndie and I were asleep in the trailer when the phone rang. It was an officer from the North Carolina State Highway Patrol. "I need you to be in Garner, North Carolina, this morning at nine a.m. Can you make it?"

"Yes, sir," I said and jumped out of bed.

Patrol school is a lot like the Marine Corps in that in the beginning there's a lot who can't take it. Recruits start leaving, climbing out the windows in the middle of the night. I found out later that thirteen people had dropped out and I was the thirteenth alternate based on my score. And that's how I got in.

I got ready in double-quick time and Syndie drove me the hour and a half to Garner. I was unprepared. As I walked into the training room with my long hair, zippered disco boots that came halfway up my shins, jeans, and a regular old shirt, everybody snickered at me. They'd already been there four days and had their jumpsuits on and their heads shaved, and here comes this hippie-looking guy. But I was there.

The highway patrol training was very physical, very disciplined, but it was nothing to me after being through Marines boot camp. This was the second time where I demonstrated that I could lead. Even though I was thirteenth on the alternate list, I ended up being one of the four squad leaders at the patrol school. It wasn't just physical training, either. There was a lot of book learning. In five months of highway patrol school you basically packed in an associate's degree in criminal justice. Right before graduation, when they knew we were going to make it, they handed out our uniforms. That was a big deal. State trooper was the most prestigious law enforcement in the state of North Carolina. It was a proud moment to wear that uniform at graduation as part of the 78th Basic School.

To begin my career with the North Carolina State Highway Patrol I was sent to Onslow County. When Syndie and my mom heard I would be working in Onslow, they were not happy. My wife cried at the thought of living there, and my mom was worried about my safety. In the NCSHP there were three counties no one wanted-ed to be assigned to because they were dangerous: Cumberland, Robeson, and Onslow, the home of Marine Corps Base Camp Lejeune. I had been a Marine, and I knew how crazy they could be.

District Sergeant Ken Hill assigned me to a veteran trooper named Cliff Bennet for extended on-the-road training. After six weeks with Cliff, I graduated to solo patrol. I found out pretty quick it was dangerous, but I thrived on it. I loved the thrill. However, I did find myself in a lot of scary situations. The worst happened one Sunday evening after I saw a guy in front of me driving all over the road. Back then you had to get a lot of DWIs—driving while under the influence of an intoxicant. It was like a quota, so you sometimes bypassed safety to get your numbers. This guy seemed to be an obvious DWI and maybe more, so I pulled him. When I went up to his window, I could smell alcohol. I got him into my car, determined he was under the influence, and then asked the protocol questions: "Do you have anything in the car? Do you have any weapons? Do you have any alcohol, any open containers?" He answered no to all.

I knew I'd got myself a DWI, but I wanted to dig deeper because I could also smell marijuana on him. I left him sitting in my car and went to see if I could find anything incriminating in his. Getting down on the ground, I stuck my head under his car seat and shined my flashlight around, but all I found was a little glass of liquor that he had pushed underneath the seat. No drugs.

It was nearly dusk, just getting dark, and as I was walking back to my vehicle I heard my passenger door crack shut. I switched my flashlight back on, walked around, and shined the light down to see why he had shut his door. Lying on the ground was a .25 automatic pistol. He had dropped it out of the car when I was walking back. All that time I had been in the car with him interviewing him and then sticking my head inside his car, he had been armed. Shame on me. Greed made me do a really stupid thing that could have cost me my life. I didn't search him. I didn't handcuff him. I put him in the front seat of my car. I was too anxious to try to get myself another charge.

When I found that gun chills ran all over me. The round was chambered. I got back in the driver's seat and waved his weapon at him. "What the fuck is this?"

He sneered. "You motherfucking cop. I was going to blow your head off and I got scared right at the last second." In that moment I went crazy and beat his ass, out of fear of what could have happened. Then, still shaking with fear, I put him in the backseat. Still today, that was the most scared I've ever been in my life.

Once you had brought blood on somebody you'd arrested, it was procedure you had to take them to the hospital. He told everybody I beat him to death, but I didn't get into a lot of trouble because the guy had a gun. It was different then.

A lot of our work involved dealing with accidents. When someone smashed up their vehicle, we had to call a wrecker to haul it away. To keep it fair, there was a rotation. If the person who had the wreck didn't specify a service they wanted to use, you were supposed to call the wrecker at the top of the rotation. It was a very strict policy. But everybody knew that it wasn't always followed. Wreckers would do you favors if you gave them more business, and every trooper had their favorite that they would feed wrecks.

My Papaw's old green truck—the one I had used to haul sewer pipe—was looking shabby, and I wanted to get it painted as a way to give back to him. One of the wreckers, a guy named Buddy, said to me, "I could probably paint your truck if I could get a few more of them accidents shifted my way." I agreed, and started to coerce people to name B&S Body Shop as the service they wanted to use when they'd smashed up their car and needed it hauled away. Buddy only did a half-ass paint job on my Papaw's truck, but I kept feeding him wrecks until I calculated the debt had been paid off.

Buddy kept pressuring me to send him more wrecks. When I refused, he went to Internal Affairs and complained that he had painted my truck and I had told him I would send him wrecks to pay for the paint job and I still owed him. Internal Affairs opened an investigation.

Sergeant Hill told Internal Affairs to back off and let him handle the situation. I was young, it was a mistake, I was an outstanding model trooper with a promising career in the NCSHP ahead of me, and it wasn't worth firing me over this. But Internal Affairs was under political pressure from Buddy's close friend and ally, the senator for Onslow County, and even though Sergeant Hill argued hard on my behalf and told them outright what he thought of both Buddy and the senator, they refused to drop the investigation.

Internal Affairs interviewed a lot of people who had "chosen" B&S Body Shop to haul their wrecks, as well as my peers. Then they came to me. Our interview went basically like this:

"We know you are guilty of doing this."

"Yes, I am."

"We also know it's going on amongst your peers. If you would be willing to give us some information, you'll be able to keep your job, but we'll have to relocate you to another county."

"I'm not telling on anybody."

There was no way I was going to be a rat, so in December 1987, three years after completing my term with the U.S. Marine Corps, I was fired from the North Carolina Highway Patrol.

Other people stepped forward to fight for me. My mother-in-law worked hard to try to get my job back, petitioning relentlessly to get me a meeting with a House representative in Randolph County. The CEO of Richard Petty Motorsports, Brian Moffitt, was an old friend of mine, and the Petty family had become friends too, so Richard made some calls and got me a meeting with the person in charge of crime control and public safety, which had jurisdiction over the highway patrol. But that didn't do any good, either.

I was jobless again. But Syndie and I weren't scared of work. She definitely wasn't. On my days off from the highway patrol we'd worked on the side washing windows in new construction. We'd look at each other, one on the inside and one on the outside, and take the stickers off with razor blades and then Windex the glass. We would get ten dollars a window. That was a lot of money back then. We would find a way.

I was disappointed and mad about my time with the highway patrol being cut short and how it

*In my North Carolina State Highway Patrol uniform.*

had ended. The whole thing had left a bad taste in my mouth. But I never saw myself working there for thirty years. It had been a good experience where I learned a lot and worked with a lot of good people. I had a lot of respect for Sergeant Hill, especially. I knew it had been a good stepping stone to keep me moving upwards.

Plus, it wasn't all bad news. Syndie was pregnant again.

# 3

## UPS

I took the Highway Patrol's offer to officially resign rather than have the firing on my record. I was depressed after that experience, but I still had to find another job. Syndie worked at Bluewater Real Estate in Emerald Isle, North Carolina, and one of her bosses, Robert Andrews, knew a high-level guy that supervised the mechanics at UPS in that area. I applied at UPS and was called in for an interview with Willie McNeil, the center manager in Jacksonville, North Carolina. When Willie asked me why I left the highway patrol, I told the official story that I resigned, but the real story was known in the area. Eastern North Carolina is a small place.

In the interview process, I was up against all the other people who had applied off the street. I had three things going for me: the introduction from Robert Andrews, my service in the Marine Corps, and my two years in the highway patrol, even though I left under "unfavorable" circumstances. UPS likes a lot of prior military, and that maybe gave me an edge.

Willie earned my eternal respect by taking a chance and hiring me as a driver. My first day was Wednesday, May 11, 1988, and I walked straight into animosity. It was almost unheard of at UPS to start out as a driver. Usually you came on part-time as a package handler. But the company's union contract said that one outsider had to come in as a driver for every three or four promoted from handler. Some of the package handlers had been waiting years for their chance to move up, but here I came off the street starting right in as a package car driver. It didn't earn me any friends that first day. But I gradually earned their respect and developed good relationships with them.

It was a relief for Syndie that I had found work. As well as having three-year-old Brian at home, she was almost seven months pregnant. UPS was also paying me more than I had been making, by far, on patrol. I started at around twelve dollars an hour, which was ridiculous back then for a new employee starting almost at the bottom.

I was a cover driver, the low man on the totem pole. I had to learn all the routes, because all I was doing was covering for people on vacation. That was challenging. They gave me a day or two of training, but the routes were complex and two days wasn't enough. I wanted to be one step ahead to do the job efficiently, so I put a lot of effort into learning how the house numbers ran, the odds and evens, and actually looking at the doors I'd be delivering to. On the weekends, I went out with a map in my own car to figure out the best way to run that particular route.

Having to deal with that challenge at the age of twenty-five, basically at the outset of my working life, set me up for everything that I've achieved since, because it taught me not to get comfortable with one situation or way of doing things.

Besides the challenge of the ever-changing routes, I didn't know how the handlers loaded the package car (UPS *never* calls it a truck or van). I had to deliver the packages to the customers, but first I had to find the right package. On my scheduled days I would go in an hour and a half early, sometimes two hours, to watch how the handlers were loading my package car.

As drivers we were always running against the clock. If the computer said that I should have an 8.7-hour day, that meant I should be able to run that route in eight hours and forty-two minutes. Every day I wanted to run under that 8.7 or whatever the engineers had said was the optimal time for that route. My goal was to shine. It was rare to run under on a cover route, and that motivated me even more. I saw this as my opportunity to stand out from everybody else. I learned those routes so well and got so efficient at running them that most times out, I ran under.

Jacksonville was what they called a bonus center. As an incentive to drivers to make the customers happy by giving them speedy delivery, if we ran under, UPS would let us go home early and still get paid for the stipulated time for that route. Also, UPS paid time and a half over eight hours, not forty. So on that 8.7 day, those last forty-two minutes were paid at time and a half. I learned fast that by working smart instead of hard, I made more money and had more free time. That first year, I made really good money.

I was so motivated, I got a little overconfident. Maybe you could say cocky. Near the end of my training period, I was out on a route and I was hurrying because I wanted to see how much I could run under by. Backing up the package car, I ran into a pole.

In ten seconds, I managed to violate two major no-nos. You can't damage a package car or have an accident, especially during your training period. And you are not supposed to back up. Ever. Not unless there's no other option.

I had been doing so well, getting pats on the back every day, and I was almost through my training period to get seniority as a driver. And then I go and back into a pole. It didn't hurt the package car that much, but from an ethical standpoint, I had to call my boss, Nicky Barber, and tell him.

"Nicky, you're not going to believe this, but I just backed into a pole."

"OK. Just keep delivering your packages, and then come on in and let's see what we can do."

He was calm and reassuring, but I just knew I was going to get fired because having an accident during your training period—you just couldn't do that. It was such a small scratch I probably could have got by without telling them. As a cover driver you change trucks all the time, and it probably would have taken them a couple of days to notice it. But I called, and I'm glad I did.

When I got in, Nicky told me we'd address it in the morning. I couldn't sleep all night.

The next morning I arrived early. Nervous, I walked in to Nicky's office. It was dull, like all UPS offices. No pictures on the walls. No windows. Nicky's expression was cold. He wanted to make sure I knew he was doing me a big favor.

He told me to sit down. I sat.

I was certain I would be fired for the second time in less than a year. I didn't know what I would do after that. I had a family, and at UPS I had the opportunity to make really good money as well as the possibility for advancement. This job wasn't a short-term stepping stone. Even though I was loving my time in operations, my goal was to get into sales.

"I've talked with Willie McNeil," Nicky said. My stomach felt hollow. "We've agreed you can stay."

Relief flooded through me.

I was determined not to waste this blessing, especially because Syndie was approaching her due date for our second child and we needed this income. From then on, I was very cautious. I still ran under the route times set by the engineers most days out. But that close call taught me that good blessings could disappear very quickly by trying to get in too much of a hurry.

A few weeks later, on Sunday, July 24, 1988, I stood beside

Syndie as she lay on a bed in the spacious delivery room of the local hospital, preparing for the greatest blessing there is in life, the birth of our child.

"Are you ready to deliver a baby?" the doctor said, looking at me.

"Yes, sir," I said.

He knew I had been in the Marines and the Highway Patrol, and so he assumed I'd had training in assisting at a birth. We had received some instruction, but it had been very high level, and I'd never witnessed a live birth. When Brian was born, I wasn't even in the delivery room.

The doctor pulled over a chair, arranged it in the right position, and motioned to me to sit in it. I was nervous and incredibly excited. I was going to actually help deliver my own son! As Syndie labored, the doctor guided me and helped with the pulling. When my boy made his first cry, I was flooded with emotion. Helping him come onto this earth from my wife was indescribably personal and fulfilling, like no experience I had ever had.

We named him Andrew Tyler Byrd, and after the Southern custom, called him Tyler.

The next day I worked fourteen hours, and Syndie told me not to worry about coming to the hospital to see her and Tyler. It was hard not to see them that second day, but this job meant everything for our family. I didn't want to create the perception that I was not motivated. When I'm trying to get something done, I go a hundred miles an hour at it. This job was such a good opportunity. I was making more money than I'd ever made in my life, and Syndie also wanted me to be successful during that training period and earn the title of being a UPS driver.

The thing I loved most about UPS in that era was that they didn't care if you had an education. They didn't ask you what college you graduated from. From day one I recognized that if you worked hard, you could earn advancement and get promoted. I also loved their attention to detail. The trucks were washed every night. Appearance was important, and so was holding each other accountable. Back then it was nothing for somebody to call you out and almost get in a fistfight over whether you had done your job right. Everybody was proud of their job. It was a great organization that reminded me a lot of the Marine Corps—very structured, very militaristic. I felt comfortable and thrived in that environment. I fit right in.

After I'd been driving for a year, Willie McNeil moved on to the Wilmington center, and Jimmy Moore came from Raleigh to take his place as center manager. As soon as he arrived, Jimmy promoted me to driver supervisor. Most drivers worked for years before being able to advance. I was in my mid-twenties, and I was really proud of earning that promotion so quickly.

But now I was supervising drivers who had been driving for fifteen, twenty, twenty-five years. At first, I encountered some resistance and bad feeling, but I earned their respect. There's a way of holding people accountable but still being a people person. Even though I only drove for a year, I knew what they were going through, and that helped me to supervise them in a way that showed I understood. In a short time I earned their trust, but I still held them accountable. I was young, I was energetic, and I wanted to keep moving up the ladder.

From the forty-five hours a week I'd been working as a driver, as a supervisor I was now putting in fifty to sixty hours overseeing my group of fifteen drivers. The on-car supervisor was the first to arrive each day and the last to leave, and there were two of us at Jacksonville, which was considered a small center. Jimmy taught me the ropes of management, and I learned a lot from working with other great supervisors. It was another piece of fortunate timing that played a role in all that I achieved later.

I got to go to time-study school, where I learned the engineering side of running the routes and was certified in being the one who went out and determined that route was a 8.7 day. I also had to certify all my drivers in the now famous 340 Methods Certification.

For the 340 certification, I had to ride with a driver a minimum of three days and a maximum of eternity until I did what was called "bring the driver in." In other words, until that third day with them, or the eighth day, or however how long it took, I had to be on that car coaching that driver until he (most drivers then were men) completed the route within the stipulated time. If the computer said it was an 8.7 day and he came in at 8.71 on the third day, I had to keep riding with him until I had succeeded in showing him that the job could be done in 8.7 hours. Going over that 8.7 was called being "over allowed."

After I had brought the driver in, then I could hold him accountable.

The drivers were union, and I had crossed that line after only a year of driving. Now I was non-union management. Because they were protected by the union, some drivers bucked the system. The number one challenge as an operations supervisor at UPS was to hold your drivers accountable to do the job in the time that it should be done in. That was the most tense part of being an operations driver supervisor, and you had to certify every driver at least once a year.

During the 340 methods certification, I stayed with that driver every minute. From the moment he punched on the clock, I was following him around, and the drivers hated that. I monitored and coached them on every detail: how they held the key to enter it into the ignition, which they did a hundred times a day; how they used the arm rail to hoist themselves into the truck; how they opened the bulkhead door. And so on for a seemingly endless number of detailed movements and decisions.

UPS had done the studies and knew that if you could cut thirteen seconds, or a minute and a half, or twelve minutes a day per driver, and they had a hundred thousand employees, then you were talking millions of dollars a year in savings. Long before it became a popular business strategy, UPS understood the huge economic value of precision time management techniques.

There was constant accountability of everything you did. The organization teaches you the correct methods of how to hold the key, how to insert the key, how to put your seatbelt on, how to release your seatbelt. They teach how to select the package and how to release the package. What are you thinking about from the time you step off the package car? On your way to the customer, what are you doing? Are you keying in the shipper number? Every step has a purpose to save time.

You had to be thinking three steps ahead of everything. What's going to happen if I knock on this door and they're not here? Where am I going to leave the package? Am I visually looking at that location? Am I making that decision now? How am I going to hide the package from being stolen? How am I going to document I left it at 213, at the neighbor's house, instead of 212? If it has to have a signature, how am I going to walk from 212 to 213 in case 212's not there? There's a constant stream of things going through your mind to work smart instead of hard.

That kind of minute detail drives a lot of people crazy, but I love it. Through the military training and then being on patrol with the NCSHP I learned how to always be cautious, always be thinking three steps ahead; I was comfortable with a structure that dictated how you were supposed to do everything. I'm the type that if you show me how to do it, I can do it. The micro-detail and training at UPS fit right into my DNA.

Along with the detail, everything at UPS has documentation. If it took me five days instead of three days to bring that driver in, then I documented it and told the driver. Six months from now, if the driver started going over allowed, I jumped back on the car with him and demonstrated again. The drivers didn't like this, and they would sometimes mess with me, playing dumb and doing things they normally wouldn't do.

One time I was riding with a driver for the ninth day doing the 340 Method. It was unheard of to go that many days, because the on-car supervisor typically wouldn't commit that much time. But I was determined to let him know we were going to keep doing this until he did it right. He got so mad at me that when we ate lunch he would not sit with me. We ate at separate tables.

Some drivers got really creative, milking another eight seconds out of the stop by initiating conversation with a customer or asking open-ended questions so I had to sit there and listen to them answer, instead of just saying, "Good morning, thank you for your business," and then turning around and leaving. "What you got planned to-day?" they would ask. Or acting like they couldn't read the label on a package, so they had to get their glasses out of their pocket. They knew very well that seconds added up to minutes, and minutes added up to hours. They knew the game. They were masters at it. They were also very smart. That's why you had to document everything. If you ever had a job performance problem with that driver with the union, you had to show in the documentation that you got on the car twice and showed them how to do it—and they did it.

That was the most challenging part of being a driver supervisor, but I was good at it. I loved getting on the car and demonstrating their capability and taking away their excuses.

My boss's boss—Jimmy Moore's and Willie McNeil's boss—was Kevin Oliver. He was in charge of southeastern North Carolina from an operations perspective. As division manager, Kevin didn't usually communicate much with the on-car supervisors. But we struck up a relationship, and one day he asked me a question.

"Keith, you've got pretty good at this on-car. What's your goal at UPS?"

During the three-and-a-half years I had been an on-car operations supervisor, I would always look at the salespeople that came into the centers. They would come in dressed to the nines, very polished, always looking sharp. In my mind, at UPS, the most polished, put-together people were the salespeople.

"I would love to earn my way into sales," I told him.

Kevin didn't say much then, but a week or two later he came back.

"Keith, I'm going to make you an offer. If you'll go to Wilmington and bring in my top three least-best drivers"—that was UPS-speak for the worst drivers—"and 340-certify them, I will put you in sales."

"Done," I said.

Syndie didn't want to move, so during the week I lived in a hotel room in Wilmington and put in long hours. I put in long hours, but I knew it was worth it.

At that time, Wilmington was a TDU center, which stands for Teamsters for a Democratic Union. There were maybe three TDU centers in North Carolina.

As soon as I got to Wilmington I saw it was going to be a challenge. They hated management, and they tested me. I knew there was no way I would get anywhere starting with the top three least-best, so to try to gain trust and traction I started with the good-natured drivers and worked my way up—or down, depending how you want to look at it.

One of the first ones I took out to certify was a driver called Tim Brock, and we quickly developed a good rapport. "Tell me about these three guys that I got to bring in," I asked him. "What do they like? What do they dislike? What do they do off the job?" I wanted to know all I could, so I could find ways to connect with them and get their guard down enough that they would listen to me and eventually respect me.

Wilmington was twice as big as the Jacksonville center. I'd gone from having thirty drivers under two supervisors to sixty. But Kevin was smart. He knew that if somebody could go in there and bring in the three least-best, then the others might follow.

The other thing about Wilmington was that the union voted it not to be a bonus center, so the drivers didn't have financial motivation to run under on a route. I knew that if I could show the advantages of doing the route under the allowed time, I could start to change the attitude of the drivers.

One day I was riding with Tim and we'd completed the route under allowed and were heading back to the center. As we approached Carolina Beach, I said, "Let's stop by the pier and we'll shoot some pool."

"Man," he said, "we're on the clock."

"We've already done our job. Since you're not a bonus center, let's shoot some pool."

He thought that was nuts. But there was no issue with integrity or ethics. If you still had your lunch break left, there was no point in going back early. I was trying to plant a seed that if you be fair to me, I'm going to be fair to you.

That was the start. Less than a year later, I had brought in those three least-best drivers. I think I also helped to make a change in that center. Once I'd done what I'd said I was going to do, Kevin stayed true to his word and got me into sales. I was tickled to death. I was twenty-eight years old.

FedEx was our rival and UPS taught us: "Let's get them packages from the competitor." It was a very positive, competitive environment. You felt your worth.

I really wanted to get into sales because I've always loved the challenge of doing something where I can see results of what I do. I loved that feeling of getting a customer from FedEx—of earning the respect of the customer and demonstrating that UPS was a better fit for their business. The whole sales cycle amazed me as far as being able to actually win an account.

I love being in front of a customer. I love the interaction of learning their business. As UPS salespeople we had to develop the relationship, learn about the customer's business, ask a lot of good questions to bring out problems that they didn't even know they had, and then try to unseat the incumbent carrier. And also retain business. We didn't just hand out discounts but also provided value-adds to help our customers grow and create stickiness with them. I love asking questions. I love stimulating conversation. I love getting in people's heads. And I love traveling and getting to meet customers. I also loved that the UPS salespeople were the sharpest-dressed, had the shiniest shoes, and were the most polished in their speech and demeanor.

Going into sales was actually a lateral move as far as rank, but I got paid more and it was the path upward for me. I was excited to begin.

One of my first sales meetings took place in 1992 at the Omni Hotel in Durham, North Carolina. That was a day I will never forget, because it's where Transportation Impact began.

I didn't know anyone. Standing at the hotel reception checking in, I turned my head and saw a guy walking down the steps who looked like a million bucks. I recognized him instantly as Travis Burt, who I'd heard about, so I went up and introduced myself. We chatted for a few moments and then went on our separate ways.

Later on that evening, I found Travis again and asked if he'd like to get dinner or drinks and talk sales.

"I can't tonight," he replied. "I'm supposed to call my family at a certain time."

I thought that was really cool, that instead of going out and having drinks, he wanted to talk to his family. From that moment Travis and I hit it off.

Travis was in Greenville, while I was still in Jacksonville, so at first we didn't have a lot of contact. When I could, I picked his brain to learn how to succeed in sales, and I also started picking the brains of all the best salespeople around me.

Not long after that conference, I had to go to account executive school in Atlanta to learn how to pitch UPS. It was a three-week program. By the time you graduated, you had to memorize the entire pitch deck, which is how sales was back then. Well, I had it memorized before I went to school. During the first three days, if you wanted to take a run at it, the instructor would let you, so of course I said I wanted to, and I was the first in the class to do it.

The UPS sales school was excellent. It was the first school I'd been to at UPS that was so structured. The amount we were expected to memorize and know was almost overwhelming. It was a different skill set for me. I knew I wanted to do it, but it was really a lot to learn. UPS over the years changed how they teach their salespeople. Back then it was about doing more talking than listening.

When I got back I was assigned to the East Carolina district, which was the eastern half of North Carolina, roughly from Raleigh to the coast. The district included operations, sales, and everything else. There were about fifteen of us salespeople, including Travis, who was now my peer. I dived headfirst into selling. I loved sales so much; I lived and breathed it. Before long, I was the top salesperson in our squad, and then in 1994, I got the kind of recognition I loved best.

There are two kinds of recognition. People like to get either money or a trophy. I am a trophy guy. Believe me, I love when the money is good, but a trophy is public acknowledgement that you can display for everyone to see.

UPS had come up with a new product called Prepaid Next Day Air letters. If a company shipped a lot of Next Day Air letters and they knew they were going to need them, they could lock in a price of seven dollars and buy five thousand to effectively prevent rate increases in the future. The shipper liked it because prices were always going up and they could count on this one thing being a consistent budget item, and UPS liked it because we were getting the capital up front. That year I was the top salesperson in the whole nation in selling that product.

For that, I got a trophy.

Bigwigs from corporate flew in from Atlanta. In front of the bigwigs and the whole East Carolina district, my boss, Denise Nichols, presented me with a plaque inscribed with my name and "First Nationwide." I was so proud. There in little Eastern North Carolina, which is probably the smallest district in the country, I was best in the whole United States. Better than Chicago, Sacramento, Houston, everybody.

The next year, corporate HQ asked for somebody out of East Carolina to go to Atlanta for six months on special assignment, and I was picked to go. Each week, I would fly into Atlanta on Sunday, come back Thursday, and have Friday off with my family for a long weekend.

The assignment was a service recovery initiative that UPS wanted to draw up. Service recovery is when you do what is necessary to retain a customer who has had a bad experience. It goes beyond simply "making the customer whole" in terms of what they paid to UPS for the delivery. For example, a customer could call the 1-800 number and complain: "The UPS overnight letter was a day late, which cost me on my house closing, and that cost me eight hundred dollars in attorney's fees."

In other words, there was a consequence to the package being late that led to another and much more serious service disconnect. Back then, UPS would tell that customer, "We're going to refund you the thirty dollars for the late package, but we can't help you on whatever subsequent costs that late delivery led to." A customer who has had a bad experience like that is going to tell everyone.

Our job was to come up with a plan to empower the frontline people to make that customer whole, so when that customer gets off the phone, they're satisfied and not telling seven other people how bad we are.

There were six or seven of us on the team in Atlanta. The leader was a big wheel at corporate called Chet Moore. The rest of us were from all over the United States. For around six months we worked on that project and came up with a plan that we introduced to the Management Committee at corporate and eventually got approved. Then we went on the road and beta tested it. We went to all the big UPS facilities, like Chicago and Philadelphia, and worked with them to implement the plan. It was a big hit, and I was proud to have been a part of it.

But though we'd successfully done what we'd been assigned to do, the assignment was not over. Chet called East Carolina and told Denise that corporate wanted to keep me another six months because the thing was really going well. She more or less said, "I'm happy to hear you want to keep him, but we need him back here. We're going promote him to area manager." So my being sent to corporate for the special assignment had been like a grooming step.

Chet called me into his office and told me what Denise had said. I couldn't believe I had only been in sales four years and already I was being promoted. I called and told my wife. I told my kids. I was so happy. After seven months on special assignment I was on my way home and I was going to be promoted.

Back in Jacksonville I got endless congratulations and high-fives. A week later, Denise asked me to come and see her. It was the first time I'd ever been into a district sales manager's office, and I could barely contain my excitement. I was dressed sharply. Denise invited me to sit on one of the two chairs in front of her huge desk.

"I'm sorry I brought you back," she said. "Things have changed. You're at the top of the list, but the promotion is going to Gregg Spence."

Between the time she talked to Chet and the time I got back, there had been some conversations and all of a sudden Gregg, who was my peer when I left for Atlanta, was being given the promotion I'd been told I was getting.

I sat in that chair feeling like all the air had gone out of a balloon. I didn't know what had happened. I'd already told my family. And going from account executive to area manager would have meant a big raise. Everybody told me to hang in there, but I was just sick about it. It was all political. What's funny is Greg eventually came to work for me at Transportation Impact. But that was later.

For the next four years, nobody else got promoted. I was still out there doing my job, still leading in sales amongst my peers, but a splinter had been placed under my skin that was to irritate me for the next twenty years.

# 4

## SURF'S UP

When I got into sales, I began sending two hundred dollars each month to Mamaw Wiley. It wasn't a lot of money, but it was enough so she could go get her hair and nails done, and other treats she never gave herself. I didn't tell anyone, not even Syndie. I wanted to do something to take care of Mamaw, because she had taken such good care of me and given me so much when she had so little. One time when Syndie and I were first married, the battery on my car went bad and Mamaw bought me a new one. When I got fired from the Highway Patrol, my aunts and my mom would tell me that Mamaw would spend hours lying on her back in the bed praying that I would find a job, because I was depressed and she was worried about me. She always believed in me. Now, I did what I could for her and for Papaw and Mamaw Byrd. Every time I went to High Point, I would buy a bunch of groceries for both households, filling the car full of staple goods that they could use until the next time I came.

Right before I went to the special assignment in Atlanta, Syndie and I moved to Emerald Isle. Syndie wanted to be close to work, and I loved the area too. Her company was marketing a new development called Dolphin Ridge, so we bought a lot for seventy thousand dollars, which was a lot of money then, and built on it. It was a move of only about ten miles, but it put Brian and Tyler in a new school district. I didn't have any worries about them, though. Both of my boys are very outgoing and likeable people, so I knew they wouldn't have a problem making new friends, and they quickly settled in. My grandparents loved the beach, so we had them to stay as much as we could. It was a special gift for the boys to have that time with their great-grandparents.

They enjoyed going to stay with Mamaw Wiley and her second husband, who we called "Dub." He was a kind, calm, and generous person. When we visited for holidays, Mamaw always prepared big homecooked meals of traditional southern food like yams and mac 'n' cheese. She and Dub had a beach camper near Bogue Inlet Pier in Emerald Isle, and when he was young Brian occasionally slept over on summer nights. He had a bicycle stored at the camper, and Dub always had a can of WD-40 to lubricate the chain before Brian set out to explore the area. Brian was one of the last to spend time with Mamaw Wiley. One afternoon he was in the High Point area and stopped by to see her. They sat on her couch and looked at old photo albums together, reminiscing about the good ole times. Looking at a picture, she told him about the people in it, where it was taken, what the occasion was. He cherishes that afternoon. Being older and more mature, he was able to appreciate her wisdom. Two days later she fell and never recovered in the hospital. She died on Valentine's Day, 2012.

Tyler was too young to really get to know Papaw Byrd, but Brian especially loved visiting and exploring in his toolshed and garage, where he kept everything from old tools to my old toys, and then roaming the small garden and climbing the apple trees. Most of the apples had holes from worms, but he had fun throwing them like baseballs. The two of them would often get in Papaw's old car to go sock shopping. Papaw would tell Brian about his time in the sock factory and the importance of a good pair of socks.

In July 1998 Papaw and Mamaw Byrd came to stay, and I took Papaw fishing. For a while, he had been showing signs of Alzheimer's. The fish weren't biting, and as I threw out his line for him I said a little prayer: "This might be the last time I get to take *my* Papaw Byrd fishing. Let him catch something good." The good Lord answered the prayer. Nobody was catching anything, and within ten minutes of casting out he caught a big old pompano that tickled him to death. That was the last time he fished.

He fought Alzheimer's for two years. It hit him quick. To see him go from being one of the smartest, most well-rounded people I've ever met, to that state, was humbling and eye-opening to what that disease can do. One minute I'd be talking to him normally, and then he'd start rambling about something that happened when he was fourteen years old. It was agony for everyone to watch the man of steel go to that place in his mind. Then it got to where he didn't even recognize me, and that really hurt. The guy I respected the most didn't even know who I was. It's an incredibly hard disease to go through and for family members to be around. It goes on and on, and then when you think they're coming out of it, they get worse again. Eventually they put him in a home. I vetted it and wasn't happy with it, so we brought him home. But then after a while we couldn't take care of him, so he went back. On May 19, 1999, he died.

Papaw Byrd helped raise me from a kid. He was my hero, a class-act guy. I couldn't tell, but my heart thinks that he was suffering. You just never know what's going on inside. It was a dreadful disease to see him go through, and I wouldn't wish that on anyone.

That Christmas we all missed him. It was like there was a hole in the family. But it was still Christmas. When the boys were small, I got really excited at Christmas. We didn't have money every year to get them a lot of presents, so the night before, Syndie and I would stay up late to place everything just right so it looked like they were getting more. It was all about the presentation. We got a kick out of seeing the boys' faces when they came down on Christmas morning and got that first look. Then we'd play all day with their new toys.

It was important to me to be a good dad. Every Saturday, the boys and I did chores together. I always had a list for them, usually of things to do around the yard and garage. I would hold them accountable, too. For example, if they had to wash the car, after they were done I would walk around the car and inspect the rims to make sure they had paid attention to detail. After that couple of hours of work, they were free to go enjoy the weekend. As they got older, we made sure they had summer jobs too. Syndie and I wanted to instill the same work ethic in them that we grew up with.

But my work ethic was also putting strain on our marriage. In sales with UPS, I was driven. I worked long hours, and I travelled a lot. It was hard on Syndie to be working full-time and also having to manage the boys without me. There were cracks in our relationship, but we were united in our commitment to our children.

I wanted to create some kind of investment for my boys. Emerald Isle was a beach resort town with a long, attractive shoreline, but many of the oceanfront lots couldn't be built on because beach erosion had taken off. I believed that one day beach renourishment would come, so I asked Syndie to find out who the landowners were of the lots that were deemed not buildable. "We'll offer them a few thousand," I told her.

"Keith, no way," she said. "There's no way I would do that." Even back then, oceanfront lots were going for two hundred thousand, if not more, and she didn't want Bluewater Real Estate associated with an offer of pennies on the dollar. Syndie was very conservative and would never want to offend somebody. I was always the one that took the chance. It was a good balance of power, which was really beneficial in our success.

I told her to give me the phone numbers and reached out to the people myself. "Look, you own something that's worthless. You're paying taxes on it. I'll give you three thousand for it." I called probably half a dozen. I came close on one but otherwise struck out, except for a couple who were tired of paying the taxes on their lot. They accepted my offer.

Brian and Tyler were young, but I really wanted them to take ownership of this project and start learning how to take care of something and turn it into a thing of value. I preached that we had to do our part in making the lot grow to where one day, when beach restoration did get voted in as I knew it would, the lot would be buildable. So, every fall, we planted beach grass on what little sand dunes there were. We also put up a sand fence diagonal to the shoreline so that when sand blew the fence would catch it, thereby creating a dune. We installed a sprinkler system, and on weekends my kids would go out and plant more beach grass, we'd put more fence up, and they got to watch the dune and the beachgrass grow and grow.

Eventually beach renourishment got voted in. Now my boys were sitting on a goldmine. As soon as the lot got deemed buildable by the town of Emerald Isle, we went to the bank, borrowed three hundred and fifty thousand, and built a house on it. In 2021, Tyler and Brian sold that house for close to 1.5 million dollars. But it was more about teaching them how to have vision and hope, and how to take care of something, put love on it, and it'll flourish. It was a great life lesson.

I was always looking for ways to be a leader and support my boys in whatever they did. Many times I volunteered to coach their sports teams, showing up to after-work midweek practices dressed to the nines. Brian played the same positions I did: catcher for baseball and running back and linebacker for football, and like me he was really a defensive specialist.

In Tyler's mid-teens his recreation league basketball team didn't have a coach one year, so I volunteered. Brian and Tyler teased me when I bought some beginner basketball books online, studied them, and drew up a few plays. One of the boys on the team was mentally challenged and Tyler was determined to give him the chance to score his first basket. Again and again in one game Tyler boxed out for him, fighting for the ball against the other team and passing it to that boy. He was going crazy out there. In one two-minute period he must have given that boy the ball probably six times. Finally, it happened. The boy shot and scored the first basket of his life. The gym exploded with cheers. After the game, I cried, thinking about Tyler making all that effort to help his teammate experience that achievement and joy.

But when we moved to the beach, the boys discovered surfing. Once they got the taste of riding the waves, that was all they wanted to do. They were always trying to improve their technique, so I would stand on the beach with a video camera set up on a tripod, pressing it on and off as they caught waves. I had to pay attention to the lineup and see when they were about to take off so I didn't miss any part of it that could help them improve. Then back at the house we dissected the fine points of their technique. I'd never really surfed, but I would tell them how to do it. Sometimes we overlaid music and made their own personal cool surf videos.

They improved quickly. After a couple of years Brian started competing, and then Tyler did too, and as a family we started travelling up and down the East Coast to contests. One of the biggest was the annual East Coast Surfing Championships in Virginia Beach. For that we would get a hotel or condo right on the boardwalk and walk down to the First Street jetty to be in on all the action.

The year Brian competed in the fourteen-and-under Menehune Longboard competition, a hurricane was pulling in really good surf in Virginia Beach. Brian was the underdog by far, and he paddled way out, further than anybody else. One surfer after another came in closer, caught a wave, and rode it in. Brian was still sitting out there, all alone. I knew he was being strategic, sitting on the outside, but the minutes were ticking by. It felt like hours. Standing on the bleachers set up on the beach I yelled at him, "Come on, Brian! Come on in and get a wave!" Still he sat there, waiting for his wave.

Sure enough, a huge wave came, way out there, and he caught that thing just perfect. All of his competition was on the inside, and Brian sat on the outside being patient and strategic, and got his wave. The crowd went nuts at his performance.

At the awards ceremony they announced third place, and then second place. Then the announcer said the name of the four-teen-and-under East Coast Surfing Champion: "Brian Byrd!" We all high-fived and hugged each other. I cried. I was so proud of him. Brian walked up on the stage and they handed him a big trophy. It was just amazing.

As he got older, Tyler started catching up to Brian in skill and strategy, and in his mid-teens he won the biggest regional competi-tion, the Eastern Surfing Association's Mid-Atlantic Championship. That was a big deal. Now we had two champions in the family.

A lot of our family vacations were tailored to Tyler and Brian wanting to surf somewhere more tropical and exotic. Those trips took us to Costa Rica and Puerto Rico, and we often invited friends of the boys to join us.

One trip, when Brian was around fifteen and Tyler twelve, we went to Tamarindo, Costa Rica, with another group of people that surfed, including one adult. Early in the morning, the group set off in a small boat for Ollie's Point, deep in Santa Rosa National Park near the Nicaragua–Costa Rica border. It was a well-known surf spot in a remote location not accessible by vehicle. They took water and sandwiches with them because they planned to stay out all day.

That afternoon, as it got late and there was no sign of the boat, Syndie and I started worrying. The time wore on. Now we were panicking. All kinds of scenarios went through our minds—an ac-cident, pirates. . . . Tamarindo didn't have a Coast Guard, and we searched to find some authority that could give us information. At last we found someone who knew something. They told us the boat had capsized and the group was stuck out at Ollie's Point. There was a rescue operation in progress. In the darkness of night, our sons and their companions finally showed up, tired, hungry, and very thirsty. Syndie and I met them on the quay, hugging them tight and crying with relief.

The boys told us that as they reached the point, the captain got too close to the swell and a wave washed in, tipped the boat over, and flooded the engine. The surf break was right next to the mouth of a river that was full of crocodiles, and they were terrified! They got to shore without running into a croc, but it was still early in the morning and all of their sandwiches and gear were wet. All day they sat miserably cooking in the sun, waiting for the alarm to be raised so someone would come and rescue them.

That was not a great experience, but it was wonderful to be part of the boys' lives as they grew up, through coaching their sports teams and travelling together for surf trips, and some of their friends from those years have also become lifelong friends of mine. There were always people at the house and everybody wanted to spend the night with us, perhaps because Syndie and I were so young. As they got older, the boys started wanting to go to parties at their friends' houses. On this topic, Syndie was generally stricter than I was. My philosophy was that they were going to drink whether we knew about it or not, so let's allow them to do it under special circumstances, so we can at least know about it, and also build that trust with our kids.

One night the phone woke Syndie and me at one a.m. It was the local police. The house party Tyler had gone to had been busted and the police had him at the station. They wanted us to come and get him. We had been partying too, so I got a ride to the station, got Tyler, and then had the person drop us at the gate of our neighborhood. As I walked my son the two-tenths of a mile back to our house, I had a man-to-man conversation with him. "It's okay to do this shit," I told him, "but you got to have boundaries. You got to be smart about it." He listened, and he understood. He still remembers that walk and talk.

# 5

## THE BEGINNING OF THE END

In 2000 at UPS a new director of sales came in to replace Denise Nichols. He was called Mike DiNovi and he was a boisterous Mafioso-looking guy from Philly. I loved him.

Soon after he arrived, Mike requested to ride with me. We visited my largest account, a company called Overton's, and then made a couple of other calls. Mike watched me interact with all of them, and then sounded me out about a plan he had.

"I need to get somebody in Raleigh where the businesses is at and shine," he said. "I've decided on you and Travis."

Mike believed that the best salespeople should be put in the areas where they could bring in the most business. Travis and I got an apartment in Raleigh and commuted home on weekends. Suddenly, in this city full of businesses, I found myself in a candy store, and I kicked ass. But I only had two months to scoop up the candy before things changed again. Mike promoted me to area manager for eastern North Carolina. Four years after the promise, I got the promotion. Mike had only been there three months.

One of the first things I did was to arrange for Tim Brock to be moved from operations onto my team. Tim was the driver in

Wilmington I had brought in on the 340 Method, and I now trained him in sales. Our team had been together for about a year when Tim told me about a "superstar" operator who wanted to be in sales and asked if I could arrange for him to make the switch.

I called the "superstar," whose name was Berkley Stafford, and set up a meeting at Port City Chop House in Wilmington. As we sat in a booth with the bustle of the restaurant going on around us, I fired questions at him to assess his character and what he needed to get to started in sales. By agreeing to bring him from part-time operator to full-time salesperson, I had made a commitment not only to him, but also to UPS. My big question was "How is this going to work out?" Over our next meetings, usually in a hotel lobby, that question was answered as we both quickly recognized that we were very much alike. Berkley and I have the blood. We love the chase. We love the sale. We love the win.

Berkley started knocking on doors and made a few small waves that got my attention. Meanwhile, I was developing my creativity in helping companies ship via UPS for a lot less money than the company would have liked them to pay. As a sales manager my job was to win business for UPS, and I realized that the best way to do that was not to try to squeeze every cent out of the customer, but instead to be their partner. In the end, both sides won.

In 2001, Tim and I had the opportunity to help win what would be a huge account for UPS. It was a company out of Wilmington that at the time would have been the largest district account for not only the area that I serviced, but for the entire district, which stretched over the majority of the state of North Carolina. I put a lot of effort into building a case to try to win that business. And I got creative.

The company shipped a lot of documents and letters, and I came up with a tactic you couldn't do today because UPS now has limits on the weight of letters. Back in 2001, you could put anything you wanted in one of those cardboard, flat-rate UPS letter envelopes. As long as you could fold the flap over and it would close, you could ship it. I took one of those huge Sunday newspapers of the time and was able to cram it into a UPS cardboard envelope and close it. I presented that to the leadership of the company to show how they could cut a lot of their shipping cost by using flat-rate envelopes, and that was a key factor in winning my team the largest account for East Carolina district at the time.

That was a massive account for our region, our center, and our group. The company had over ten locations around the country and more internationally, and I had to put a team together to work with them to implement the switch from FedEx to UPS. I needed people I could count on. I thought about Berkley. It was a big risk to take a junior salesperson and suddenly put them in a position to help implement one of the largest accounts that our region had ever won, but my sense of him told me he could contribute in a positive way. I decided to give him a shot.

I had to travel to the company's U.S. locations to train their employees on how to transition from FedEx software to UPS software. It was crucial that the implementation go well, so with the help of some colleagues, I built an elaborate plan that also involved Berkley traveling. At UPS it was unheard of for an area sales manager like me to travel. It was unimagined that a junior salesperson would travel.

We were getting underway with the implementation, when one day my phone rang. It was Berkley. A UPS higher-up had questioned why he, a junior salesperson, was traveling. "I'll do anything you want me to do," he told me. "Tell me how you want me to handle it." I heard the panic in his voice. We bled UPS Brown. We were company men. Berkley was just starting his career and he saw it all disappearing before his eyes. I had to reassure him so he could keep working, and I also knew this was my responsibility to handle. I was the one who had put him in this position.

"Don't worry about it," I told him. "I'll go into a sword fight with a butter knife for you."

I'm a company man, but my people come first.

There were signs now that UPS was stepping up their game. Not only in the philosophy and the strategy of selling, but also in the caliber of the salespeople. They weren't taking people from operations any more. Now UPS was hiring people off the street who were polished and experienced in sales and had college degrees. In so many ways in my time at UPS, I was blessed with the luck to be the right person in the right place, at the right time. By the 2000s, a Keith Byrd, who's an on-car operations supervisor and good at holding people accountable, would have had no chance at getting into sales.

They also started coming down hard on those of us who had come from operations into sales. Anybody who was in sales, they wanted to have a degree, so the company paid for us to take courses at an online university called LaSalle (important note: not to be confused with the two other legitimate and highly regarded La Salles), and our managers pushed us into doing the degree program. UPS had vetted the school, and the company paid for the program.

The degree program was a joke. It was basically pay to play. The school would even take your work experience and add it to your credits. It was so easy, I took a week of vacation, took all the tests and everything else they required, and came back to work with a four-year degree. Later, I saw a report about an online university that had been busted for not being accredited and being a sham. It was LaSalle. So my degree is worthless, but it allowed me to keep working in sales at UPS.

After Mike DiNovi promoted me to area manager, Travis also moved back to Greenville to work for me, and over the next few years, a fantastic team formed. Travis, Chris Burns, Tim Brock,

Neal Newhouse, Mike Fross, Gregg Spence, who ironically had moved laterally from area manager to another role in sales, and Berkley. At UPS, we always led everything. Through working together day after day for years we became really close, and even more important, I knew everyone's skillset. Eventually, I recruited every single one of them to join us at TI.

As an area manager, I was officially in business development, and I was responsible for making sure all the accounts under my charge stayed compliant—their profitability, shipping trends, and other metrics had to stay within the range stipulated by our agreement with that company. This brought me into occasional close contact with John Howard, a supervisor in the finance department who was responsible for monitoring compliance. Every now and then my phone would ring and it would be John on the other end to tell me that one of my clients had dropped significantly in revenue and therefore the margin was negative. To bring them back into compliance, John always wanted to either increase their rates or find a way to pull costs out of servicing that client.

We were on opposite sides of the fence so our relationship was adversarial, but I quickly developed a lot of respect for John. I learned that he always talked straight. I was on the coast, the only area sales manager not in Raleigh, so John became my inside guy that I trusted. You hear scuttlebutt in the field. I could pick up the phone and call him and he would tell me what was going on.

After a while in finance John moved to the regional business development team, and our relationship did a one-eighty. From being adversarial, we were now working very closely together. At least once a week, I drove in from the coast to Raleigh and we met face to face. We also had continual conversations about my accounts and about various dynamics within the business development function. We had a lot of coordinated conversations on how we could make my team better and able to more easily achieve objectives and goals. We worked truly side by side. John would help me make a business case, whether I was selling to a customer or internally. We developed a deep trust and camaraderie that later came to play a pivotal—I would say a crucial—role in the success of Transportation Impact.

Around that time, UPS came out with a different way of selling. From all-talk, no-listen, they flipped completely to a strategy that was all about asking questions, stimulating conversation, and listening to skillfully uncover problems. It was based on the book *SPIN Selling*, by Neil Rackham, which is a great book. The acronym SPIN stands for Situation questions, Problem questions, Implication questions, and Need-payoff questions. It's a philosophy that teaches you how to ask open-ended questions to create conversation that will lead to a customer realizing they do have a problem and they need you to help solve it. This system taught people how to improve or hone their sales and negotiation skills.

Every year, we had to do a SPIN assessment. It was hard. You really had to know the SPIN method. It was one thing that I was very good at, and of the whole sales team, I would do the best. My team also scored the highest each time because I was able to break down SPIN and teach it to them in such a way that they could understand it. We dissected each letter of the acronym on a whiteboard, and then we role played until each person understood the purpose of each part of the acronym. SPIN doesn't sound hard, but it requires a different way of thinking.

The other thing that changed at this time, yet again, was my relationship with John Howard. Now it became even more adversarial than it was in the beginning because John moved to the revenue management group. He was responsible for giving the discounts that we wanted to get for our customers, and so we had to present our business case to him. As long as you came prepared with a solid business case, then the conversation would proceed fairly well. Otherwise you'd hear, "Keith, we got to do this to your customer or you can't have those discounts. You're not going to get that. You've got to sell value." It was always very respectful. John is best defined as a strategic thinker who's a problem solver. He was a good, solid thinker and always gave me a good, solid response.

At least the meetings with John were purposeful and productive. It was different in the rest of the company. Now it was all about conference calls and meetings on what you're going to do differently, why you're not making your numbers. We would find ourselves having a conference call to get ready for a conference call to get ready for another conference call. It was stupid. Here was our competitor, FedEx, actually getting their people out on the street in front of the customer, while we were bogged down in meeting after meeting and conference call after conference call to explain why we weren't making our numbers—instead of being out in front of the customer to try to make our numbers!

I was a leader, so I had to manage how I thought and communicated and demonstrated myself. I was setting the example. But the way the organization was changing was getting ridiculous, and I was really getting perturbed.

One day I was in a meeting with two other area managers, Jan McVeigh and Darryl Smith, and our boss Chris Adkins. Chris was a sharp guy who had replaced Mike DiNovi a couple of years earlier when Mike went to Boston. There were some department heads there too, and we were meeting with the district manager, George Willis. Now, at UPS, the district manager is like God. The district manager is over all of operations, all of sales, and all of the other functions for an entire district. There were only about fifty in the whole U.S. To say an area manager is not even allowed to look at a district manager—let alone talk to him or her—is facetious, but it's also almost true.

We were sitting around that table, and I'd had it up to here. The year before, my team had been the best in the country, and this year we were not doing well. At UPS, when you had a really good year, they would stack your plan for the next year. Our plan had been stacked so high, there was no way we could make those numbers. They were unachievable goals.

There were about ten people at the table, and most of them were my superiors several layers above me. Each person in turn was talking about their results and why they were good or not good. It came around to me, and I looked right at the district manager.

"Look," I said, "I can't ask my people to do what I can't do."

I explained that the numbers we were being asked to make were impossible. I wasn't being disrespectful, but I was making an excuse, which nobody did at UPS. It was a legitimate excuse, and I believed in that because I didn't want George Willis to think my people were bad. Plus I knew I was in the right because we were still way over last year's numbers. At UPS you always go to a problem with a solution, so I told him my proposed solution. If they wanted to fire me or push me out, I was willing to accept that because I knew I was doing the right thing.

You could have heard a pin drop. George Willis stared at me. He was a former Marine, like me. It was all he could do to keep from coming across the table and beating my ass, but he held his cool.

Afterwards Chris Adkins came up to me in the bathroom and said, "God, I love you. You handled that perfect." Chris understood. You can't assign a task that's virtually impossible from a numbers perspective. Not to mention, here we were in yet another meeting defending our numbers, when we could have been out on the streets taking business away from FedEx.

Word got out immediately that Keith went nuts and he was probably going to get fired. I didn't get fired, but the splinter that had lodged under my skin in 1996 when I didn't get the promotion I had been promised now had a few other splinters for company, and the irritation was growing. I didn't know yet what my next step would be, that would give me both freedom and success, but somewhere in my mind a break had been made.

Around 2005 Tim Brock came across an opportunity to win a mul-timillion-dollar account from FedEx in Wilmington, just down the coast from us. The company was called United Care Pharmacy, and they sold Viagra, diet pills, and sleeping pills online, somehow doing it halfway legally by running everything through a server in Costa Rica, but shipping throughout the U.S. This was an opportunity even bigger than the one I'd got in trouble for having Berkley travel to implement, because it was all Next Day and Second Day Air. Air products are premium products; they bring in more revenue. UPS back then was still mainly a ground company, so it was a big deal to win an account that used mostly premium services. Tim and I worked hard and convinced the company to switch their local business from FedEx to UPS.

Then we found out there was an opportunity to pick up a lot more volume from UCP's other locations, which were still using FedEx. Normally the credit for an account goes to the local UPS district, but I got creative and set it up so that the accounts in other parts of the country all tied back to an East Carolina district account. For example, the UCP office in Dallas was shipping out of Dallas, but Dallas wasn't getting any credit. In my mind, we won the business, so we deserved to get the credit.

The CEO of United Care Pharmacy, Tom Russo, asked Tim and me to fly to Costa Rica to talk to some of his vendors and explain the value that UPS brought. He implied that if we went, there was a chance to win two hundred more premium-service packages a day. This kind of travel was unthinkable for an area sales manager and a sales rep, but blinded by the flashing dollar signs, UPS agreed to let us go.

A rusty old Isuzu Trooper driven by armed guards picked us up at the airport and took us to a restaurant that was closed to regular customers. Tom was making three hundred grand a week selling Viagra and diet pills, but as we seated ourselves in the empty restaurant, he made it clear this dinner was going on my expense account. He started off by ordering a five hundred dollar bottle of wine. *How am I going to explain this to UPS?* I thought. UPS was notoriously restrictive when it came to wining and dining customers. In fact, forget wining and dining. Getting a pizza or a few donuts was sometimes an issue. Not to mention, Tim and I didn't even drink wine, normally.

The night went on, we had a good time, and the hundreds of dollars piled up on the bill, but Tom assured us we would get the extra business because we had made the effort to come down to Costa Rica.

I was fascinated by his business model. At that time I didn't know it was illegal. It seemed everything was legit, because FedEx had already been servicing UCP. On the way back in the plane I asked him how he'd got involved in the business. He told me he'd gone from working as a floor guy at Home Depot to making three hundred thousand dollars a week. Enthralled by the success, I told him, "One day I'm going to strive to be like you and come up with a good business model."

He looked at me and said, "The only thing you need to do is to get creative and do something somebody else has not done."

Over the next days I thought about what Tom had said and came up with a plan. I called and told him I could get him an additional three or four percent as a rebate if we got the additional two hundred packages per day. He hadn't been expecting that. "I told you to get creative, and then you went back after I beat you up on rates and got this rebate," he said. A sudden understanding hit me. If I could save customers money and share in the savings, that would be a great business model.

Around this time, UPS changed the way they divided up the districts. We went from being the small district of East (North) Carolina, to all North Carolina and South Carolina being together one district, and we reported to the people in South Carolina. My boss, Chris Adkins, went laterally to corporate, so I had a new boss, and the management layers were even thicker because the district was now so big. The spirit of the company had changed a lot, and it seemed like every time you turned around, you wound yourself in more requirements and restrictions.

Travis and I for a long time had been close friends. In the years since that first meeting at the Omni Hotel in 1992, he had worked for me most of the time, and our families spent a lot of time together. He also was frustrated with the changes in the company's culture, with one in particular causing him to really question the way he had to work.

About a year and a half earlier, Travis had sought my advice about a change UPS had made that was almost a moral issue. Previously the sales reps had sent in their requests for customer pricing via email—maybe fill out a few spreadsheets, submit a few handwritten notes. That hodgepodge system was bogging down the pricing groups, who were overwhelmed, so UPS had moved to an online pricing platform. Now the reps could see the savings they could get for their customers, without having to go through the pricing groups.

Travis saw that he could save one of his customers twenty or thirty percent. But he was a newly commission-based salesperson—another change UPS had made. So if he saved UPS a bunch of money on that customer, he got paid better. The double-edged sword was that if he did the right thing for the customer, who he had developed a real relationship with, he was taking money out of his own pocket. Either he did the right thing by the customer, or he did the right thing by his employer and his family, or he found some middle ground, which only partially did the right thing by everybody. It disturbed him so much, he was losing sleep.

The first time he saw this issue, he called me and we discussed it extensively. I was his boss and I was also a commissioned salesperson, with my commission based on the sales of my team. So it also affected me to do the right thing. Then it happened a second time and a third time, and I remembered the idea that Tom Russo had sparked. It was something new in the industry and it would solve the problem of how to do the right thing by both our company and our customer—as well as ourselves and our families.

Travis and I were both goal-oriented, and he had wanted for a long time to go into business with me. Over the following months, we tossed around the idea, but without being really serious about it. Then a long-time customer of Travis's called to tell him they were switching to FedEx. Then it happened again. After it happened a third time, it hit hard that this work was no longer about relationships. It was about bottom-line dollars. We had reached the tipping point. It was time to take our destiny in our own hands.

We did such a good job of protecting the margins at UPS. What if we did the same thing, but took our skill set and knowledge and acted as a consultant for the customer? We would be doing the right thing by the customers and our own company—and through our company, our families. UPS would still make plenty of money, and we could create our future.

It was a great idea. We just knew it was going to work.

# 6

## WHITEBOARDING THE DREAM

I had a beach cottage in Emerald Isle, second row from the ocean, that I rented out as a vacation cottage in the high season, which runs typically from May to September. The cottage was called Simon Says. The offseason had just started, and I was living in Simon Says because our marital issues had reached the point that Syndie and I had separated.

The beach cottages in Emerald Isle are like upside-down versions of regular houses. On the bottom, opening out onto the pool area, is a recreation room. Above that, on the middle floor, are the bedrooms, and then on the top floor you've got the kitchen and living room, so you can see the ocean from the living spaces. In fall 2007, after we hit the tipping point, Travis and I adopted Simon Says as our brainstorming HQ. The off-season gave us seven or eight months when we could come and go as we pleased. Travis lived in Greenville, almost two hours away, so most weeks he arrived Friday night and slept the next two or three nights either with me or at the vacation-rental condo he owned.

I can't learn from a chalkboard, but to think anything out I have to write it down, and when there is more than one person, the best way to do that is on a whiteboard. Travis and I had a lot of thinking to do, so I bought a couple of whiteboards and stuck them up on the wall in the living room with yellow masking tape.

Saturdays and Sundays we covered those whiteboards with ideas. I couldn't talk fast enough with everything that I wanted to do for this company—the things I had learned from research and other companies' websites, and the thoughts that just popped into my head. We soon filled the first couple of whiteboards. We didn't want to erase any of it, so I kept buying more whiteboards and sticking them up on the walls in the kitchen and living room with yellow masking tape. Eventually most of the painted walls were covered with whiteboards, at least thirty-three of them. It was a good thing I owned the house. Later we had to repaint the interior before I could rent it out again.

That fall, winter and spring, we hashed out the business model, the challenges we were going to have, and how we were going to overcome the challenges. Throughout the weekend, fueled by Crown Royal, the enthusiasm would carry us into fervent optimism and belief, high-fiving each other and filled with excitement. Then Monday morning rolled around and we asked ourselves, "Are we nuts? We've got good-paying jobs. What are we thinking?" It was such a big move to leave a company that was giving you that kind of insurance, that kind of 401(k), that kind of stock options.

All this time, we continued to do exactly what UPS expected of us, what they were paying us for. It was not what we were passionate about anymore, but we honestly earned our salary, which at that time was around a hundred grand a year.

Travis and I were both goal-oriented and wanted to make more than we were making. For me, it went even deeper than that. Since I was young, I'd had the vision I was going to make a shitpot full of money one day. I knew one day I was going to do it. I just didn't know how.

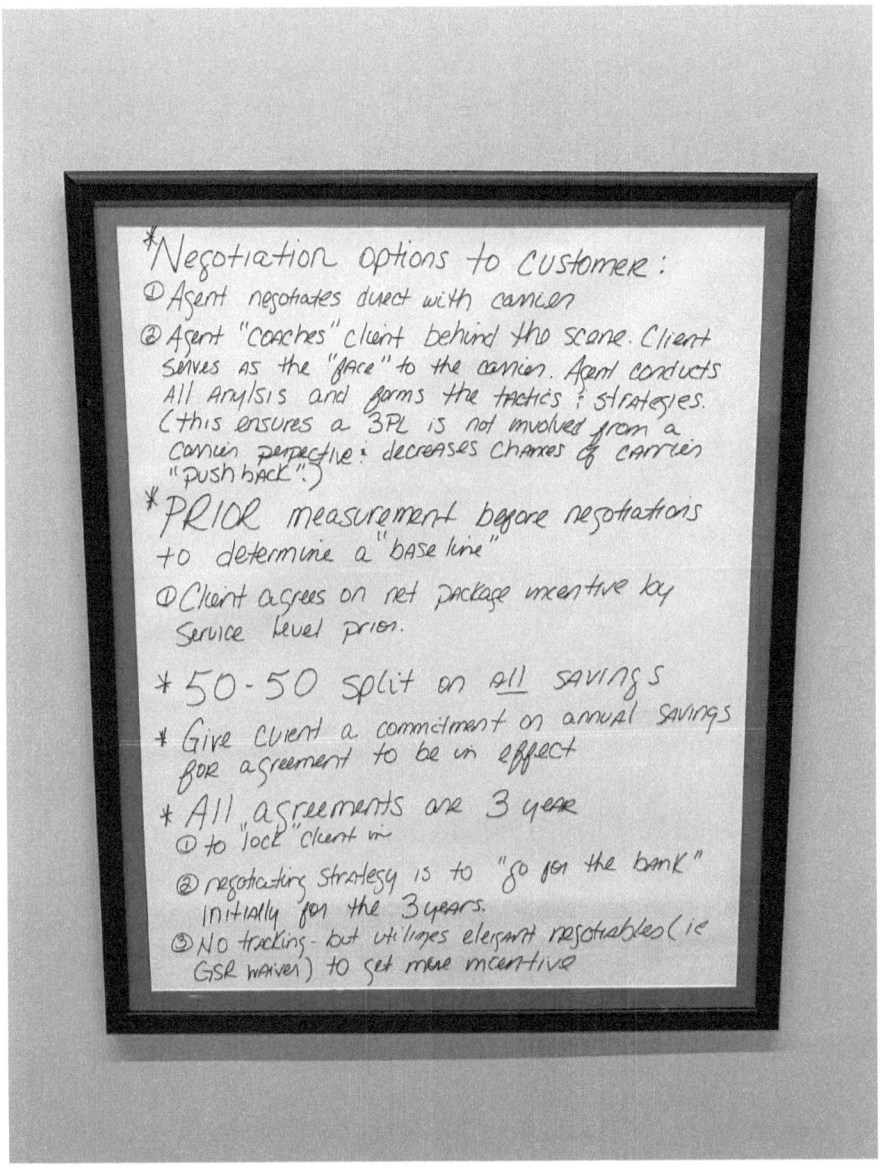

*Negotiation options to Customer:*

① Agent negotiates direct with carrier

② Agent "coaches" client behind the scene. Client serves as the "face" to the carrier. Agent conducts all analysis and forms the tactics & strategies. (this ensures a 3PL is not involved from a carrier perspective & decreases chances of carrier "push back".)

* PRIOR measurement before negotiations to determine a "base line"

① Client agrees on net package incentive by service level prior.

* 50-50 split on all savings

* Give client a commitment on annual savings for agreement to be in effect

* All agreements are 3 year
① to "lock" client in
② negotiating strategy is to "go for the bank" initially for the 3 years.
③ No tracking - but utilizes elegant negotiables (ie GSR waiver) to get more incentive

*The whiteboard that shows two of the key elements of our business plan that made TI so successful: 50-50 split on the negotiated savings, and locking the client into a three-year agreement.*

What I loved about Travis and I going into business was that we could make whatever we wanted. We knew the sky was the limit because the customers were there. Ecommerce was just coming to fruition. I would not have been satisfied at UPS even if things had been glorious, because getting passed up on that promotion after they brought me back from Atlanta put a bad taste in my mouth and demotivated me. UPS is a great company with great benefits. They were known for being a company where you could go as far up as you wanted to go as long as you had the work ethic. You didn't have to have a college education back then. But I could see that UPS was changing when the company went public. You had to make the numbers. You were no longer a person. Instead of being about working hard and earning a position, it was about politics and numbers.

In late spring 2008, we stood in the living room at Simon Says and gazed at the whiteboards all around us. We were pretty sure we had it all figured out. We had drilled down to everything. What bad could come out of it? What good could come out of it? What would be the consequences? How would we handle it? We were confident we had thought of every possible challenge or negative and countered it with a solution or changed the business model to avoid it.

For one last sense check, we decided to run our idea by a customer who could use our services. Early in my sales career at UPS a skateboard distributer in Wilmington called Eastern Skateboard Supply became my customer. ESS was founded in 1985 by professional freestyle skateboarder Reggie Barnes, who had sharp business sense. When I was his rep, his company was really growing.

I called Reggie and asked if he'd meet us for lunch. He chose one of his favorite places, a sushi bar called the Bento Box. Travis and I both hated sushi. Now we both love it! But we only ate it that day because we had great respect for Reggie as a businessperson and a great relationship with him, and we knew that if he saw the value in our idea, then that was the last confirmation we needed. We were candid with him. Reggie negotiated all of Eastern Skateboard Supply's agreements with UPS, and when we had finished explaining our business model, he called it a "no-brainer," a term that we later used liberally in our marketing and sales materials.

Reggie also said that yes, he would be our first customer. That was the last shot of confidence to finally kick ourselves over the finish line and say, "Let's do this."

At some point in late May, I got so fed up with the way UPS was going that Travis and I decided it was time. We were going to do it. We were going to quit UPS and launch the dream that was laid out in black ink on those whiteboards. I would go first.

But first, we went to Travis's dad's house. Travis's dad is a life-long entrepreneur and savvy businessman. He and I are a lot alike in that we get out of bed every morning wondering how we're going to put food on the table. Every day we are thinking how to improve our life. No backward steps, ever.

We told him our plan, and he got so excited he was running sideways around the kitchen. We explained to him all the things we were going to do. How the idea was a no-brainer from a financial perspective for our potential clients. We explained our business model. We do a free analysis of the customer's small parcel spend, with no commitment. Then we come back to the customer and say one of two things: Either we can save you money or we can't. And if we can, then we get paid from the savings we generate. We planned a three-year, fifty-fifty deal with clients. We lock them in for three years, and each year we split fifty-fifty the savings on their UPS or FedEx spend that we have helped them negotiate. The savings is found money for them—it's money they wouldn't have gotten without our knowledge and assistance—so we figured that any C-level executive would be smart enough to see the value in splitting that with us. The three-year agreement gave us guaranteed income and allowed us to squeeze every drop of savings we could from the client's small parcel agreement over that time.

When we had finished explaining, Travis's dad asked us one question. Only one.

"What are you going to do at the end of three years?"

Travis and I looked at each other, and then back at him. We had thought hard about this question during our whiteboarding sessions, but we didn't have a clear answer for him. We knew it was a problem, and we would have three years after signing the first customers to figure out the solution. But still, him asking that question at that moment was like popping a balloon. For a hundred and eighty straight minutes in that kitchen we had slathered all over him, and he zeroed in on the one key point we were still unsure about. Dream crusher!

But it didn't change our decision.

I thought I was doing a great job of not showing that I was thinking of leaving the company, but later one of the guys who had been on my team and under my mentorship said that, looking back, he could see the signs. He had worked for another company before coming to UPS, so he had perspective—he knew there were great business and career prospects outside of the Brown. He said that in the last couple weeks before I quit, I went really quiet. At one point in that time we had lunch and I was supposed to ride with him, but I said, "I got something. I got to go. I'll talk to you later." He thought I was going to go work for somebody else.

But as far as I knew, no one outside of our families had any clue. There were a few UPS people I trusted, and John Howard was one of the first ones I told.

Every year, a whole lot of hairdressers descended on Myrtle Beach, South Carolina, for a convention. Of course, most hairdressers then were women, so for a bunch of us at UPS it was a great joke to make a "boys trip" to Myrtle Beach that weekend. This was the weekend, and eight or ten of us headed south for our annual boys trip to play golf and have a break. The group from UPS included

Travis, me, John, and Neal Newhouse, and my old high school buddy Dennis Rebert also came along.

At some point on the Saturday I got John in a quiet spot and told him what Travis and I were planning. I wanted him to come with us. We could really have used his operational and financial skill, not to mention his overall steadiness and organizational talent. But John was and still is very risk averse. What we were doing was too big of a jump for him.

Two days later, Monday morning, June 9, 2008, I stood at the countertop in our kitchen, picked up my UPS-issued cell phone, and called my boss, Sophia Shoate. I told her I was resigning because I wanted to go a different way. I did not discuss what I was going to do. She was obviously shocked. When I hung up the phone, excitement filled me.

To celebrate, Travis and I took our families to lunch at a hole-in-the-wall restaurant in Emerald Isle called ChowdaHeads, which obviously was known for its chowder. We were in a great mood, although our wives were naturally worried about the future. I don't think either of our families had believed we were that serious, because let's face it—we had a vision of what we wanted to do, but Travis and I both were scared to leave UPS. Mentally and emotionally I had been back and forth, back and forth. But this time, I was forth, and I knew it was forever.

At the end of lunch, Travis's wife, Cass, said to me, "You motherfucker. This better work. You hear me?"

"It's going to work. You just got to be patient with us."

"If it doesn't, we're moving in with you!"

Overall, though, Travis's family had been supportive from the beginning, even with him spending all those weekends away while we drilled down to every detail of the business model. That must have been hard for Cass.

A few days later, I woke up on my good buddy Neal Newhouse's couch to a phone call from Sophia Shoat's boss, Rich McArdle, the well-respected district manager. Rich more or less said to me, "You better not do what you think you're going to do." I managed my information skillfully and listened more than I talked. "Yes, sir. No, sir," I said, but didn't commit to anything.

From what Rich said, I figured out they must have gone through my laptop. As good as I do some things, in this case I was stupid. During those months that Travis and I were drilling down to all the details, I had a graphics guy design a logo for us, and that logo was on my UPS laptop. I had also downloaded customer information to a thumb drive.

Rich's call was just the beginning of the unpleasant consequences. When I left UPS, it was like I had cooties. They put the word out that Keith Byrd was going to start a company to harm UPS and take away its margins, and people I had known and worked closely with for years suddenly wanted nothing to do with me. Even people I considered good friends. The culture of UPS is cultlike. It's not quite brainwashing, but it's close, in a good way. "Bleed Brown" isn't just a catchphrase; it's how UPSers actually feel about their relationship with the company.

UPS knows how to develop a businessperson, period. From A to Z. But everybody is scared to leave because of the security. It's a great job. You've got some of the best entrepreneurial minds in the world working for UPS right now. Bravo to UPS for building that culture. Their retention rate is high because they sell you on the fact that you're working for the best company in the world. It really takes a lot to leave UPS, and when someone does leave to start their own business, people shake their heads and call them crazy.

Syndie and I were back together, but there was tension because she was a real estate agent, and in mid-2008 real estate was in full crisis. Not long before I quit UPS, we had paid seven hundred thousand for our lot in Emerald Isle. We couldn't afford it. But land in 2007 was going nuts. People were making hand-over-fist money on real estate. Soon after I quit, that lot was not even worth two hundred thousand.

I spent the next few weeks planning an execution path to attack certain of my UPS customers, with Eastern Skateboard Supply at the top of the list. Travis still wasn't ready to make the leap, but I knew he was close.

Late one afternoon, right before Fourth of July weekend, Travis called to tell me he'd done it. He'd quit. He said that morning he'd woken up and thought, "Today's the day."

Travis has always had very strong faith, and he had been praying to know what was right. He called his manager and told him he was quitting and wanted to leave on peaceful terms, and then he asked where he could meet to turn in his UPS-provided credit card, cell phone, and laptop. The call went dead, and thirty minutes later his UPS credit card wouldn't work at a gas station. His manager couldn't reach him on the cell phone that the company had cut off. Then he logged into the UPS network on his laptop and got what's called a blue screen. They basically fry your laptop because it no longer means anything to them. They'll fix it later.

UPS doesn't care who you are. Once you quit they're not going to keep you around. We were both more than willing to make a transition, but we knew UPS wouldn't go for that. Once you quit, they want your shit right now, that day. There's no such thing as a two-week notice at UPS.

Knowing this, Travis wanted to take his leave of some of his best customers, so he made a couple of his scheduled visits to say thanks for treating him so well. Then around 4 p.m. he went to the Rocky Mount building, which was what the UPS building was called.

This is how Travis loves to tell the next part of the story:

A supervisor from the security department was walking up and down the catwalk at the UPS building, saying, "I don't know where the hell he is. We cut off his damn phone. How the hell am I supposed to find him?"

I said, "Hey, I'm here."

"I got him!" he said, and then turned to me. "I didn't ever think it'd be this peaceful."

"When you decide to go," I said, "you're gone. And I had a calm come over me this morning. Today was the day. And so I chose to drive my equipment here to Rocky Mount."

And it really was that simple.

Now Transportation Impact could begin.

But we were far from through the fallout. Rich McArdle had made allusions that I had taken a lot more information than just some customer details. Then after Travis quit, UPS put the word out internally that we had taken data that could have included employee information and social security numbers. Nothing could have been further from the truth. But that black eye stuck. And UPS didn't just spread that misinformation to a hundred people, they spread it to eight thousand people, and they did it in three days. It was like they had the direction from corporate for the whole district to paint us as the bad guys. We couldn't get anybody to talk to us. Which, looking back, is really funny, because beginning in about 2013, everybody we knew who left UPS or retired wanted a job with us.

But that was later. Travis's best friend at the time, who was also the godfather to his children, was a UPS driver. For twenty-five or thirty years he and Travis had the closest friendship possible be-tween two grown men. After the company's misinformation cam-paign, this man refused to talk to Travis for months and months.

UPS poisoned people against us, and the company culture is so strong that even the closest friends did not give us the benefit of the doubt. It hurt our feelings. But we had a lot more to worry about than hurt feelings and lost friendships.

Saturday, July 5, Fourth of July weekend, I was lying in bed when I heard the doorbell ring. I got up, walked to the front door, and saw a cardboard UPS Express Delivery envelope lying on the mat. I picked it up and tore it open. Inside was a single sheet of paper. I slid it out. "Alston & Bird LLP" was on the letterhead. I read it, and then went back to my room, put on a pair of slip-on shorts, came back, slid my feet into flip flops, and walked next door.

My next-door-neighbor was an attorney on the real estate side for Ward & Smith, a legal practice with an office in nearby New Bern. After reading the letter, I understood enough to know that I needed a professional opinion. I knocked on my neighbor's door. He invited me in, and I handed him the letter. He was a real serious guy, and he read the letter without changing expression.

"Do we have something to worry about?" I asked.

"Yeah," he said. "Yeah, you have something to worry about."

My heart dropped.

Without cracking a smile, he said, "You need to contact my office Monday and I can get you to a guy."

# 7

## JOUSTING WITH THE BIG BROWN BULLY

UPS, one of the largest corporations in the world, was threatening to sue Transportation Impact, a company that barely existed beyond a name on a legal document.

They sent the letter UPS overnight Saturday air delivery. Our lawyers told us they purposely did that to ruin our Fourth of July weekend, and they did exactly what they intended to do. That Saturday was a bad day. We figured there would be some kind of blowback, but nothing like this. That letter scared me to death.

After talking a bit more with my neighbor, I walked back to my own house and picked up the phone to call Travis. He and his wife and teenage kids were at his parents' lake house for the holiday weekend. When I called, everybody was out in the boat with no cell signal. I left a message, and over the next few hours I left a few more messages.

I was so nervous. I knew UPS was a big company that had a lot of money. While waiting for Travis to call me back, in my mind I went through everything that could possibly happen. At last, around lunchtime, he called. After they'd got back in to shore, he'd walked to the top of the hill to get a signal and his phone had blown up with all my texts and voicemails. I read him the letter and told him what my neighbor had said. We agreed I would call Ward & Smith first thing on Monday, and then he went back to his family and their holiday weekend at the lake. Every time Travis was available by phone, we ran things off each other, but otherwise we could do nothing.

Here's one of the ways that Travis and I are very different. He felt a pit in his stomach, but he didn't see that the letter needed to ruin his weekend, because there was nothing we could do until Monday anyway. He was able to live with the pit in his stomach and still enjoy relaxing with his family. I'm more of a worrier. My mind spins on what we can do to fix the problem. I want to make sure we are doing everything we can to be proactive. That weekend, my mind spun at top speed.

First thing Monday I called Ward & Smith and they set me up with one of their attorneys, Rex Willis, who we got to know very well over the next years.

Travis and I drove together to the Ward & Smith office in New Bern. The military taught me to always be early and never be late, so we walked in to the reception area ten minutes early. Ignoring the chairs at the sides of the room, while we waited we walked around reading the accolades and partner bios hung on the walls. I wanted to learn what I could to get a feel for who was going to represent us.

After we'd paced around and around for about twenty minutes, the receptionist showed us into Rex's office. Sitting behind a large desk was a good-looking older gentleman, like Matthew McConaughey playing one of those good Southern lawyers worked to death, plus a hundred pounds and suspenders. He's that guy who looks like he walked out of *GQ* magazine, but he also looks like he stayed out at the bar the night before.

We came to love Rex. He had a way of sitting back and smiling as you were talking. He was serious, but at the end of the conversation, you felt comforted, like it was going to be okay. Whenever I would get down and out and talk to him about something, he would let me know this is serious, but here's how we're going to combat it. You just felt good after you got out of a meeting with him. He retired several years ago and is still held in great esteem at Ward & Smith, which is one of the most highly regarded law firms in North Carolina. Before he retired, he trained another attorney who he considered to be the next bulldog to handle our account, and Lee Hodge has been with TI for over a decade now.

For us, Rex was a rock star, our hero. He was the guy that was facing off with the big brown machine. To this day, I've got a lot of respect for Rex Willis. He kept us from jumping off the cliff, because we were really close to jumping off the cliff many times during that period. UPS scared the shit out of us.

Rex invited us to take a seat, and then for the next three hours he sat back and listened before giving us his thoughts. As we walked out the door, he said, "Fuck UPS. They're big, but they're not that big."

Walking to the car, Travis and I were speechless. We were both thinking, *I don't think Rex understands how big UPS is.* We had our heads between our legs, and Travis had another pit in his stomach. But still, Rex had an attitude about him that exuded a happy ending regardless of the way the meeting went in his office. He had his chest pumped out so far that even though we believed we were going to jail, we still felt good walking to the car.

Rex was our knight in shining armor.

Thanks to my relationship with a family member who worked at a bank, we had exactly five thousand dollars on a credit card to start the business. The very first thing we ever charged on that card was the meal when we told our families that we were leaving UPS. The second thing we charged on the card was the whole five thousand, because that was the retainer fee for us to be able to even sit down and talk to the folks at Ward & Smith. Three weeks after we started the company, we were one hundred percent in debt.

Those were some terrifying times. UPS can be a big bully. I love the company to death—they put my two kids through college and taught me a heck of a lot about business and sales—but they can be a bully, and they put a lot of stress on us.

Add to that stress our perfect timing of taking the leap to quit secure jobs and start a business at the exact moment that the U.S. and most of the rest of the world was diving headfirst into a recession. Travis and I were determined that our families wouldn't feel the effect of our decision, so we planned to sell our UPS stock as needed until Transportation Impact was supporting us fully, but there was a lot of tension in my household. Syndie believed in me, though, and continued to support me.

While Rex was bulldogging with the bully, he told us to lie low. Under no circumstances were we to go out knocking on doors to get customers or do anything else that would be visible to UPS. So now we had no job and we couldn't go out and bring in business for our just-born company. Under the radar, we did what we could. We spent hours on LinkedIn studying potential customers, and we made a lot of phone calls. Behind the scenes we gently worked the list that we thought we had, the customers we thought we would be able to engage with, just to check their interest.

The crux of the issue was that legally UPS could ban Travis and me from contacting any company in the territory where we had worked for UPS, which was North and South Carolina. In other words, our home territory. UPS could also prohibit us from dealing with clients and customers we had called on or done business with in the past, wherever in the U.S. they were. We had counted on those relationships to give our business a jump start. Now, after twenty years of sales and leadership, we had to go back to square one and start knocking on doors like junior salesmen, and we had to get on the road and go out of state to do it. And right now, we couldn't do even that.

That wasn't the only difficulty confronting us. Not long after

Ward & Smith took on our case, we got word that UPS had computer forensics investigate my computer and go through our emails. They found email correspondence about developing our TI logo as well as the logo itself, which was an image of a dollar sign being crushed by a vice. But that was a relatively small thing compared to my loading customer information onto a memory stick. I did not deny it, but I did point out that we had never opened the stick after loading the info onto it, and I immediately returned it to UPS. The forensics ultimately confirmed that we had never opened it.

The integrity of not using that information was our saving grace. I loaded the information onto the stick a long time prior to us leaving, and I didn't think I was doing anything wrong; I didn't do it with that type of mentality. But I obviously didn't think it through like I should have. In fact, I had the stick for over a month after I left before UPS even found out about it, and I never opened it. If I have any regrets about this whole journey, that is the only one: Not being as smart as I should have been. I should have had a cleaner break.

But UPS's main issue was the confidential information we had in our heads. The knowledge that we had, they couldn't take away from us, and that included our knowledge of all the customers whose info was on that memory stick.

Rex reassured us that legally, UPS could only restrict us at most for two years. In negotiating with the company's lawyer in Atlanta, his focus was on what we could do, not what we couldn't do. Despite his reassurances, I was nervous. What had I done to my family? UPS had a pocket full of money for legal action. I second guessed what I'd done. But when it came down to it, I knew I hadn't done anything wrong.

Despite Rex's reassurances, Travis and I were scared to death. We brainstormed every harebrained idea we could come up with to prevent our business from being closed before it even opened. In the end, we agreed with Ward & Smith to make a list of UPS customers in North or South Carolina that we had prior relationships with that UPS couldn't legally stop us doing business with. For example, Travis had worked for Parker Overton for five years before he started at UPS. When UPS told us that we couldn't go into Overton's, we said, "You can't tell us that we can't go into Overton's, because Travis knew him through means other than UPS." Or there was another person who Travis went to church with, who was a decision maker at a company on the list.

For each customer we put on that list, it took Rex days to get a definitive yes or no from the UPS lawyer. Their tactic was to distract Rex and rack up our legal fees. Over the next months, through Rex we went back and forth with UPS's legal group in Atlanta negotiating that list. We threw a thousand accounts at them, because we knew they'd instantly pare it down to a hundred, and then we'd have to fight from there.

We were pretty sure we'd be able to get Eastern Skateboard Supply on the "okay" list, because in June, right around the time I left UPS, I'd partnered with one of the guys on my sales team who was a big surfer, Doug Starcke, to buy a surf shop in Emerald Isle called 58 Boards. We paid seventy-five hundred dollars each. Back in the day it had been called Sweet Willie's and everybody loved it. It was an old school surf shop, an institution in town, but it was in danger of going out of business, and we wanted to reinvigorate it so it stayed part of the community. Because I co-owned a surf shop, Eastern Skateboard Supply was a key vendor that I did business with. We counted on that being a strong enough argument to keep ESS on the list of companies we could approach.

They *had* to let us keep ESS. I thought about the trust Reggie had placed in us. Right after I quit I took him up on his promise to be our first client. He was nervous that working with us as a third party to negotiate his UPS agreement could harm his relationship with the carrier, which he counted on heavily as a key component in keeping his business running smoothly and his customers happy. But our relationship was strong enough and he believed in our idea enough that he took the chance of signing with us. He knew he was going to be our guinea pig and there was no way to know for sure if the strategy we had devised on those whiteboards would be successful.

Reggie was smart. He knew that UPS would make money on him, no matter how good a deal Travis and I were able to get him. He understood that it's got to be a win-win, and that because we knew how the UPS pricing worked on the inside, we knew how far we could push. He wanted to go all the way to the edge as far as the absolute best pricing he could get while still keeping UPS profitable. What none of us knew was how UPS would react to Travis and me inserting ourselves between the company and its profitable customer.

Reggie signed exactly the type of agreement Travis and I had planned in our business model: three years and a fifty-fifty split of the savings on his UPS spend that we negotiated for him. As I watched him sign our simple one-page contract, I was overjoyed. Now, just a month later, I was racked with anxiety. We had our first customer on the terms we wanted, but we had to stall until we had permission to work with them. We took baby steps, learning about Reggie's business and studying his existing agreement, but Dorrie, his logistics manager, was getting frustrated at the delay. We obviously didn't want to tell her we were fighting for our lives not to be sued into nonexistence by UPS! Mumbling something about "legal issues" getting the business started, we left it at that.

The months dragged by. We worked LinkedIn, stalled with Reggie and Dorrie, sold UPS stock to pay our bills, and lost sleep. I struggled with depression. One day I didn't bother getting out of bed.

Travis came over. "Keith, buddy, get up."

"What have I done? We left this company. We left these pensions. I have a family."

"Try to get up. We're going to go make some calls. We're going to get on the road."

I got out of bed.

Finally, in mid-fall we settled with UPS by agreeing to stay out of North and South Carolina for two years, with the exception of the twenty-six customers on the list that Rex had negotiated. We were immensely relieved—to say the least! UPS could have tied us up in legal action for years. For us, getting permission to approach those twenty-six UPS customers was a true blessing and a tremendous win. We had no idea how big the win was for the birth of TI. We thought that of those twenty-six customers, if we could get a few to sign with us, we would be able to run the business long enough to figure out our next steps. We were looking to go month to month to keep afloat and see how we could pay our bills a year from now.

We also had to pay the most important bill: Ward & Smith's. Rex was our knight in shining armor, but he wasn't jousting with UPS for the love of it. In the end, Rex's four months of battle with the largest small parcel carrier in the United States cost us about fifty grand, which we paid out of our personal savings.

Now at last we could do battle with UPS our way—renegotiating Eastern Skateboard Supply's parcel shipping agreement!

# 8

## ON THE ROAD AND
## KNOCKIN' ON DOORS

Jimmy Johnson was the UPS rep for Eastern Skateboard Supply. Jimmy was on my team at UPS, and at the time I left he still reported to me. So right off the bat, in our very first negotiation, we were going to have an awkward dealing with someone who had been a teammate and friend and was now our adversary. When we finally did sit down at the table together, it was weird.

But first, we had to get UPS to the table.

Reggie notified UPS that he had hired us. We now all had to sign a nondisclosure agreement. Even back in the iron age days of 2008, an NDA could be fired off in twelve seconds with a few clicks on a computer. It took UPS three weeks to sign the NDA, yet another of their delay tactics. Every day that UPS kept Eastern Skateboard under the old contract, UPS was making more money. It also made us look bad because "we" were further delaying ESS getting their new, better rates.

Now it was late October, more than four months after I'd gone to Reggie two days after quitting UPS and got the signed agreement from him as Transportation Impact's very first client. That day I was so excited—it felt like everything that Travis and I had brainstormed and debated and planned to the tiniest detail was about to come to life. Then it stopped.

I was still excited, but I was also wary and a lot more aware of how many challenges we still had to get through to make this business a success, and not to let UPS bring us down. But I was determined. My nature is to fight to the end for what I believe is right, and I knew that what we were doing was right. It was the right thing for the customer, I believed that it was the right thing for us and our families, and ultimately it was the right thing for UPS, because we understood how to negotiate discounts that the carrier was already prepared and able to give while still making a good profit. Most of all, though, I was relieved and (very!) impatient to finally be getting started.

After we at last got the signed NDA, we engaged with UPS on behalf of Eastern Skateboard. There was a lot of back and forth by email. We had already asked Reggie and Dorrie questions that allowed us to determine where we could get savings for them and what would be the best approach to take with UPS. The pre-engagement strategy we took with this first customer has ended up being the blueprint for every single one of the thousands of negotiations Transportation Impact has done since. Before even making contact with the carrier, we learn as much as we can about the company, their shipping patterns, plans for new products, and many other details, so that we are able to engage in the negotiation as if we were a stakeholder in the company. The brilliance of this strategy is that with our knowledge and understanding we are able to play both roles: UPS pricing expert and customer company executive.

In any negotiation, it's always useful to bring in competitive pressure, so we also approached FedEx, because Reggie said he would entertain an offer from FedEx, although he didn't really want to switch. We met with the FedEx people out in the open, the same way we were doing with UPS.

Again UPS was dragging its feet. The emails went back and forth, and there were two or three in-person meetings, until finally, after weeks of this, we had in hand an offer from UPS.

Travis and I have completely opposite strengths, which is why we're such a great team. I'm the sales guy and strategic thinker, and Travis understands numbers. He's a mathematical genius and extremely good at details. We individually scrutinized the offer from UPS, and then Travis came to me.

"I've found a mistake in the calculations," he said. "What UPS is offering is actually going to cost Eastern Skateboard a lot more than they're stating."

"Are you sure, Travis?"

"Yes, I'm sure."

"Are you completely sure?"

"Yes, I'm sure. Look."

UPS had come in with a rate cap, and they were telling us how much money they were going to save ESS, not at the beginning of 2009, but over the course of 2009, 2010, and 2011, thanks to this average rate cap. In their calculations, UPS had applied the cap by basically building three spreadsheets and increasing the rates over the years. But based on what we knew UPS actually *did* as opposed to what their memos and press releases talked about, Travis was able to show on paper that the rate cap was actually going to cost Eastern Skateboard a lot more money than UPS was telling them they would be saving.

It's smoke and mirrors. Every year, UPS announces a four or five percent rate increase. So when UPS tells a customer that they're going to have a 4.9 percent rate cap—in other words, less than the stated increase—that implies to the average person that their rates will only go up by 4.9 percent. But that is not the case.

Travis proved mathematically that with the rate cap that UPS was offering, Eastern Skateboard's rates would actually increase by seven or eight percent.

He showed me his calculations, and then for the next several hours we debated. I quizzed him hard. We had to be one hundred percent accurate, one hundred percent certain that what we were about to tell ESS and UPS was correct, because we were putting our reputation on the line with this very first customer. It felt like this was our all-or-nothing, make-or-break moment.

We told ESS and UPS what we had found. UPS insisted their calculations and the promised savings were correct. We scheduled a meeting to discuss it.

We met at the Eastern Skateboard office. Sitting at the table across from Travis and me were three UPS people: my former team member Jimmy Johnson; his boss, who was from West Carolina; and the pricing guy from UPS who had been brought in from Columbia, South Carolina, to explain why the mistake that Travis had found wasn't a mistake. Reggie and Dorrie completed the group. Travis and I were excited as hell, because we were about to prove we knew what we were doing, and we were finally going to bring in some revenue, but the atmosphere was really awkward. Jimmy was probably feeling betrayed, Reggie and Dorrie were worried about their relationship with UPS, and to Jimmy's boss and the pricing guy, we were the bad guys that UPS had been telling them about. They had to negotiate with us because the legal agreement secured by Rex said they had to.

We laid out what we'd found, and the pricing guy tried to explain it. He tried this way and that way, but in the end he couldn't, because Travis was right. We saw in his eyes that he knew we were right.

I also saw in Reggie's eyes that the light bulb had gone on for him. I could almost hear him thinking, *Damn, this is why I know your business model is going to be so great, because you just uncovered something*

*I would never have.* It was a very embarrassing meeting for UPS. The pricing people at UPS tell the reps, "It's this way or the highway. You've got to trust me on this. This is a good deal." We proved them wrong. Jimmy and his boss were looking at the pricing guy like, *Are you kidding me? We just got embarrassed like this?*

The pricing guy sputtered to a stop, and in the silence that followed, Dorrie looked at everybody around the table.

"This has all come full circle for me," she said. "When your contract is thirty-one pages long and has a lot of fluff in there, so I can't figure out how much money I will spend sending a package from here to South Carolina, it might benefit you more than it benefits us."

That was a matter-of-fact way of saying: "You've got a lot of smoke and mirrors. If you made your contract three pages, instead of thirty-one pages, I'd probably like it more. It's obvious you've got a bunch of crap in that language in that contract. We're glad we hired TI."

Travis and I were triumphant. But the triumph had a sour taste. Jimmy had worked hard to earn Reggie's trust, and now that was damaged. Travis and I knew we were going to get paid, which was a blessing, but it was obvious the UPS people had a bad taste in their mouth. Nonetheless, at the end of that meeting, I felt so much better about the success we were just getting ready to have. That meeting proved the validity of our business model.

Reggie was very happy too, because we saved him fifty thousand dollars a year, so for each of the next three years, the life of our agreement with ESS, we could count on around twenty-five thousand dollars in revenue from the fifty-fifty split of the savings, unless there was a significant change in his shipping. Revenue! At last!! Although not yet. We had originally hoped we could start billing in September, but it was the middle of November before we were able to send the first invoice. After that memorable meeting, we still had some issues with the language of the agreement because UPS had made a few minor mistakes. Sometime in October we all agreed in principle, and then we had to wait a month to bill ESS. We were anxious to have the new rates in place by then, because the Christmas period was Eastern Skateboard's peak season and we knew they were going to have a spike in volume. More packages shipped equals more savings equals more money for Transportation Impact.

Reggie was so happy with the savings that he fell in love with our business model. He couldn't believe we had been calling on him all those years when we were with UPS and that much money had been on the table. He knew we were trying to build our business, so as a friend he started making phone calls and spreading the word about Transportation Impact within the surf and skate industry, where he was well-known, highly regarded, and trusted. His recommendation was especially powerful because he was speaking from personal experience. We had proven we could save a business money—and not chump change, either—and who doesn't want to save money? Reggie's enthusiastic recommendation over time gained us headway in an industry we hadn't really considered as one to target. But first, we had more hurdles to jump.

In negotiating Reggie's agreement with UPS, we hadn't had to deal with costly accessorial charges such as oversize or additional handling, because Reggie's boxes were quite standard in size and shape and not particularly heavy, so they were very profitable for UPS. But then, out of the blue, we got a customer who shipped very ugly boxes, from a UPS standpoint.

I was on my front porch on a Saturday morning when my cellphone rang. The man on the other end introduced himself as Billy Powell, founder of Powell & Powell, a company in Fuquay Varina that manufactured the type of pop-up canopies that are used for events like weddings and tailgate parties. UPS hated that kind of box because they had trouble handling it in their routine sort every night and it was awkward for the drivers to handle. This was about the time UPS started saying, "If these boxes are going to cost us a lot of money to handle internally, we're going to start charging the Powell & Powells of the world for the extra expense they're causing us." So UPS had implemented an additional handling charge for ugly boxes like Billy Powell's, and Mr. Powell was very ticked off.

He said he had heard about us and got my number from someone local. On the phone we set a date for a meeting. I was overwhelmed. That was the best phone call in the world. I immediately called Travis. "You're not going to believe this. We just got our second customer."

We met with Don Hutchinson, the CFO, grilled him with our questions, and got a sample of his shipping data so we could analyze it and find the savings opportunities.

Not long after, my phone rang and it was Neal Newhouse, who was still in sales at UPS.

"Keith!" he said. "You're meeting with Don next Tuesday."

"Yeah. I knew you were going to find out, but I was going to let you know."

"Yeah. *Okay.*"

Powell & Powell was Neal's account. He said Don had asked him if he knew a couple of guys called Keith Byrd and Travis Burt, because we were coming in the next week to talk to him about his shipping costs. "Oh they are, are they?" Neal replied. And then he called me.

Of course I knew that Powell & Powell was Neal's account. We had told Don that we knew Neal, but we didn't say anything about how well we knew him or that I had been his boss. I didn't give Neal a heads up because I didn't want to conflict with UPS, even though we were best buddies. What made it even more awkward was that when we left UPS, Neal knew what Travis and I were doing and only half-jokingly he told us, "Stay the hell out of my accounts." And here we were, with our second customer, going into one of his biggest accounts. This was business, though. We viewed Neal as being in the middle at best and probably leaning a lot more toward

UPS, because he was doing his job. From our perspective in this context, Neal was the enemy.

We agreed as a courtesy to get together and touch base before the first meeting at Powell & Powell. We met at a café over a convenience store in Fuquay Varina. We did not want Neal to know what our strategy was, but we wanted to give him an idea of the lay of the land.

We told him: "Here's what we're doing, as you know. You know what we do. Yeah, we're engaged in your account. You need to sharpen your pencil. Don't think we're bullshitting when we say FedEx is in here," because we were giving FedEx a chance to get that business too. We wanted him to tell UPS there was a competitive threat. The conversation was very professional.

We also gave him a heads up as to what we had found.

I said to him, "Buddy, I'll tell you, there's twenty-plus percent left."

He looked incredulous. "Are you shitting me? That's two hundred thousand dollars!"

"Yeah, man."

He didn't believe it, but it was real. For this million-dollar shipper, Travis and I had found twenty percent in savings that we were going to negotiate hard for.

For Neal this was a blow in more than one way. First, he had genuinely believed that when he told Don he had the best rates since sliced bread, it was true, because that's what the UPS pricing team had told him. Second, it would affect his commission. Neal felt threatened, upset, and pissed.

Not surprisingly, the meeting between the four of us was weird. Don reassured Neal that he hadn't signed an agreement with us yet, so Neal went back to UPS to run through the pricing. As he puts it, it was "the usual dog-and-pony show," and he ended up having to write a statement saying that a consultant had come in and found savings. UPS replied they wouldn't deal with a consultant. "Well, we're going to lose the damn business," Neal told them, "because the consultant said there's twenty-some percent on the table."

Powell & Powell did hire us, but we soon discovered we also had been misled, by Don himself. He was in the process of selling the company to a private equity group, and he had led us to believe he had a lot more power in the decision-making process than he in fact did. After the first two or three meetings he took a backseat to the new decision makers.

We put out the bid to both FedEx and UPS. UPS ended up keeping the business, but only after stepping up to the plate and doing what they had to do in terms of agreeing to what we had found, part of which was a reduction in the additional handling surcharge. The people at Powell & Powell thought we would never be able to negotiate that out, but we managed to get it reduced by about fifty percent. Back then, additional handling was eight or nine dollars a package, so for a high-volume shipper like Powell & Powell, even a small reduction quickly added up to big savings.

The bottom line was we succeeded again. We saved the customer exactly what we said we would.

Around this same time, we started talking with a company in Greenville, North Carolina, called Hammock Source. We had managed to get Hammock Source on the list of local companies we could approach thanks to Travis's long-standing relationship with the CFO, John Farley. We knew that Hammock Source had a lot of the same issues as Powell & Powell as far as "ugly" packages. They had previously solely done catalog sales, but they had just opened several online businesses, which was increasing both their sales and their shipping costs.

When we got him on the phone, John Farley told us, "I'm getting ready to take a fifty percent increase because of this eight dollar charge on half my packages going out the door." We explained how we could help, and he agreed to meet. John wasn't keen on hiring us because he was worried about his relationship with UPS, but after we showed him what we'd done for Powell & Powell, he begrudging-ly signed an agreement.

Once again, the UPS account executive was a guy from my sales team. During our whiteboarding sessions, Travis and I had discussed the likelihood of dealing with UPS sales reps who had been teammates. From our perspective that was an advantage, because we knew their strengths and weaknesses.

In that negotiation we managed not only to get the additional handling charge reduced, we also got Hammock Source a discount on the large package surcharge. After not wanting to hire us, John was very pleased with the results.

Transportation Impact: three for three.

We continued working our relationships with the twenty-six companies in North Carolina on the approved list, and in late fall 2008 we landed another one, Neil Medical Group, a medical supply company based in Kinston.

Travis had gently touched the decision maker at Neil Medical, Bobby Adams, with a couple of messages and got no response. Travis called him again one day on his way home. He was on a two-lane road trying to have his great sales hat on and be intentional in the conversation when, right as he went through a bad cell area, Bobby said, "Look, Travis, I'm not going to lie to you. This is like the fox guarding the henhouse."

Bobby Adams was probably the smartest customer we had dealt with up to that point. He was highly analytical and he understood minimums, pricing, surcharges—everything. When we met with him, he basically told us, "Keith and Travis, you're trying to get me to sign a contract with you. I believe in your business model. But you used to be my UPS rep. Now you tell me there's half a million in savings? You've been screwing me all along. I got a problem with that."

That was a tough sell. We had to walk on eggshells and convince him that two or three years ago in 2005 and 2006 when we sat down with him, we were the devil in the room. We were UPS and we were getting paid to manage margins, but his account and several others like it were the reason that we considered this business model.

"Bobby," I said, "whenever the pricing guy tells me something, I got to believe it. Travis and I started this company because we found out that the shit the pricing people were telling us was not right. You're saying that I screwed you for those years, but I was doing what I was told to do, because I didn't know any better. I didn't dig into it. I had to trust my pricing guy. Now we've cracked the code. We started peeling back and doing the numbers. This might hurt a little bit on the front end, but understand this is going to benefit you in the long term."

We finally convinced him, and Bobby signed an agreement with us to negotiate with UPS on behalf of Neil Medical.

Again here, the UPS rep was a guy who used to report to me. It was not surprising that the UPS account executives of these local companies had been on my sales team, because this was my area, but it was still weird and awkward and kind of crazy sitting across the negotiation table from people I had trained and mentored. Still, this was business, and we took full advantage of knowing the strengths and weaknesses of the sales executives so well.

And again, UPS dragged out the negotiation over multiple meetings. We knew it could be done in three weeks, but instead every time it was taking months. Negotiating out in the open was not the best way, it was clear, but for some reason we kept doing it. Perhaps we had so much else going on that we just didn't have the time to sit down and figure out a better way. Yet.

The last engagement in 2008 came from a cold call by Dale Morris, an ex UPS sales rep that I was training to do sales for us, working strictly on commission. I had gone out on the road with Dale and we were in Midlothian, Virginia, a little south of Washington, D.C. Just east of Amelia, the county seat, we came to a business with a bunch of trailers behind it. We got out of the car and went in.

The business was called ISC Sales and it was the genuine As Seen on TV. They were doing the fulfillment for Walgreens and others, and the shipping volume had massive swings. They might ship three packages one day and three thousand the next day.

We started talking in late 2008 but it was early 2009 before they signed with us. This was a challenging negotiation. For once the UPS rep wasn't from my team, but because of the wildly variable shipping characteristics, we couldn't go to the carriers with a monthly or even seasonal volume projection. In the end, when we put the bid out to UPS and FedEx we gave an annual volume projection, and we secured good savings for ISC Sales.

Momentum was building, but because it took so long before we could bill our first handful of customers, revenue was not. Total taxable income in 2008: $0.

Our first six months of business we worked our asses off within the constraints placed by UPS, and we had nothing in the bank to show for it—and no salaries to show our wives. Next year had to be better.

But for it to be better, Travis and I had to get out of our comfort zone and really hit the road.

We didn't have a lot of money, and flying was out of the question unless it was for an outstanding opportunity, so we got in the car and drove. We couldn't even afford motel rooms, so we deployed mostly from Travis's dad's lake house up on the Virginia line, because we could stay there for free and it was a strategic location for the states north of us. Or else we'd sleep at my dad's house in Greensboro, but that was west. We headed first to Richmond, Virginia, and from there rolled out to D.C. Then we started into Maryland and down into Georgia. Virginia, D.C., and Maryland we hit pretty hard because they were closest. We then moved into West Virginia and Florida.

We knocked on the door of any company that seemed like they could use our services. Referrals have always been important, and they were like gold in 2008, 2009, 2010. Anybody that knew anybody that knew anybody, we'd make a phone call, and then if they expressed interest we'd go and visit them. But those were few and far between. Anywhere we saw a UPS or FedEx trailer backed up, that was a leading indicator of a potential big customer, so we immediately stopped and went in and pitched our service.

That was another challenge. With UPS, I was selling a brand and I had a proven service. This was new to walk into a customer's business and them not really know you. First of all, you're asking for their data to analyze. So there's the trust factor. Then you're coming back and saying, "Hey, I can save you eighteen-point-two percent. That equates to four hundred twenty-two thousand dollars a year." They're like, *"Right."*

Being complete unknowns and pitching a service no one had heard of forced us to polish our skills to win over the customer, not only to earn their trust to get the data so we could show them how much we could save them, but then to hire us and let us prove our worth. That's what made us who we are today, I think, having to get out of our comfort zone and not count on relationships, but actually go out and sell the business model. But the first few years it was really difficult and frustratingly slow.

In January 2009 we were making a cold call on a company called Emtech Laboratories Inc. in Roanoke, Virginia. For some reason that I don't remember now, we had stayed at a motel the night before, and Travis managed to hurt his back when he twisted to pack his T-shirt in his overnight bag that morning. So to say he was not in a good mood for the drive to Emtech is an understatement.

At this point, we'd probably been together every day, morning, noon, and night for about three weeks, including weekends. Driving back to Emerald Isle after the call, we got as far as Charlotte when we got so frustrated and irritated with each other that Travis told me to let him out of the car. I pulled over as soon as I could, slammed on the brakes, and said, "Get out!" Saying he'd get a rental car,

Travis slammed the door shut and I drove off, leaving him standing by the side of the road. Just like a married couple, we'd finally had enough and needed a short separation. During the early years when the stress was so high, we could have killed each other a million times behind closed doors. But we never lost sight of TI being bigger than us. To me, it was growing pains.

At Emtech, we walked in, explained our mission, and the owner and CEO agreed to meet with us. His name was Moses Nakhle. We explained what we could do for him, and then I said, like I said to everybody, "If UPS came in and saved you a hundred grand and FedEx saved you four hundred grand, would you switch?"

"Hell, no!" he said. "I'll never go to FedEx. You guys just need to use FedEx to get UPS in line. UPS has been too good to me for too long."

Moses was persuaded that we could help him, though, and he gave us a sample of his data that we took back to Emerald Isle. Over the weekend we did the analysis. Monday morning we had the results. UPS was playing hardball, but they were the incumbent. We were playing both sides, and FedEx was really motivated to win that bid, so we had FedEx up to a certain dollar amount. We didn't want to drive all the way back to Roanoke to deliver the results if Moses wasn't going to go for the best deal we had so far got for him, so we called him first to sense his interest in what we had done for him on the FedEx side.

Right before I dialed his number, I turned to Travis and said, "We're getting ready to find out the willingness of this customer to switch, because we just heard three weeks ago, 'Hell no, I'll never go to FedEx.'"

I called Moses. "We can save you three hundred and fifty thousand, but you'd have to switch to FedEx. Would you be willing to do that?"

"Hell, yeah!" he said. "What do you think I am, a retard?"

We were a little shocked by his phrasing, but pleased he was willing to take the best deal we could put on the table, even if it meant having to change carriers. Now we could start playing hardball back with UPS. We set up a meeting with Moses and drove back to Roanoke.

Emtech made hearing aids, and their shipping container was a Next Day Air pack, which is big flimsy paper. I am lucky in that I have always had a strategic mind. Getting out of the box is easy and fun. I wanted to figure out a way to move Emtech from an overnight pack to an overnight letter, because the value of the goods being shipped was under a hundred dollars. In their conference room, I brainstormed with Moses and Deede Vermillion, the controller. Deede was great to deal with and ended up giving us a testimonial that we were still using a decade later.

I had an idea. "Let's go after UPS and FedEx and see if they will allow you to take that hearing aid out of a pack and put it into a letter, which is a fixed-rate, low-value item, and then we'll also go negotiate a better letter rate. We're going to double dip."

Everybody in the conference room looked at me like it was the greatest thing they'd ever heard. We agreed on that strategy, and we said we'd call them when we heard from the carriers.

Walking back to the car, I turned to Travis. "We can do that, right?"

That happened a lot in the early days when Travis and I were together on the sales call. I was known for committing to everything, and then when we were walking out the door, I'd say, "We can do that shit, right?" I never said no to a customer. He'd always laugh and say, "We'll figure it out."

This was how it worked. I say to the customer: "If I'm able to talk UPS or FedEx into letting you put it in that letter, rather than that pack, that's an immediate three dollar per package savings, and I negotiated nothing. You're going to pay me a dollar and a half of that three dollars, right, Mr. Customer, if I'm able to do that?" The customer replies, "Yes." That was such a big deal. Now, not only are we going to take their discount from forty percent to sixty-five percent, we're going to take them out of a flat rate of eight dollars into a flat rate of five dollars. It's a double whammy.

That's how creative we were back in the early days.

But the creativity also increased the complexity. Add to that, as the carriers started adding more surcharges, we were also able to negotiate better rates on surcharges. But the more creative we got with our solutions and the more surcharges we negotiated discounts on, the more complex it became for Travis to accurately calculate the savings so we could bill the customer. We lost many nights' sleep over the integrity of measuring the savings we had negotiated. We never wanted the CFO to find one penny off in our billing. When we handed a bill to a customer, we knew it had to be right.

For example, for Emtech, first we had to rerate their packages at the published rate for the pack, and then compare it to the published rate for the letter, and then determine the savings for both. That wasn't in a billing file. We had to do it manually because of my idea to save them in two ways on that one package. And Travis was doing all of this on Excel spreadsheets after downloading the billing info from the carrier websites at the end of each week, which took hours and hours over our household-grade internet connection.

That was one of the things we talked about on the drives up and down the eastern seaboard. The days were long, and at times we got irritated with each other, but mostly we were excited. We took it very seriously because we had to put food on our families' tables. The first three or four years we never thought of giving in, because we couldn't. It was a huge learning time for us, too.

When we left UPS, we really thought we knew how to read a UPS bill and how to understand all the surcharges. When we started billing the first few customers we learned just how mathematically involved the discounts were—how, for example, the fuel surcharge was calculated. During those drives we would talk through the math and the language in the UPS contracts.

We also talked about the business. How to overcome the objections that we weren't anticipating. Always trying to expect the unexpected. I learned quick. When I did all those stupid things out of enthusiasm before I left UPS, that was a turning point for me. It was a life lesson to always expect the unexpected. I always have tried to go through the bullet points of what could happen in every situation. But that really taught me that you can't only be two steps ahead; you need to be ten steps ahead of everything.

So we utilized those hours on the road to not only expect the unexpected and talk things out—What are we going to do? What's the bad that could come out of it? What's the good that come out of it?—but also to problem solve things that were coming up from a mathematical and a language perspective in the contracts that we hadn't understood before. We were paranoid about the integrity of our bill to our customer.

# 9

## THE FAMOUS BROOM CLOSET

When we weren't on the road, Travis was still in Greenville working out of his house, and I was in Emerald Isle. We spent many hours on the phone with each other. When we needed to meet face to face, which was about once a week, our meeting point was the Hampton Inn in Kinston, which was an hour for me and about forty minutes for him. Their lobby breakfast area was our boardroom.

Doug Starcke and I had by this time revamped the old 58 Boards and named it South Swell Surf Shop, because the surf rolls in from the south to break on the long east-west Emerald Isle shore. Doug had also quit UPS and come to join Travis and me in Transportation Impact to be managing partner of TI's sister company, First Flight Solutions, and contributed significantly to our ultimate success. Now that there were three of us, it was getting crazy having us all working from our homes and driving to meet up—this was before all the telecommuting tools that make remote working so easy now! I wanted structure, and since two of us were in Emerald Isle it made sense to use South Swell, 8204 Emerald Drive, as our office base.

At the back of the shop was a broom closet. It was a pretty decent size, twelve feet by eleven, so we cleaned it out, painted it, and put carpet in. To create a worktop we could all use, we went to the local granite store and bought a used piece of granite, and then we found a bitty 15-inch TV. We installed the granite and the TV, and we had an office! We were so proud of that space.

Every morning we walked through the surf shop into the closet, sat down, and then spent the rest of the day searching on LinkedIn to try to get leads or working the phone trying to get in front of a prospect. We even handwrote letters to potential customers and sent them via UPS Next Day Air or Second Day Air. It was expensive and we couldn't really afford it, but we did it so the recipient felt compelled to open it. Whenever you get an overnight letter, you always wonder what it is, because someone paid a lot of money to send that.

We also got creative. For example, if the company made picture frames we'd write, "My wife is a big customer of yours. Here's a product that she just bought. Please give us a chance to earn your business," and we'd put a photo of the wife holding the product. We tried to create that personal connection so they felt obligated to re-spond. In the early years we sent out a lot of handwritten letters ev-ery week, because that's all I was doing during the week. If I wasn't knocking on doors, I was writing letters. The hit rate was amazing.

However, after getting in the door at Emtech in January 2009, it was three months before we got our next signed agreement. Then two months after that a lead from a satisfied customer got us a small shipper called Red Tag Crazy. The following month, July—Transportation Impact's one-year anniversary—we got two new customers.

Every customer we had engaged with so far had unique shipping characteristics, so Travis and I were challenged in finding the best way to bring their costs down via more favorable terms in their car-rier agreement. It was fun. I love being challenged to come up with a creative solution that I know is really going to make a big positive impact on the customer's business. Most of them were low-volume shippers, but no shipper was small to us in those early days. If we could save a shipper thirty thousand dollars annually, that was huge for us! Fifty percent of thirty thousand is fifteen thousand, and if you stack up enough fifteen thousands, you can stay in business.

Then we got a piece of luck that seemed like it would be our breakthrough moment.

Starkey Hearing Technologies is one of the largest hearing aid companies in the world, with global headquarters in Eden Prairie, Minnesota, about twenty minutes southwest of Minneapolis. Our old family friend Richard Petty had a business relationship through NASCAR with Starkey. He wanted to help us out, so he secured us a meeting with the vice president of global supply chain at Starkey.

I was incredibly excited. This would be a breakthrough deal for us, if we could sign this client. Unusually, the VP of supply chain sent us sample data before meeting us so we could run an analysis. I am sure the only reason he did that was because of the Richard Petty connection, and it was a real gift because it allowed us to calculate that we could save them over a million dollars a year. Travis and I couldn't afford to fly to Minnesota, but it was such an incredible opportunity we found the money for two round-trip tickets and flew up there. All the way to Minneapolis we were checking our figures and strategizing about how we would present our services and what we could do for Starkey.

At the airport, we rented a car and then drove twenty minutes due west to Starkey HQ, a group of single-story red-brick buildings surrounded by manicured lawn and gardens. We left the car in the huge parking lot, found the main reception, and then were escorted to the office of the VP of global supply chain. He didn't smile as he greeted us. In fact, he was very short with us and allowed us to give only a condensed presentation, not the time that we wanted to fully demonstrate what we could do for Starkey and how and why it would be successful. When we finished, the guy looked at me and said, "When you get some name brands, when you have somebody bigger than a hammock manufacturer on your website, come back and see me."

I couldn't believe it. We had flown all the way up there and we were offering him over a million dollars in savings, and he wrote us off because we didn't have the logos of any name brand customers. That was a light bulb moment. From that moment I understood the power of demonstrating credibility and capability through marketing. As we walked out of the office building into the sunshine of Eden Prairie, I felt crushed, but I was determined to do whatever it took to get that big name customer. And when I did, I would put their logo all over our website and our marketing materials. I was determined to show that guy one day that he had made a mistake.

Years later, when we did have name brand logos all over our marketing and our website, I came across him on LinkedIn and sent him a fuck-you message listing all the big companies we had as customers. I never did hear back from him.

After we returned to Emerald Isle, I dived right back into finding and following up with prospects. There was a company in southern Virginia that I had been persistently emailing and calling. Seated at the granite worktop in the broom closet, I called again, and at last the president agreed to meet with me. We set a date and time, and in August Travis and I got in the car and drove three and a half hours north to Sedley, Virginia.

Sedley is a spot on the map in a large swath of green with a population of around five hundred. It is also home to Hubs Peanuts, the company that introduced gourmet Virginia peanuts to the world in 1954 via Dot Hubbard's family recipe. It was now run by Dot's eldest daughter, Lynne Rabil, who met with us in her office.

Hubs was started as a mail-order business before FedEx existed and before UPS offered service in Virginia. When UPS came to their area, Hubs signed up, but UPS could only deliver two packages a day to businesses—so Hubs shipped two cases one day, two the next, and so on. One of Lynne's high school jobs was manually writing addresses and doing zip-to-zone conversions. Over the decades, the two companies had literally grown together, and Lynne and the rest of her team were not at all interested in switching to FedEx. They had always had good relationships with their UPS reps and received excellent service. Even though UPS never really negotiated off the base price, Hubs always got discounts.

But their UPS agreement was up for renewal, and FedEx had been persistently knocking on their door and making increasingly appealing offers. Sitting in her old bedroom, just down the hall from the kitchen where her mother had cooked the batches of peanuts and created the business, Lynne listened to our pitch. She didn't expect anything to come out of the meeting, but after she heard what we could do for Hubs, she and her team decided they didn't have anything to lose, so why not go through our process? Lynne understood clearly that our inside knowledge of UPS sales and pricing would give Hubs an advantage in the negotiation that they'd never had before. She signed a three-year agreement for the standard fifty-fifty split of the savings.

We solicited bids from both UPS and FedEx. Sedley was so small, we met with the carrier reps in the community college boardroom in Franklin, a town about fifteen minutes away. Again, there were multiple meetings and a lot of back and forth that dragged out over months. The FedEx rep would come in, and then the UPS rep would come in, and then they'd all go back to the drawing board. The UPS rep obviously thought there was no way that Hubs would switch carriers, and I don't think Lynne did either, at first. But in the negotiations, FedEx came in with such strong incentives that it was hard for Hubs to look away from them. Lynne was surprised that we would push for FedEx, since we had been UPS representatives, but for us, the best deal for the client was the best deal.

What FedEx was offering was a real opportunity, but we also understood the significant costs in terms of operational changes and other pain points of switching carriers, so we took Lynne to Greenville to show her the operations of Hammock Source, because they had switched to FedEx. We introduced her to the management and others involved in the shipping, and they showed her how their operation was flowing and talked about what it would be like to transition. That allowed Lynne and her team to weigh up the pros and cons, and they decided the opportunity for the savings outweighed the pain of making the transition. Once that decision had been made, we were able to engage fully with FedEx, and the negotiation went really well. Twelve years later, Hubs Peanuts is still with FedEx.

The Hubs Peanuts negotiation had dragged out over months, and we sensed the growing resistance of UPS to dealing with third-party consultants. Most of the negotiations took three or four months, when we knew it could be done in three or four weeks. I felt like UPS was trying to test us to make us look like an idiot in front of the customer. The more face-to-face meetings they could get with us, the better chance they had of showing us up. With every negotiation where we all sat at the same table, the tension got greater. It was creating animosity, which got in the way of us being able to get the absolute best deal for the customer. The carrier felt like they'd lost a relationship with a customer, and they were holding back what was really market appropriate. Something had to change, but it took another two negotiations out in the open before the light bulb went on for us.

Later that August we took our skill of negotiating a discount on the additional handling charge (AHC), which we'd developed and sharpened at Hammock Source and Powell & Powell, to Vulcan Tire. Everything this company shipped was hit with AHC, and we were able to get them a significant discount on that surcharge. It might have even been a hundred percent.

At that time, UPS's policy was to charge additional handling on anything that wasn't in a corrugated box or was beyond a certain length. For example, a fishing rod got hit with AHC. After our highly successful experience with Vulcan Tire, we started attacking the tire industry hard because they were all getting whacked with additional handling, and we were getting them anywhere from fifty to a hundred percent off. It was a big hit. Eventually, we had probably a dozen tire companies, and we were hitting homeruns.

The carrier would pitch the AHC charge to the customer: "You've got a unique package. We can't put it on our traditional belts. We've got to put it in a golf cart and take it across the warehouse." But in reality they still threw most of those packages on the conveyor belt. It was a legit charge, but it was also a big marketing ploy because most of the time UPS did not special handle that stuff. Whether it was in a corrugated box or not it went on the belt, the same belt as the corrugated packages went on. We knew this because when we worked at UPS we used to see those AHC packages going down the conveyor belt.

Vulcan Tire had come to us through a referral from a company that provided an online platform to do automatic audits of UPS and FedEx invoices, to find mistakes that the shipper could get refunded for. They wanted us to use their audit platform. It wasn't right for us, but instead we came to a partnership agreement with them. For every referral they provided us, we would give them a percentage of our portion of the savings. It was awesome. It was like having a new sales force without having to train them or deal with any of the human resources responsibilities. This was the way to go—working smart instead of hard!

Now if we could just figure out how to work smart in the negotiations to get rid of the carriers' resistance. Doing them out in the open, we could tell that we weren't going down the right road. The carriers felt like they had lost their relationship with their customer, because now the customer was listening to Transportation Impact and not to UPS or FedEx. There was also a lot of tension because the carriers didn't like us getting a piece of whatever discount they gave, and the customer could see the tension.

In business, you have to stay three steps ahead of everything. I could feel that this was not going to be sustainable. Travis and I decided it was time to implement the alternative strategy we had laid out on one of the original whiteboards. We would conduct the negotiation the same way, but we would stay behind the scenes, coaching the customer what to say, and coaching them with the math to show the carrier they knew what they were talking about. The key was going to be to pick the right person to be the "bad guy" or "hammer" in dealing with the carriers. Doing it out in the open, the onus was on us to have the strategy and play the role of the hammer. We were the one talking to the carrier, so there was not as much pressure on the customer. We had all the knowledge and we knew how to use it in the negotiation to the customer's best advantage. Once we were out of the picture, someone in the customer's company had to be able to play that role.

For example, if the UPS rep has been dealing with Joe in the back for eight years, and Joe's not that smart when it comes to accessorials and minimums and things like that, and now all of a sudden Joe is brilliant, if we didn't play it right, then they were going to know something was going on. We decided on two ways to approach this challenge.

Ideally, we'd have somebody high up in the company who had never met the UPS rep be the hammer. Somebody who didn't have the relationship, so the carrier didn't know how knowledgeable they were with regard to the language in the contract, minimums, accessorials, etc. In the other scenario, if Joe still wanted to be the contact person, we would make it look like the non-incumbent carrier had gone in there and educated him—not Keith and Travis behind the scenes at TI. As if the non-incumbent carrier had come in and said, "Joe, I haven't had your business in eight years. I have nothing to lose, so I'm going to show you where your cost drivers are. I'm going to offer you market-appropriate discounts." So now Joe had the knowledge and hard numbers and he was pissed off that the incumbent carrier had been screwing him over for eight years, and he wanted the same deal he could get from the non-incumbent, or better if he could get it.

Which strategy to use, we would discover during our information-gathering session with the stakeholders in the company, when we asked a lot of questions like "Who owns the carrier relationships? Have you ever met a high-level UPS person at a NASCAR race? What's your marketing plan? What's your growth? Do you have any new products coming out?" In these two- to three-hour sessions we were honing the skill of creating dialogue to provide us with information that would help in the negotiation. Now we would also need to use it to find out who was going to be the hammer. Our biggest concern in doing it behind the scenes was losing control of the negotiation. We saw that picking the right person was going to be critical.

Soon we had the opportunity to try out our new strategy.

The audit company sent us a lead on a coffee roastery in Oakland, California, called Sweet Maria's. The roastery had been started by Thompson Owen and Maria Troy as a mail-order business in Ohio in 1997. Now they had a warehouse in Oakland that was packed to the ceiling with coffee and merchandise. Maria ran the business side of things, and I secured a meeting with her.

By now we could afford a plane ticket for me to fly from North Carolina to Oakland. I flew out, met with Maria, and flew back with a signed agreement in my briefcase, along with all the information I had gathered from Maria. Travis and I spent the next day brainstorming and devising the strategy we would use with this first negotiation where we had to pull the strings from behind the backdrop. Once we had a good plan, I flew back to Oakland to get Maria's buy-in on the strategy.

Our analysis showed she could save a large amount of money.

When she saw how much, Maria was pissed, because she felt like she had been getting screwed all along. The problem for her and Tom was that they didn't know how to do the math to figure it out. It's just so complicated. The carriers know contracts and the discounts and the accessorials, and they deliberately make it all difficult to understand. Once I told her the dollar amount, Maria was a champion because she had it in her gut. She did everything I asked her to do, and we got everything we told her she was going to get.

The other great part? It was all done in three weeks. Start to finish.

There was no question. This was our new business model.

We had negotiated out in the open with thirteen companies—the thirteenth being a printer parts company in New Jersey—and we had finally learned our lesson and discovered the secret sauce. Must have been lucky thirteen.

# 10

## THE ONE BIG NAME

We hadn't started making really good money yet. But damn, I was out there selling the hell out of it. At this point, Travis was starting to do more of the billing than sales, because selling is important, but measuring the savings and sending the invoices is equally important. The thing was, we didn't have any technology to help with calculating the savings and making sure they were accurate to the penny.

Specific to each client, we generated invoices to show where they were before we walked in the door and where we had taken them to after the negotiation, using their own data that the carriers provided to them, which were basically CSV files. For the calculations, Travis was using a very simple set of rules that we had in Excel, but it wasn't at all automated. He had to go through the UPS or FedEx billing file, pull out the info we needed to calculate the savings, and then input that into the spreadsheet. And then it had to be checked very carefully.

For the first nine months, maybe a year, we were able to use Excel to show the customer the savings. When we made our agreement with each client, we got them to sign off on this very simple before-and-after comparison, which basically said: "I understand the way that you're going to present the savings." That was the first buy-in from the client.

We were using only a percentage of what was available to us in the carrier-provided billing files to drive home a hundred percent of the savings that we had generated for the customer. In the early days, it was very much focused on rates and rates only.

Even though we were only measuring a few items, it was a slow process, especially because we were paranoid about the integrity of our commitment to hold true to exactly what we had promised the customer. The one thing that kept us up at night was the integrity, to make sure we could measure the savings we had negotiated. We never wanted the CFO to find one penny off that showed we had misbilled something.

As the number of customers grew, the pace of the billing and the incoming revenue slowed. That led to trials and tribulations between Travis and me, because he wasn't billing fast enough in my opinion. We look back and laugh at it now, but in any business, at the point when you go from nothing to billing fourteen customers, and then you've got to figure out how you are going to do it, it creates tension. It was good, clean, healthy tension, though, and it made us both better.

Part of the slowness was on the customer's end, and we couldn't do anything about that. When we sent a new customer our first invoice, they had to sell it internally. Once it was approved, they would put our invoice in the queue to cut a check. Over time, as they came to trust us, they would pay the invoices more quickly, but at first there could be a delay of several weeks or even months.

The other part of the slowness was on our end. It was a meticulous, time-consuming process to send out a bill. As the carriers added more surcharges and accessorials and we negotiated better rates on those surcharges and accessorials, the complexity of calculating the savings grew exponentially. I knew I could count on Travis to be precise, but I also knew we had to get him some help with the billing and ultimately to automate it as much as we could. As we gained momentum, it seemed like there were so many things that needed to be done and they all needed to be done right now.

At some point in late 2009 we brought in someone I knew and trusted, along with a buddy of Travis's, to help with the billing. It would take the three of them all weekend to download the data at the download speeds possible at that time with our household-grade setup. Then late Sunday evening, for the more difficult billing customers, or some time on Monday they sorted through the files to try to get the bills out Monday, Tuesday, Wednesday, so Travis could hopefully help out in other ways on Thursday and Friday. It didn't bother us a bit to work fifty or sixty hours a week, just as it never bothered us at UPS.

As the months went by, we started negotiating more things outside of a true rate for our customers. The additional handling surcharge was the first big one, and there were many others after that. The carriers were getting cleverer about finding ways to charge a few more dollars for each package, so we had fun creatively keeping up with them in the discounts we negotiated. One that became big for us was the delivery area surcharge (DAS).

Let's say our customer sent a lot of Next Day Air packages and we had negotiated a sixty percent discount for them on Next Day Air. Well, UPS started saying, "Oh, by the way, Mr. Customer, that shipment was going to a ZIP code that UPS considers remote. You are getting your sixty percent discount on that package. However, we've charged you another two dollars for that package at published rates because of where you're shipping to."

The DAS is probably one of the top three surcharges that the carriers use to boost their bottom-line profits. UPS has stated internally that thirty or forty percent of their profits came from surcharges. That's a significant percentage. UPS actually goes to those ZIP codes every day, but they try to make it seem in the customer's eyes that the more remote ZIP code is a lot more costly because it's further from the main hub. Another common surcharge is for delivery to a residential address. That is a tremendous cost driver at UPS. It's called delivery density. If the package is going to a business, there can be two or three packages being delivered at one time. UPS would much rather have five packages going to one place than one package to each of five places. The drivers do the same amount of work, but it takes less time. Of course, FedEx has the same mentality.

When we started Transportation Impact, only a few delivery area surcharges existed at UPS and FedEx. As they got smarter about finding creative ways to add surcharges, the carriers went from two DAS to four, and then from four to eight, and in 2021 there were twenty delivery area surcharges. UPS and FedEx keep more clearly defining the more costly ZIP codes and making the shippers pay for it.

So we figured out quickly that we needed to measure things other than just the rates. Every time the carriers came up with something that that was less beneficial for the shippers, it made it easier for us to go to our customer or potential customer and demonstrate value. There were more and more ways we could show them: "This is where you're not getting good value. We can help you."

We were also using Excel for the analysis to calculate how much we could save a potential customer. It was manual, but it gave us and our sales contractors some insight as to which service levels our customers used and which ones they didn't. The analyses were even more detailed than our invoices, because we had to be as educated as UPS and FedEx on what was important to our shipper. When we walked in to meet with that CEO or CFO, we had to understand exactly how we could help them, because they never took time to dig through their billing files. They had the data available, but they didn't understand the value in correlating those files and the information they had at their fingertips, and how it all related to them negotiating a better agreement.

When UPS and FedEx provided an agreement, typically they would offer discounts for anything. For example, the rep would say, "We got you a seventy percent discount on a Next Day Air Residential letter." They wanted to leave the customer with a perception of how great that agreement was. But if our customer didn't use a Next Day Air Residential letter, that seventy percent meant nothing to them. That was part of the carriers' smoke and mirrors. Travis and I were trained the same way. You focus on what makes you look good.

At Transportation Impact, the magic we had with customers is that we could say, "That seventy percent sounds good, but you don't use that service at all. Let's focus on what you're actually shipping out the door right now, which is a ten-pound Next Day Air *package*, not a letter." We focused our efforts based on what we had learned about our customer through our analysis: each specific review, each unique client, exactly what they were shipping. We could go in with a laser focus and negotiate agreements on their behalf that were very beneficial to them. There was no smoke and mirrors in the stuff we asked the carriers for behind the scenes. It was customer-specific. They all realized pretty quick that we knew what we were doing.

By mid-2009 we had outgrown the Excel spreadsheet. To help us build an automated system for calculating the savings, we hired a developer named Brad Whaley. Brad was also a former UPSer, so he understood what we were measuring and how it had to be done. He and Travis used the Access database platform to create our very first in-house software, which we called TidBit ("Tid" stands for Trans-Intelligence Dashboard, as in "I'm going to run these files through the Trans-Intelligence Dashboard").

Sometime in 2010, Brad told us he could no longer keep up with our growing needs and introduced us to another coder who could help us long term. He brought her up to speed, and she and Travis worked together nights and weekends. She did a very good job for us; she was just slow, because you have to be very, very thorough when it comes to coding. What you code in is what's going to get spit out. Also, she didn't have a UPS or FedEx background, so there was a learning curve for her to understand what exactly we needed and how to make that happen. It took maybe twelve months to get TidBit 2.0 out, and it was still limited by having to be on somebody's laptop, typically Travis's.

While Travis was dealing with everything on the back end, I was relentlessly focused on sales, and I knew that industry trade shows were an opportunity we had to start taking advantage of. Among shipping industry trade shows, by far the biggest was Parcel Forum, held each fall. In 2009 it was in Chicago, and at the last minute we decided to go.

We arrived in Chicago unprepared. We didn't have any kind of collateral, and we really didn't know what we were getting into. When we flew up, we weren't planning to exhibit. We thought we were going to walk the halls and sign up customers left and right. When we got there, though, we found out that when we registered we'd signed up for a booth, but we only paid to attend. Somehow I ended up meeting with the heads of the show and they allowed us to have a booth. They wanted to give us a little help as a start-up company, which was very generous of them.

We had brought nothing with us, so we took a white bed-sheet from the hotel room and put it over the table the organizers gave us. Travis hurried down to Fast Signs in Morton Grove and paid three hundred and fifty dollars for a generic 3' x 3' sign that said "Transportation Impact" and had our logo of the dollar sign being crushed by a vise grip. Then we stood behind the table with our hands in our pockets and waited for the people to come flocking. Everybody walked past, hardly giving us a glance. It was embarrassing and discouraging. Sure, it was an impromptu decision to go, but the bottom line was we were not prepared.

That evening, Travis and I went to Gibsons Steakhouse, which we couldn't really afford, sat at the bar with a couple of Crown and Diets and said to each other: "If we're going to do this, we're going to do it right. Look at us. We've seen what other people are doing. We're out of our league, here. We've got to get professional." Everybody at that show had a professional-looking booth, and we had a white bedsheet and a redneck logo that we thought was awesome.

That experience was a big lesson. We were never unprepared for another trade show. In fact, it was the opposite. If anything, from that time on we were overprepared. We already overprepared for every sales call, and what was a trade show if not a giant sales call?

Attention to detail. That was the lesson.

We did three more successful negotiations behind the scenes to close out the year, and as we turned the corner into 2010, the company seemed to be turning the corner too. The money was starting to flow in, although Travis and I didn't take salaries in 2009. We were still living off our UPS stock and savings.

But now we had the secret sauce. With each negotiation taking only weeks instead of months, and the customer not having to worry about damaging their relationship with the carrier, selling our service was easier because we'd removed two of the main objections. We were also gathering testimonials and getting referrals whenever we could.

In fact, we got a great lesson in asking for referrals from an early client. We had finished the negotiation for them and were presenting the results. Travis and I were sitting across the desk from the CFO, and we said: "Here's what we did. Isn't it great?"

She agreed and said, "Can I call anybody for you?"

I looked at Travis and then back at the CFO. "Huh?" I said. "Do you need me to call someone?"

"I don't understand what you're talking about."

Patiently, she explained. "Would you like me to pick up the phone and call a potential customer and tell them what a good job you do?"

"Oh!" I said. "References. Referrals!"

"Yeah," she said. "That's what I would do for you, because you did such a good job."

There were two other huge advantages to doing the negotiations behind the scenes. First was the value of the savings we could get our customer. When we were negotiating out in the open on the customer's behalf, the carrier resented us as a third party that had come between them and their customer, so they held back on the discounts or other concessions. Once we were no longer visibly in the picture and the carrier was negotiating directly with the customer (coached by us), that resentment was taken out of the equation and we were able to negotiate to the full extent of what was viable for the carrier. For example, let's say we could see that the customer should get sixty percent in savings over market rates, double their current thirty percent. Negotiating out in the open we'd be able to bring them from thirty percent to forty-five percent. But now, behind the scenes, we could get them all the way to sixty percent, or maybe even more.

The other big advantage was the scalability. Now that we weren't having to be there in person for every negotiation, there was theoretically no cap on our potential for growth.

Along with referrals from customers, we were still being fed leads by the sales guy at the audit company, and they were quality leads. Because of the way the company loaded their customers, that one sales guy had a good relationship with everybody the company did business with. That was important, because he would call and say, "Hey, owner of ABC Company, here's Keith Byrd of Transportation Impact. This is what they do for a living," and then I would take over. Thanks to the relationship and the personal introduction, we were almost guaranteed to get at least a follow-up call, and usually a meeting. The other thing was that when we walked in the door, we already knew we could save them money. By the end of 2009, we thought this audit company was the best thing that had ever happened to us.

We learned a lot from that company. Number one, we learned that's the way to do it. Work smart, not hard. Partner with anybody that has a sales force and a customer base. The second thing we learned was that we definitely had to get in the audit game, because it's a much easier sell than the negotiation service and it would give us access to the customers' carrier invoices. Once we had access to their shipping data via the invoices, we could uncover the savings and cross-sell them on the negotiation. With that as our channel to market, we could explode.

The audit technology analyzes the customer's carrier invoice for errors, including service errors, and then secures the refunds on the customer's behalf. The customer doesn't have to do anything. For example, if a package was supposed to be delivered by 10:30 and it gets there at 10:35, we obtain one hundred percent of that re-fund and then split it with the customer. Another important part of the audit is the dashboard, where the customer has at their finger-tips the ability to see all the characteristics of their parcel shipping. Before they walk into a staff meeting, if they need to know anything about their shipping, the audit software can produce it for them.

At that time we didn't have the skillset or the people to build our own audit, so in early 2010 we were on the lookout for an audit pro-vider to partner with. It wasn't long before we met someone from Veriship and soon came to an agreement with them.

Right from the start it was a really good relationship. They were willing to give us a fair split on the share of the customer sav-ings that we got in our agreement with our customers. That was a game changer for our business model, because it overnight put us on the board as a best-in-class company and legitimate logistics service provider. We blind labelled the Veriship software, so on the dashboard it said "Transportation Impact" with our TI green and our logo. It was run through the Veriship servers, but it had a Transportation Impact URL. We sold the hell out of that audit. I was personally selling three to five a week. It was nuts. Before I knew it we had three hundred customers.

I developed my boilerplate pitch to sell the audit—"This is a nonintrusive invoice-based audit that secures refunds on behalf of the client and provides business intelligence to the client"—and we immediately became Veriship's biggest customer. It got so they had to dedicate two of their employees to Transportation Impact, because they were having to give so many presentations. I would get the customer on the virtual meeting and Veriship was responsible for the presentation of the audit software. We even had a 1-800 dedicated line for us in their office, so when a customer called, the Veriship person answered as Transportation Impact. They also handled all the billing and the service calls.

Once we had a few months' worth of a customer's data from their carrier invoices via the audit, we analyzed the savings we could get them through negotiation and then went to them and said: "Mr. Customer, thank you for signing up with me on the audit three months ago. I took the initiative on running an analysis. I've only saved you sixty-eight dollars for the last three months, but let's go out and get the three hundred and sixty thousand in annual savings."

We were crushing it. The customers loved it. Talk about a channel to market. That audit was the biggest thing that provided us with explosive growth.

We knew we had to develop our own audit platform, and instead of being simply a good platform, it would be great, because customers told us what they didn't like about the Veriship platform. A couple of years later, when we were building our own audit, we took all that information and made ours a world-class product.

Veriship also had the two criteria for a good partner for us: a sales force and a customer base. They didn't have a relationship with their customers the way the other company had, so they couldn't provide personal introductions, but they had ten times the customer base. We came to a partnership agreement in addition to the audit, and they fed us leads. The hit rate was lower, but the volume was much higher. They were giving us five leads a week, and back then that was all we could handle in terms of the analysis. Now we do an analysis in fifteen minutes. But we just didn't have the software back then.

As our business was growing and we were doing more and more free analyses, we started seeing what was in the market and how we had been misled all those years by our own pricing people when we were at UPS. They would tell us, "On thirty pounds and up you can't get that fifty-seven percent discount." But once we were analyzing tens and then hundreds of companies' shipping data, we started seeing sixty-three percent or more out in the market on packages that were uglier than what we'd been asking the pricing people about on behalf of our UPS client accounts.

Here's a great example. Big Rock Sports was one of my accounts when I was with UPS. When we left UPS in 2008, I told Travis there was no use pursuing Big Rock because they had great rates. I don't think we even put them on the list that Rex negotiated. Once we knew what was really out there, we went back to Big Rock and saved them 1.3 million dollars a year. That's how brainwashed we were. I didn't even want to walk into Big Rock to sell Transportation Impact because I had been their UPS rep and the pricing people had told me that Big Rock was at the limit. They don't show the salespeople the math. They just tell them: "Here's what's available." But now we knew what was really available.

As our growth was exploding via the audit, I was still searching for that one BIG name to put on our marketing materials and our website. I never forgot what that guy at Starkey in Minnesota said.

Brian Moffitt, the CEO of Richard Petty Motorsports since

2011, is an old friend of mine. During high school summers when I worked doing plumbing with my dad, Brian often worked with me, so we became good friends. One day Travis and I were in Richmond, Virginia, for a sales call, and I asked Brian if he could get us in the door at Reynolds Packaging Group—known to everyone in the country as Reynolds Wrap. The company had a plant in Richmond, and I knew Brian had a connection with them through NASCAR. He managed to get us a meeting with Debbie Tiller, the company's director of global transportation.

Debbie was interested in what we had to say, but she wasn't sold, and also she wasn't the ultimate decision maker. We had to get her full buy-in and persuade her to introduce us to her boss, Gerald Cantwell, VP of global supply chain. But she was interested enough that we were able to set up a meeting with her and the manager of Carrier Sourcing, Allen Thornton. After another meeting or two, Debbie and Allen were sold on the value we could bring to Reynolds Wrap, and at last we got a meeting with Gerry Cantwell.

Gerry was a very smart, shrewd guy. He asked all the right questions, and then he agreed to work with us. But there was a catch. He negotiated us to a flat fee of around thirty thousand dollars for the carrier negotiation. That was a barely noticeable fraction of what we would have made had we gone even ninety-ten on the split, but that didn't matter to us. The name was what mattered. The name and the relationship. I knew that this one name was going to make us millions. We probably would have done it for free just to be able to brag about having Reynolds Wrap as a client, but the thirty thousand was nice. Plus we managed to get them on our audit platform, so we would earn a percentage of everything they saved for the lifetime of our agreement with the company.

And then something happened that skyrocketed the value of the relationship.

When we were preparing the strategy for the negotiation, as per usual practice we had the customer give us a list of all their locations.

Travis noticed immediately that some of the account numbers were not part of the company's consolidated pay plan. We investigated further and saw there were account numbers that did have shipping activity and were not tied to any contracts. The discrepancy went back six or seven years. The only explanation we could think of was that when Reynolds had acquired other companies, these accounts hadn't been transferred and for years they had been paying published rates instead of Reynolds's negotiated rates.

In our next meeting, we told them what we'd found. "If you average the spend of these accounts and their discount, that's a large sum of money UPS owes you. UPS can tell you exactly how much."

We put it back on UPS, because we didn't have the data that went back six or seven years, and they didn't have it either. We knew UPS would do the right thing. Sure enough, UPS came out and wrote Reynold's Packaging Group a check for around a hundred and thirty thousand dollars as reimbursement for all the years' worth of discounts they hadn't gotten on those accounts.

When we got the news, Travis and I whooped and high-fived each other, because we knew that this was going to be a success story. Then about five minutes later, we looked at each other and said, "Why in the hell ain't we getting half of that?" Our lawyers got a call from us to modify the language in our simple agreement to make sure that in future if we found retroactive savings, we would get our portion of it.

But more importantly, it showed Reynolds Wrap that we knew what we were doing, and we hadn't even started the negotiation yet. So we immediately gained a lot of trust.

Forever afterwards, we told that story. If one of our salespeople is in front of a customer tomorrow, they will act like we just saved Reynolds Wrap a hundred and thirty thousand dollars on one finding. It's a natural part of our pitch now: "The value add we bring, Ms. Customer, is we're always auditing your bills. For an example, Reynolds Wrap's a big client of ours. We found that several of their account numbers were paying published rates. Because of our findings, UPS had to write them a check for a hundred and thirty grand."

As we developed the negotiation strategy with Gerry, Debbie, and Allen, they requested a lot of face-to-face meetings, more than most customers, because they wanted to make sure we coached them right and they had the strategy down. They were very particular, and we learned a lot from the questions they asked. That was another thing that paid off for years to come. We incorporated what we learned from them into our strategy, and it made it stronger. Also we didn't mind putting in the extra time and effort with them, because we knew it was important to develop the relationship, so they would pick up the phone and be a reference for us.

Here, we succeeded beyond our wildest hopes. Allen was so impressed by what we had done for Reynolds Wrap that he became one of our biggest advocates and a huge asset to our company. For all the years afterwards, we would end our pitch by saying, "Call this guy. He'll share his experience with you," and we'd give them Allen's cellphone number. Every single time, Allen would answer that call and tell that prospect how we negotiated a best-in-class agreement and, by the way, we found them a hundred and thirty grand. It was like it was just laid in our lap.

# 11

## WE UNLEASH THE POWER
## OF MARKETING

While we were getting ourselves established as an audit provider, a million-dollar gift landed in my inbox.

In early January 2010 we engaged with SCOTTe-VEST on the renegotiation of the company's UPS agreement. We had to overcome a lot of reluctance by Scott Jordan, the founder and CEO, because when we told him what was involved, he thought it was going to cost him a lot of work and time. But we persuaded him, and his negotiation went really quickly, only three weeks from start to finish.

Scott was shrewd. Once he understood the strategy, he played it out perfectly. Scott was famous for getting into it with Mark Cuban on *Shark Tank* to defend his rights as a successful entrepreneur—that episode is one of the most controversial and most watched in *Shark Tank* history—so he was perfect to play the part of the hammer with UPS, because he's that kind of guy.

About a month after the negotiation was concluded, we had an early morning call with Scott. He was not in the best mood, probably because it was so early, and he wasn't entirely nice to us. An hour or so after we hung up, a video voicemail from him popped into my in-box as an apology. I hit "play."

SCOTTeVEST has one big sale annually, in the last week of February, and the savings we helped him negotiate on his UPS agreement came into effect in time for his biggest shipping week of the year. Scott was so pleasantly surprised with how easy the whole process had been and thrilled with the savings that he spontaneously recorded a testimonial video for us.

We couldn't have scripted that video, and if we had scripted it, we couldn't have done it better. It was like the best commercial I'd ever seen in my life. In less than two and a half minutes he told a story that hit every pain point about giving us the data, how efficient we were, how little time he spent on it, how successful the negotiation was, and how we saved him thousands of dollars in one week. He nailed it.

"This is huge," I said as the video ended. "This is what's going to get us over the hump."

I got a tech-savvy person to figure out how to get it download-able, and from that point on for big presentations when I was in front of C-level people, after going through everything, I would hit "play." Scott would come on the conference room screen, tell his story, annihilate every pain point, and prove everything I had just said about the benefits of working with us. That video has made us millions of dollars.

It also became the bible of our marketing material. We picked it apart, just taking it out of the customer's mouth and feeding it back. It was the perfect problem-solution, and Scott gave it to us.

I could feel momentum building, but we were still scrambling, and every customer call was a big deal. After our experience at Parcel trade show, I was acutely aware that we had to up our presentation game. Our presentation skills were lacking because we were used to UPS producing everything for us when we were in sales. We had no collateral. So when I got a hit on a lead with a huge, global company called Eaton and Travis and I were contemplating flying out to Arkansas to meet with them, I looked to find someone who could help us with the presentation. My wife said that the real estate firm she worked for used a local business called The Print Fish.

We put a PowerPoint together and hurried to The Print Fish, which happened to be right down the road from the surf shop. The Print Fish occupied a small space upstairs, and when we walked in the owner was standing behind the counter. His name was Brian Dobler. He asked what we needed, and we told him we had a big presentation and by the way it was tomorrow. "Alright," he said. "Let's get it done." We handed over the thumb drive with the PowerPoint.

Brian pulled up the presentation on his large screen and after reviewing it for a few moments in silence, he said, "Let me clean this up for you, boys," which was a nice way of telling us our PowerPoint looked like shit. He asked us questions to learn about our business and edited the presentation. The first version he handed us looked good, but we could see he hadn't understood exactly what we did.

"We're not a trucking company, and you've got an LTL truck on here," we said. "We're small package."

That was a small thing, though. I was just amazed that he was willing to stay late and make our presentation pretty for us when he didn't even know us. He even told us he wasn't going to charge us anything because he knew we were starting up and didn't have that much money. I was so impressed by Brian's desire to help us that we went across the street to Kathryn's, a little martini bar and bistro that would also come to play a role in our story, and bought a hundred dollar gift certificate.

After a couple of hours of dedicated creative work, Brian printed out our presentation and handed it to us. Wow. He had transformed our amateur PowerPoint into a professional presentation that not only looked slick but also told a story that led the viewer through to the conclusion that working with us was a no-brainer. That was exactly what Reggie Barnes had said and what Scott Jordan said in his video. It was a no-brainer. I instantly fell in love with that presentation. I knew it was going to be the presentation of the future for us because of how it looked and the story it told. I was so proud. What Brian Dobler did with this presentation sparked the first of many "Keithisms" that became familiar throughout TI. "I need a pretty version!" I would say, my redneck way of asking for a finished product that was best in class, just like Brian had made for us.

I told him how thrilled I was, we shook hands, and then we handed him the gift certificate. "Here, this is for you. We really appreciate you goin' the extra mile."

As we walked out of the shop with our wonderful presentation, I knew that Brian was going to be a big partner of our company. We had found Madison Avenue right here in little Emerald Isle, and it was a heart connection for both of us.

When Travis and I were making all our plans on the whiteboards down at the beach house, marketing never came up. We never thought we would have to have marketing. We thought that people would be knocking down the doors wanting our service. We thought we would just walk in to a company and a few hours later walk out with a signed agreement. The light bulb came on when we were sitting at the bar drinking Crown and Diets after Parcel trade show, where we observed the professional collateral that people in the logistics world had. I was amazed, and I knew that we had to change the way we presented our services. Now we had found our marketing department. It was the perfect fit. How lucky we were to have this guy right down the street.

That was in March 2010, and over the next two months our relationship with Brian rapidly developed into his becoming an indispensable part of our team.

We had him print some business cards, and when he delivered them to us in the back of the surf shop, we spelled out to him more clearly the nature of the service we were offering so he could understand better, and talked about having a brochure or a sell sheet. Then he looked at our logo and said, "It's really not a logo. It's more of an ad." A few days later we went up to his office and chatted about what he could do for us. He set up his studio lights and took professional photos of us to put on the business cards and to use in ads. Over the next weeks we were back and forth, in his upstairs office or our Control Center, as he called it, bouncing ideas off each other and sparking mutual creativity for how to market Transportation Impact.

Most days now there were two of us in the broom closet, sitting at the granite countertop among the metal storage racks and boxes of T-shirts, working LinkedIn and the phone to drum up sales. It got to the point where we were having a lot of meetings, and we just couldn't do it. With two people in the office doing two or three phone meetings a day, we were talking over each other. One of us would have to go out into the surf shop to take his call. We knew that soon we had to get a proper office where we could all shut our doors and have a professional atmosphere.

It also seemed silly, or at least inefficient, constantly going back and forth between Brian's office and ours. All the time we were bouncing things off each other. We would find ourselves doing more brainstorming than him actually bringing stuff. We'd go to dinner for two hours and talk about how we could go to the next level, not just in what he was doing for us, but in terms of the business as a whole. We fed off each other. Besides Brian's Madison Avenue skills, what impressed me most was that he was actually interested in our business model. At that time, we were still pioneers in this space, and it was hard for anybody to understand what we did. We even had to invest the time in educating our attorneys so they could understand the fine details. We got our elevator speech down, eventually, but for a long time most people thought we shipped packages.

Brian, though, soon knew our business model as well as we did.

He was constantly asking questions. It was great to be around some-body that was interested and that added value from a creativity per-spective. He was not scared to say, "Hey, this is okay, but this ain't what you need to be." He would actually call our baby ugly, and we loved that. I want you to tell me my baby's ugly and what we can do to change. Answering Brian's questions was a great investment, because he would produce an end product that got attention.

It developed into a great friendship. We loved being around each other; we all had the same fire. It was remarkable that we could find somebody else like that right there in Emerald Isle. The relationship was mutually beneficial, a rising tide that floated both boats and also lifted us personally.

I'm a big gut person. I can read people. If it's in my gut, I'm of-ten right. There are two things that are important with whoever I'm dealing with: trust and loyalty. You've got to have those two things. Loyalty is 99.9 percent of everything; the other tenth is not measur-able. And trust is the foundation of loyalty. When Brian and I got together, I knew he had those two things, and that's why we trusted him. We'd give him a project and say, "Look, we've got to win this account. Let's see what you come up with." It was that trust factor.

So when it was clear we had grown out of the broom closet and needed to find a proper office space, it seemed logical to ask Brian to move in with us. We could save a lot of time going back and forth to each other's offices and instead brainstorm "in the moment" right there on the spot—and he could share the rent. We were still very frugal, and Travis and I were not ready to commit to taking on the full responsibility of renting an office space. I knew Brian was look-ing for a bigger space, so moving in together seemed like a win-win.

We heard there was a spot open in the strip mall beside Kathryn's, the martini bar and bistro where we had bought the gift certificate for Brian when he made that first presentation for us. That was only three months ago, but it seemed like he had already been part of the TI team for ages.

It was a big place, much more than we all needed. But it was Emerald Isle; you get what's available. The rent was around thirteen hundred dollars a month, and the thought of being responsible to pay that much rent every month scared me to death. I arranged a date with Brian and we went over to look at it. My idea was that he would have the front part for his copying machine, and we would retrofit the back into four or five offices, plus a small conference room. I pointed out to Brian the space that he would have, and then told him how much the rent was and that TI would take on two-thirds of it. We both pressed our foreheads against the glass, holding our right hands above our heads to shade the reflective glare so we could see.

"Brian," I said, peering in beside him, "are you sure you can pull your part of this thirteen hundred dollars a month? You've got to guarantee me you're going to pay your part. We can't carry this."

It was a big move for us. We were going from two guys in the back of a surf shop to six individual offices and a conference room—and a sign out front with our name on it. Transportation Impact. We would be official. To be fair, from Brian's side, if we didn't pay our portion, he'd be stuck with a much bigger rent than he signed on for. But we had already bonded, and he knew that I was the kind of guy who would make this thing work, no matter what.

So in May 2010 we moved in together. It was funny. It was like a whirlwind courtship, where we'd met only a few months ago and now we'd got married.

It was also very exciting. We had the renovations done, and then it was time to furnish the space. TI had won some business with a North Carolina furniture company, so I grabbed the company checkbook and went shopping. I don't like to do things halfway, so I ordered really nice furniture, including a desk and chair for Brian. I wanted to show my appreciation for his taking so much unpaid time to immerse himself in our business.

Trucks full of furniture pulled up outside Suite B, 8002 Emerald

Drive, and I hired a surfer we knew to put everything together at night. That afternoon we left an empty space with beige walls, and the next morning we walked into a fully furnished office. It was just like a movie.

When I think of something creative, I want to talk about it right now. So it was a game changer when Brian and I were within arm's length of each other. Now the creative juices went from flowing fifty percent of the day to eighty percent of the day. Instead of getting in the car and going that dreadful quarter of a mile and up the stairs to see Brian, we could pop next door to Kathryn's, grab a drink and some food—it would lead us off task, I admit.

But Travis and I were still paranoid about making the rent. We were afraid we were going to use the conference room very little, so we had the brilliant idea to rent it out as a revenue generator and went all out turning it into a first-class space. At Mike Denmead's shop, Artisan Granite & Marble, we bought a whole slab of granite for the conference table. I was so proud of that granite. Mike told me he'd never put a piece that big on a table. Then I bought and installed a big-screen TV. When it was all done, we thought that 14' × 10' conference room was the coolest thing in the world. We were going to tell Emerald Isle Realty and some of the other businesses: "Look, ya'll need conference space. We've got it for you!" But that lasted all of two weeks because our business started blowing up, and we didn't want anybody in the conference room because we were always using it.

Just as soon as we moved into that space with Brian and the supercharged creativity, our business went nuts. It shows how important marketing is to salespeople. Because let's face it, sales drives revenue, but marketing boosts sales.

In those early days, there were a lot of times we would work late—really late—together, because it was so hard to get time in front of a potential customer, and once I'd seen what Brian could do, I went nuts. I was working easily twelve, fourteen hours a day, and then traveling, because if I could get a meeting, Brian and I would sit for however long it took to get the presentation perfect. I only had that thirty or forty minutes in front of a customer, and Brian helped me to maximize the impact of every one of those minutes.

To this day, that is a big part of why we've been successful. We went from not being prepared, not having collateral, no marketing, to a best-in-class, professional presence. When we got in front of customers, we looked like a much bigger company than we were. In fact, some early clients who actually visited us at our office, like Lynne Rabil of Hubs Peanuts, said how surprised they were to find us in a suite in a strip mall.

For years, everywhere we went, every C-level that we presented to, everybody was blown away by our collateral. We had competitors coming up, asking, "Who is your marketing team?" They couldn't believe it was one guy in a room at the front of our suite in a strip mall.

*Travis in his office in Suite B, 8002 Emerald Drive.*

Another thing that was instrumental to the success of TI is that we adapted very early on. We didn't just stick to the usual things everybody else did to try to get in front of a customer. For example, we would go out and buy their product, and then we would all put on that customer's product and go down and stand on the beach and Brian would photograph us. (He was not only great at marketing, he was a great photographer too!) Then we would send the customer the photo with a handwritten letter that put it back on them: "Hey, I'm a client of yours; be a client of mine."

When Brian brought us creative, out-of-the-box, risky ideas, I loved it because I knew it was going to make our company shine; it was going to be a differentiator in the market. I love when you look at something and go, "Wow!" Those were the kinds of things he produced. Sales flows through my bloodstream, and I love the strategic side and being noticed. Thanks to the incredible creative energy of our relationship with Brian, for a long time I was fully engaged with our marketing.

We are also grateful to Brian for lighting the bulb in our head that we didn't want to piss off UPS and FedEx in some of our marketing efforts. We really didn't think about that side of it until Brian brought it to our attention. From then on, we were a little more measured, let's say. We could have filled a few chapters in a guerilla marketing book. Sure, we didn't win them all. But the important thing was that we were not afraid to push and poke the market. We were risk takers, and Brian was, too.

Perhaps our most famous one was the money bag. We had a trade show coming up, and I told Brian I didn't want to look like everybody else. I wanted something that would get people's attention and make them remember us.

Our business was about savings, so he had a local lady sew a giant canvas bag, and on the side of it we printed really large: "FedEx and UPS Refunds." On his big machine, Brian printed a whole lot of giant hundred-dollar bills, and then laid them on his garage floor and hosed them with a light mist to make them look used. We hauled all this to the trade show along with a few packs of balloons and handed everything over to the staff to set up. They must have loved us. But it was awesome, and it got attention. The canvas bag was filled with balloons almost to the top, and then the rest of the way it was stuffed with the hundred-dollar bills so they poked out of the top.

People came by, saw "FedEx and UPS Savings," and grabbed a hundred-dollar bill as they walked past. The brilliant part was that on the back side of the bill was our one-pager, so hundreds of people at the trade show took our info and we didn't have to do anything. Some people even wanted their photo taken with the money bag. These days it would be pretty corny, but back then it was cutting edge and cool. It was a hit. It was risky too. It was edgy, because here we are at the same trade show as UPS and FedEx, and we're throwing it in their face with a bag of money. Before we hit the Go button on that, we really had to think about it. But we ended up using that money bag for years.

Always in the early years, we had to be so careful about how far to push the ten-thousand-pound gorilla. UPS could have shut us down. Brian learned how to walk along the edge with us. I was paranoid about that line in the sand. I didn't ever want to cross it. The money bag was something small, but it was really effective with customers. However it took a lot of thinking to do that. There were times where Brian would pitch an idea and we'd say no, that's crossing the line. Eventually, he knew the line better than we did. We never wanted to go to where it was obnoxiously in your face. It grew to the point where if Brian had a couple thousand dollars in a marketing idea, we had ten thousand dollars in legal fees to see if we could do it. It wasn't just about some creative idea or the next thing. We had to get in the shoes of UPS and FedEx and ask ourselves: "How are they going to see this?"

*Perhaps our most famous risky promotion was the money bag. I wanted something that would get people's attention and make them remember us, and Brian Dobler delivered beyond expectations, as usual.*

We never forgot that there wouldn't be a Transportation Impact without FedEx and UPS.

Even with the worry, though, the creativity and energy that came from our partnership were exciting and a huge amount of fun. You can't put a price tag on that. Plus it brought results. So many times we would come back to the office after a sales call and say to Brian, "We landed it. It was that brochure you made!" Of course, it was never just the brochure. Our business model made sense to smart people. But I know that our presentation played a huge part in making smart people pay attention to us and take us seriously. It said: "We know what we're doing, we're a player in this game, and you can trust us." What Brian produced for us immediately gained us credibility and professionalism. And he kept expanding his portfolio, from trade shows to one-pagers to magazine ads to digital marketing.

However, there came a day when I discovered he wasn't perfect.

I was at a trade show. It must have been a late decision to go, because Brian hustled and quickly made a couple of brochures. It was Saturday night. I was handing out Brian's creation at the show, loving people's *wow* reaction to it, when one of our competitors came up to me. He held up our brochure, pointed to it, and said, "If you can't even audit your own brochure or spell a word right, how are you ever going to handle a client's multimillion-dollar audit?"

I was mortified.

After he walked off, I grabbed a brochure, circled the misspelled word, took a photo of it, and texted it to Brian, telling him what the competitor had said.

He was at home having dinner with his family, and when he saw my message and the photo of the misspelled word, he almost threw up on the table. I think he felt even worse than I did. He described that moment as a nightmare in his soul, and I didn't want to hand out any more brochures. After that, he hired a proofreader to go over everything he created for us with a fine-tooth comb before it went out.

But I think that experience cemented our relationship, because we saw in each other the same reaction to that one small mistake. It wasn't just perfectionism. It was the do-it-right attitude, and living up to your word. Those two things have from day one been the driving force behind Transportation Impact: Attention to detail. Do what you say you're going to do.

# 12

## TI BECOMES A "REAL" COMPANY

Now we were in an official office where we each had our own space with a door we could close, we had a top-notch marketing team in the form of Brian Dobler, we had a big-name logo on our website and a growing client list, and now, even working sixty or seventy hours a week, we could no longer cope with everything that needed to be done with the help of the few contractors we had. It was time to hire our first employee.

There was a young woman in town who had gone to school with my younger son, Tyler, who I thought would be great as full-time office help. I discussed it with Travis, and we decided to make the leap to taking on the responsibility of an employee.

Erin Klein was in her early twenties and not long out of college. When I offered her around the same hourly rate as she was getting at the realty company where she was working part-time, but with us it would be full-time, she soon agreed to join us. On June 21, 2010, Transportation Impact's first employee started work. Erin jumped right in to doing whatever needed to be done, including helping Travis with receivables, and immediately became a key member of the TI family.

By this time we also had three sales contractors, people who we knew and trusted and had persuaded to join us. The first to come on board was Chris Burns, who worked remotely from his home in Greensboro, North Carolina. Although he had been in business development at UPS and wasn't a natural salesperson, Chris immediately understood our vision and the potential for it to be hugely successful, and his belief in TI and his loyalty have never wavered.

Then in January 2010 our sales team got a further boost with two more contractors, Tim Brock—the Wilmington UPS driver I had brought in so long ago and then helped to move over into sales—and Bob West, a logistics professional we knew from the industry. Like Chris, they both worked remotely.

We trained them in our strategy and set them to work. We hand-picked the people we chose to work with us because we wanted people we could trust and who would do whatever it took to get the end result. In sales, that meant they had to have persistence. They had to have tenacity. You can't be afraid of hearing No. You have to keep trying. Eventually the person is either going to tell you to go away forever, or they're going to say, "OK, I'll give you ten minutes." And then you'd better make the most of those ten minutes.

I'm incredibly tenacious. I don't give up until I get a "No, and don't bother me ever again." Like the time we were at a trade show and I saw a guy I'd been emailing but getting no response from. At trade shows, most people are there to sell and I'm very cognizant of that, so I keep my pitch to about ten seconds. We went up to the guy and stood there until he turned his attention to us.

"Keith Byrd, Transportation Impact," I said. "I've been emailing you. I'm not here to buy. Here's what I want to do."

"Damn," he said. "You are relentless. I will give you thirty minutes if you promise to quit emailing me."

We didn't get that one, but my persistence was about to pay off. Big time. For months I had been emailing the COO of Pandora, Scott Burger, but not getting a reply from him. I really wanted

Pandora as a client. As a global jewelry company with a great reputation, they had very high small parcel volume, and I knew we could save them a lot of money. Their headquarters at that time was in Columbia, Maryland.

In midsummer Travis and I found ourselves in Maryland, and I decided to try to get Scott to at least talk to me. Strategically, I got a hotel room next to the Pandora headquarters where I could see him pull up. Out the window, I watched as he arrived, got out of his car, and walked into the building, and then I called his direct line.

"I just watched you walk into your office," I said. He thought that was kind of weird. "I'm not trying to be weird. I came all this way, and all I want to do, if you'll take another thirty seconds and come right back out to that reception area, just let me hand you something and shake your hand. I promise I'll never bother you again." He agreed to do that.

Travis and I raced downstairs and across to the Pandora reception area. When we got there, Scott wasn't there, so we introduced ourselves to the receptionist and said we'd like to talk to Scott Burger. She walked us to an interior office, knocked on the door, opened it, and said, "Scott, these gentlemen asked if you had a couple minutes."

I didn't wait for him to reply. Stepping past the receptionist I entered his office, with Travis close behind. We introduced ourselves, explaining that we were the owners and founders of Transportation Impact, and sat down.

"I decided to come and see you myself, because the guy who's been emailing you hasn't managed to secure a meeting," I said jokingly, not mentioning that I was the one who had been emailing him.

"Boy, I thought the last guy was annoyingly persistent, but you're taking it to a whole new level." But he was smiling, and I knew the door was open.

"We think this can be hugely beneficial to you," I said. "Let me make you look like a hero."

We started to explain how the model worked and how the payback came, but I wanted to demonstrate so he could see. Real numbers in ink get people's attention faster than all the talking in the world. Scott didn't have any windows in his office. Instead he had two whiteboards stuck on the pinkish-beige walls, a little one behind his desk and a big one. I got up, walked over to the big one, picked up a marker, and wrote a large number showing how much the company could save.

"How does this look?" I said. I crossed the number out. "We can make it more favorable for you." I wrote another number, bigger than the first one. "What do you think of this?"

I saw in Scott's expression that I had got his attention. Later he told me that it reminded him of going shopping over in Thailand, where the people in the markets don't know English, he doesn't know Thai, and both sides just write numbers on pieces of paper and cross them off.

Scott asked a lot of questions to understand exactly what Pandora's responsibility would be, and we used the whiteboard to hash out the broad terms of what our agreement would look like.

Eventually we were all comfortable with this initial mutual understanding, and Scott stood up. It was time to go. He escorted us to the lobby, we shook hands, and Travis and I walked outside. I looked at my watch. Our unscheduled meeting had lasted almost two hours.

We had five or six more meetings to nail down the fine points and make sure Scott was well prepared for the negotiation with the carrier, because he was going to be the contact. Our strategy of guiding the negotiation from behind the scenes was likely the key factor in Scott agreeing to sign with us. With FedEx and UPS being a duopoly, and both of them critically important to Pandora, he was very protective of the fact that Pandora had very good relationships with both of them, and he didn't want to "inject an adversarial third party who was just focused on squeezing every nickel out of it."

To determine the exact savings to be gained, we asked for access to Pandora's shipping invoices. They handed us a pile of paper. We were aghast that a company that shipped as much as Pandora did was not using electronic billing. After we pointed out that it was archaic, they pretty quickly migrated from paper to electronic billing.

The moment he saw the invoices, Travis became very excited, whipping out a calculator and piece of paper and doing back-of-the-napkin math. In those rough calculations, we quickly saw that we could save them a significant amount.

The negotiation was the most complex one we had ever done, because for the first time we were working on behalf of a company with a global presence. In our strategy we had to manage negotiations for standalone agreements for the two or three major countries in which Pandora had a presence, including an intra-Europe agreement. It was complicated, but Scott handled it perfectly. He's a very smart man.

Within about a month, Pandora had a new carrier agreement that reduced the company's annual shipping cost by over a million dollars. As usual, we delivered almost exactly what we had said. Scott didn't tell us then, but at first he had the same concern that Lynne Rabil at Hubs had: "How do I audit the auditor?" In the early days, his team double-checked the math on our invoices a lot, but as the relationship went on and he built up a much higher level of confidence, they checked less and less.

It was a big deal to us to have a client with an international presence. Back at our strip mall HQ I would say, "We're global now!"

Joking aside, it worked to our advantage. The complexity of the negotiation in combination with how successful we were helped to create stickiness. That first negotiation was the beginning of a long and mutually profitable relationship between our two companies that has continued through Scott becoming CFO and then president of the Americas for Pandora, and then leaving the company. Over the years, Scott helped us a lot by being willing to be a guinea pig for new ideas for ways to save our clients money. We have re-mained personal friends, and Transportation Impact had an equal-ly great relationship with Scott's successor, Kevin Conklin, and his team, who continue to take full advantage of TI's ever-evolving and deepening data analysis capabilities. (Kevin left Pandora in April 2021, but our relationship with the company continues and Kevin remains a close personal friend.)

Travis and I were working easily sixty, seventy hours a week, and I was travelling constantly, but we managed to relax in the hours we weren't at the office or on the road. Right from the beginning, we lived the TI motto: Work hard, play hard.

Dolphin Ridge, where Syndie and I lived, was a gated commu-nity marketed as a "private vacation and family environment," and we spent a lot of our free time relaxing at the swimming pool and clubhouse that were only about a minute's walk from the beach. Our sons were both at college, and they used to bring their friends to stay with us. Brian's college roommate, Brandon Staton, had vis-ited many times and was staying again this summer.

One July afternoon we were at the pool, lying on the loungers, enjoying a beverage or two and getting in the water when we got too hot, when Brandon started quizzing me about TI. I explained it the way I always did, but he kept asking more questions, and then he asked me for a job.

Brandon was about to graduate with a journalism degree and I had no idea what he would do for us, plus I wasn't sure we could take on another employee just yet, so I didn't respond enthusiasti-cally. But he persisted. Then out of the blue he said, "I didn't know you went to LaSalle."

I grinned. He had obviously been doing his homework, which meant he was serious about wanting to work at TI. One of my fa-vorite questions to ask in an interview is "Tell me about our compa-ny. Tell me what we do." Anyone who wants to work for me needs to come prepared. He must have studied my LinkedIn profile. I explained the degree had been required by UPS and I never actually went to LaSalle, and then told him I liked that he'd done his homework.

After a few hours in the sun we all moved into our downstairs rec room, the main hangout spot. There was a pool table and a big screen TV with stadium seats. We installed ourselves in the stadium seats to watch some sporting event on the big screen, and Brandon continued bending my ear about working at Transportation Impact. Finally he said, "Just give me a chance." That resonated with me. I knew what it was like to want someone to just give you a chance to prove yourself. But I still wasn't sold.

"We just started this company," I said. "You have no experience. You didn't work for UPS. I don't know what the hell you would do."

He didn't know, either, but he said, "Just give me an opportunity. Please."

I talked to Travis. "Let's just see where this goes," I said. "He's a family friend. I know we don't need anybody, but I would like to find something for him to do. I believe in him." Travis agreed it would be good to at least have Brandon come in for an interview. We discussed a possible assignment for him, and came up with a great idea.

Brandon came into the office and we all gathered in our bedroom-sized conference room for an "official interview," but really it was an unscripted employee orientation. We had decided Brandon's main responsibility would be selling a new service called NPoD, which stood for non-proof of delivery, meaning that the package did not have a scan proving it was delivered (although in many cases the package was actually delivered). The carrier's stance was that the data accompanying the package was as important as the package itself.

For certain types of customers that shipped high volumes,

especially express shipments, which tend to be more expensive than ground shipments, NPoD was pretty lucrative as an audit point that could generate revenue. There was a real opportunity to save our customers money and generate revenue for our budding business. Brandon's job was to sell the customer on the idea of filing to claim the refund and then satisfy the carrier's requirements to credit our customer for those claims.

We spent an hour giving Brandon all the information he needed to get started, and then I asked if he had any questions. He said he had one.

"What the hell is NPoD?"

We laughed, and I cleared up his confusion. I told Brandon he would be reporting to Travis, and the interview was over.

We filed out of the conference room and headed toward the refreshment area we had installed at the back of suite B. As we were all together in the confined space of the corridor, Travis said, not lowering his voice, "When we started this business, I told Keith one thing. I said I didn't want to manage any damn people."

Fortunately he didn't mean it in an unkind way. I don't think Travis has an unkind bone in his body. He did tell me he didn't want to manage employees, but I was travelling so much, I just did not have the time to train and manage Brandon on a day-to-day basis. We still laugh about Travis saying that. In truth, we were all learning as we went. The employees were learning what their jobs entailed and how they could help the company grow, and we were learning how to manage employees. We didn't have a concrete plan. We just put people in positions to explore what worked.

In the Marine Corps, I absorbed the fourteen leadership traits and became a believer in them. Ever since, I have tried to stay true to those traits when I deal with people in both professional life and personal. I've always believed in leading by example. Practice what you preach. I also think it's important to challenge people to help them get things out of themselves that maybe they didn't know they could.

My one notable negative is lack of patience. Sometimes I assigned a task or asked somebody to do something and didn't really give them time to come up with a solution. Or change in people's behavior didn't come fast enough for me. Whatever it is, I want it to be right, and I want to keep moving, and I want attention to detail.

What we had assigned Brandon was basically a crash course in claims processing. At the time, he was living in Chapel Hill, a hundred and eighty miles from Emerald Isle, so we agreed he would work from home.

The month of August passed, and nothing much happened on the NPoD front. I wondered if it had been a mistake hiring a journalism major who admitted that he had not been a very good student. In early September, we asked Brandon to come into the office so we could discuss his progress, or lack of it. We were paying him three hundred dollars a week and we needed him to bring in revenue. Bringing in revenue from NPoD should have been a slam dunk.

Travis and I met with him in the conference room and told him how unhappy we were with his performance.

"I'm trying," he said, "but the problem is I don't really know what I'm doing. You guys are trusting me to call on decision makers at companies and ask them questions that might be stupid. I don't have any background. I don't know what an invoice looks like, I don't know what the service is, I don't know anything."

I sat back in my chair. "Well, you better figure it out, or I'll find someone who will."

"I need to be here," he blurted. "I need to be in the office so that when I have questions, you guys will see me working."

We found him an office space with a desk and a telephone, and for the remainder of 2010 he commuted the hundred and eighty miles each way. Occasionally he'd stay with me, but most days he would drive to Emerald Isle and drive back to Chapel Hill. In the last three months of 2010, he put ten thousand miles on his car driving back and forth. I watched as he stepped up and did what it took to get the job done, and he earned my respect.

We were fortunate with Erin and Brandon that they could get thrown in the deep end and learn as they went. We were trying to grow the company and still properly service the customers that we had, and we didn't have a lot of time to spend on training our two brand new employees. We weren't trying to add five customers a year—we wanted fifty new customers a year, which were tremendous growth goals; but really, we would take any growth.

One thing we did every time we finished a negotiation—after learning from the client who had asked us if she could make a phone call on our behalf—was to take the client out to dinner and ask that CEO or CFO: "Tell us what we did right. Tell us what you'd change." And then we said, "By the way, if you'll call one or two of your CEO and CFO buddies, why don't you tell them in your words what we did for you?" We always offered to reduce their bill or pay them a referral fee or give money to the charity of their choice.

When one CEO calls another CEO and says, "Look, these guys said they were going to cut my costs thirty-five percent. I couldn't believe it. You need to at least sit down with them and see if they can help you in some way," that's all it took. Then doors start opening very quickly.

Travis and I were on planes all the time. Tim Brock, Bob West, and Chris Burns were travelling. If it was a big opportunity, Travis and I might go together, lining up three or four sales calls in one day. We still had to run the company and deal with the day-to-day. There were always employees knocking on the door, seeking guidance to grow their piece of the business, or to better understand and learn what they could do to help us. With sales, there was always something going on. In the early days, we all participated in a lot of things all the time, because it was very good cross-training for our staff; nobody's ever overly trained. We did a good job of exposing the younger, initial staff members to a lot of the business in a short period of time. It was all part of a wonderful dance.

Right from the start we had cell phones. We understood the value in being able to do business from anywhere, anytime. Lack of mobility was one of the big constraints with TidBit. Whoever used it had to be in the office. So for the next version of the analysis and audit software we created, Travis was determined it would be cloud-based so he could get on an airplane on Saturday afternoon, go watch his son play a football game, and when he had a break, he could take care of all the bills for the prior week. We kept taking steps toward not being tied to the building, although it took us years and years to get fully free.

Travis is a mathematical-technological genius and I'm a natural at sales and strategizing, but neither of us is strong on record-keeping and file organization, plus we just didn't have the time. Travis and his team were meticulous with the billing, and we had one lady doing basic bookkeeping, but we could see it was time to get a professional accountant on board. We were growing so fast. My wife recommended a consultant who worked with Bluewater Real Estate. His name was Richard Brown. He had been doing higher education finance for the past thirty years and had also worked with BDO, an international CPA firm, so he was someone we could trust to put our accounting systems in order.

We met with Richard and hit it off, and in late 2010 he started work with us on a contractual basis. His whole life was budgeting and projecting and accounting and finance, and he had some unique skills that fitted in well with a growing organization. He arrived at suite B and we showed him where the records were and left him to it. What he found, he told us, was "a general ledger that made no sense and accounting systems that really didn't work very well." We had no budget and none of the things that he would have expected to see in a sophisticated business.

The first thing he did was recreate the general ledger to represent what actually was going on in the business. It was basically cash-driven, so it wasn't too complex, but he had to reconcile everything back to cash and get a general ledger that made sense. The second thing he did was to create a disciplined budget model. Travis and I were always very focused not spending any cent that didn't need to be spent, so we stuck to Richard's budget religiously for all the years he was with us. Every month, he produced a new report and we sat down and discussed it. That was the main way we kept control over where the business was going and how it was growing. It was exciting to watch that budget increase as the months went by and our client list grew.

We really appreciated the financial and administrative discipline that Richard was bringing us, as well as the ability to project and budget and control expenses. We also valued the peace of mind, especially now we had employees and had to deal with regular payroll as well as social security, workers compensation, unemployment insurance, retirement plans, and everything else that entails. It was always very important to us to have everything legal and financial be absolutely straight.

I think Richard found our office scene to be very casual. We all showed up to work in flip-flops and shorts, and people's roles were not clearly defined. Brandon's main task was NPoD but he also helped Travis with billing and analysis; Erin's main task was anything and everything, including helping me with sales—trying to secure a meeting for me by making forty phone calls a day; Travis did the billing and technical development; I was hyper focused on sales; and everybody piled into the conference room when it was time to whiteboard out the negotiation strategy for a new client.

I thought of it as the TI family, where we all did whatever it took to grow the company, and when we weren't working, we had fun. Right from the start, even before TI was born, when Travis and I were in the beach house whiteboarding our business model, we had a work hard, play hard approach. When we were on, we were on, and when we were off, we were still on, and that came with us into suite B, next door to Kathryn's Bistro & Martini Bar. From day one, we built that culture. We didn't care if you needed to go watch your kid's baseball game—go watch it. If you needed to go to Walmart and run errands, go do it. We trusted you to get your work done.

# 13

## THE SECRET SAUCE

If I had to point to one single factor that was responsible for how fast we were growing, it would be switching from negotiating in the open to coaching the client from behind the scenes. When we were at the table with the UPS or FedEx representative during those first thirteen negotiations, it created tension that the customer could see. Also, because the carrier was unhappy that we had come between them and their customer, they held back on truly market-appropriate rates and limited the discounts we could get our clients.

At last we realized it had to change, and we developed our coach and counsel technique. Once we took away the bad vibes, the negotiations went a lot faster, everybody was happy that relationships weren't being damaged, and we were helping our clients get better discounts. The constraint of all the bad vibes forced us to come up with what in the end is a better business model.

In the year-plus since that very successful first behind-the-scenes negotiation with Sweet Maria's, we had been modifying and tweaking our strategy. A lot of the improvements we made thanks to learning from clients who asked questions and put scenarios in front of us that we hadn't considered. They really made us fine-tune our delivery of the whole process, because they were as smart as we were with regards to what we were pitching. I can probably count on one hand the customers that really helped make us more polished in our delivery and how to expect the unexpected, because not many understood about things like minimums, DIMs, and contract language. These few, really smart customers pushed us to improve not just in pitching our service to try to get them to sign a contract, but once we got the contract signed, how to explain what was entailed in the delivery and how it would go. By challenging us and asking knowledgeable questions, some of the smart customers early on helped us develop a better roadmap to success from A to Z.

Once a new client has signed their agreement with us, we go in like a forensic scientist, meeting with the stakeholders in a multi-hour session to gather every detail that we need to create the negotiation strategy. To this day we still do these external strategy sessions (we also have internal ones) the exact same way. The first step is to get all the stakeholders in the room, so we can ascertain what's going on in the business.

Before going behind the scenes, our biggest concern in not being in the room during the negotiation was losing control of the situation. But that made us very good in learning how to ask better questions during that external strategy session to cover all the bases, so we maintain control over the negotiation, even though we're not there in person. For these sessions, we developed a questionnaire that started with fifteen questions and grew to twenty-five. And those twenty-five questions will stimulate twenty more that aren't even on the page. As we kept getting creative and changing the strategy, it would bring up questions that should be asked at every strategy session. Those early customers also prompted us to add questions we hadn't thought of. The questionnaire has become like a bible that our salespeople use to stimulate conversation pertinent to the success of the negotiation.

In the meeting with the stakeholders, we say, "Forget about UPS and FedEx right now. What's your three-year marketing plan? What new products are coming out? How are you going to market them? What other cost initiatives are going on in the company right now? Have you changed any kind of providers, from corrugation providers to phone providers? What's your M&A plan? What's your growth plan this year?"

It's very important to know the whole picture of marketing, any acquisitions coming up, what their mission statement is. We study their website before we meet with them. We study LinkedIn. Who are the players? What do they like? What are their hobbies?

For the first hour and a half, we talk about what's going on in the company. The next hour, we talk about their relationship with the carrier. "Who negotiates the contract on your end? Who's gone to NBA games with the UPS rep? What's the highest-level person at FedEx you've ever met? Any new C-level people that could be the bad guy during this negotiation that don't have a relationship and have never met the rep?"

One of the reasons we have to ask so many questions about the relationship with the carrier is that it's really important to find the right person within the organization that's smart enough to be the point person in the negotiation. You can't take the sixty-two-year-old guy who doesn't even have a high school education, but that's who the UPS rep calls on, and all of a sudden, him be a damn genius. The rep will know something is going on. If we're dealing with that guy, for us it's a creative sales job to get him to buy in that we have to use somebody else. In this kind of situation, ideally we want someone who has never met the UPS rep.

It's always going to be somebody high in the organization, but who has never really had a relationship with the carrier. Probably seven out of ten times, that's how we do it. The other three times, the person who regularly deals with the rep is smart enough to be the bad guy and carry out the strategy. And because that person is smart enough, the UPS or FedEx rep's not going to be alarmed when they come up with the analysis and start asking knowledgeable, sharp questions.

So in that first session with the client, we ask questions all over the board to stimulate conversation that can throw up nuggets of gold. The more questions you ask, the more likely it is that something will surface. Like the time we had gone through our entire questionnaire with a client, for two or three hours sitting in the room together, asking questions and listening to their answers, and right at the very end, we found out that one of the C-levels had gone to a NASCAR race with the number three guy at UPS.

Brandon and I stared at each other for a split second and asked, "Do you have his card?"

The guy searched around, found the card, and handed it to us. It actually had "Call me any time" handwritten on it.

"Damn!" I said. "That's going to be our contact."

We centered our whole strategy around this guy, and we went straight to the number three at UPS. We got everything we wanted.

That's happened probably two dozen times, a scenario about a business card or some relationship that somebody had. Whenever we found that out, that was like putting a big smiley face on us. We knew we were going to be successful. At UPS and FedEx, VPs and above love when a customer goes to them, because now they can beat their chests to their peers and say, "I've saved this account." All a higher-up like that does is pick up the phone and say, "I don't care what it takes, don't lose this account," and then hang up. And it tears everybody's ass.

Our questioning can seem very intrusive, and in the early stages some customers want to know "Why in the hell are you asking me that?" But then a few weeks into the six-week negotiation, they suddenly understand. They tell us, "I had no idea why you would ask for all that off-the-wall stuff. But as the six weeks collapsed, it all came together, and it all happened exactly like you said it was going to happen. It's kind of magical."

It's a blessing to hear that. I'm not bragging. It's just how good we are at what we do. We've perfected the art and craft of the behind-the-scenes negotiation. Attention to detail, that's what got us here.

Once we've got everything we need out of the meeting with the stakeholders, we go back to the office and everybody gathers for the internal strategy session. This is where we craft the strategy for how the negotiation with the carrier will go. Before we left that two- or three-hour meeting, I would already know my strategy while I was walking out to the car, but we would still go dedicate a day to developing it.

We would crowd into our itty bitty conference room with the awesome granite slab table and go over everything we'd learned from the client, throwing out ideas, drinking lots of coffee, and getting takeout from Kathryn's Bistro as we whiteboarded out the strategy. That's my skill set. I love that strategizing of once we've got a customer signed, how are we going to be successful? How are we going to take it from A to Z? Many nights we stayed there till eleven o'clock or midnight just having that strategy session.

We've got to get creative, because nine times out of ten, if we tell a customer we're going to save them eight hundred thousand dollars, the CEO says, "Keith, I really like the savings, but I'm not going to switch carriers." So we've got to do a really good job of creating a competitive environment so that the incumbent carrier works as hard as possible to keep their customer.

If the client will not entertain switching carriers, then we explain that we have to create the impression of a competitive threat to get the incumbent to give them the rates that we know are market appropriate. To do this, we craft emails for our client to send to their carrier representative. It's crucial that we get these emails perfect—the tone, the style of writing, the style of logic and reasoning, the type of language, even down to the smallest details of punctuation and the signature—because we can never give any clue, not even an indefinable sense of something "not right," that a third party is involved in the negotiation. If we didn't copy and paste their signature correctly, that could derail it. If the carrier suspected we were involved, that could have significant repercussions for our client because the relationship would be damaged. Our clients are dependent on a good relationship with their carrier to keep their business running and profitable, from receiving supplies to getting their products to their customers on time and intact. A damaged carrier relationship would likely result in unhappy customers at best and notable revenue loss at worst.

In fact, John Howard told me that certain groups within UPS actually had training to try and identify when a consultant might be involved, and how they were supposed to respond if they sensed that a third party was engaged.

So when we build the strategy, it is unique to that client and to the people we're working with at that client. If we used the same template or approach for all our clients, eventually the carriers would call us out. After asking all our questions, we know and understand the client's business and parcel shipping well enough that we can think about it like them. Our creativity and attention to detail are crucial to success.

The first step is to find out how the client typically communicated with the carrier. Most of the time it's done in person or via email, but we've done a few just via text message. We had a big customer in California where the guy we were dealing with was smart enough to be the bad guy. He told us he had never met his UPS rep. All they did was text back and forth. So we conducted the whole negotiation via text message and sending pictures of the analysis and other evidence to back the case for better discounts. And we hit a home run!

Almost all, though, are by email or sometimes in-person meetings. With the emails being the make-or-break point of the negotiation, we give them a lot of time and attention. Hours and hours. We start by asking the client to send us their last six or twelve emails to their carrier rep, so we can study the style and tone. Then we mimic that style and tone in the emails that build the business case for the discounts. Because these email chains are documentation of a competitive threat, they get forwarded up through the hierarchy at the carrier to get the customer the rates they should have.

It's not right that the carriers take their existing customers for granted and don't reward them for their loyalty with the best possible discounts. We make sure those companies get the discounts they deserve. That's why, after we stepped out of the picture in the negotiation, our success rate went really high. Once you take out the middle guy, the carrier feels like they still get to be the hero. We've just got to coach them to be the hero and give them an opportunity to do the right thing.

So we also have to be inside the carrier's head. How is the rep going to respond to each email? What will the carrier's next move be? What objections will they raise? What smoke and mirrors will they use to try to distract the client? What doubts will they try to create in the client's mind? What fears will they try to plant?

Then we craft the emails, or if the client usually meets with their rep in person, we write a script. As a team we brainstorm and role play. We go through every possibility: What if the carrier says this? What if the client says that?

All those hours and the painstaking attention to detail pay off. One client contact who was the "bad guy" in the negotiation later came to work for us at TI in sales. He believed in it so much that he wanted to sell it, because his experience as a TI client blew him away.

Once we have the strategy crafted, then it's time for our last sales job of this process: selling the client on the strategy. I always looked at it as two sales. We've got to sell the customer on the service and on the savings. That isn't easy, because they can't believe the dollar amount. They think it's too good to be true. Then the harder sale is once they've hired us. They know they don't have to pay us unless they allow us to do what we're suggesting. So we have to sell them on the strategy, and this strategy is in a lot of ways counterintuitive for them—most people are non-confrontational. Most people have a good working relationship with their carriers. We've got to be prepared for their objections, the what-ifs, and tell them what the carrier's next move is going to be at each stage. Some people feel like their job is in some ways on the line in these situations, and so the best thing is when we send an email that we craft on their behalf to a client and they don't want to edit anything. That's when we know we have done our job right, down to how many spaces they put after a period, what font and color they use, their email signature, whether or not they misspell words.

That is really the magic. Being able to sound like the client, yet still communicate the point such that the carrier looks at the email and thinks: "I'll be damned. My competitor's been in there and told them everything. We're going to lose this business."

When we have a sound strategy, and we have the buy-in from the stakeholders within the company of how it is going to go down, the whole negotiation is a lot easier and more successful. But we still have to make sure we stay in control.

I once flew out to Phoenix, Arizona, to click "send" on an email. I was so worried it was going to go wrong. This was a big deal, too. The guy we were working with was the owner of the company, but he was a scatterbrain. He was everywhere. It was hard to get a commitment out of him. Someone else in the company told me, "That's asking too much. Go get behind the desk with him." So I did.

Attention to detail. We will do whatever it takes. None of us are scared to get on a plane. What we do has to be perfect. That's why perfection is one of our core values. There's no room for error.

For me, that care extends to relationships. In B2B, relationships are everything. I have always tried to establish and maintain good relationships with clients, employees, anybody I interact with. It pays off, and sometimes it pays off big.

Steve Huntley was a unique individual who really knew the freight game. He had worked at a huge Fortune Top 100 company but ended up going out on his own and doing much the same thing we did, but in the truckload and less-than-truckload (LTL) world. Steve also understood the importance of relationships, and he had a whole network of them in southeast Florida because that's where he lived. One day, he reached out to us, proposing that he could introduce us to customers in return for a commission on the sale. As soon as we met him, we knew Steve was one of us—his demeanor, his goal, his approach.

One of Steve's relationships in Florida was with Office Depot. The giant office supply company's global corporate headquarters was right in Steve's playground, outside of Deerfield Beach, Boca Raton. Steve managed to connect us with Brent Beabout, vice president of global network strategy and transportation for Office Depot. Over the next weeks, we had a few calls with Brent to discuss the opportunity for Office Depot, and then, at last, he agreed to meet with us.

We knew we were going to be meeting with several people, so we needed a perfectionist note taker. Brandon with his journalism skills fit that bill. He was also going to be integral as far as formulating the strategy, so we wanted him to listen to everything that was going on. This was going to take a team effort to be successful, and it was incredibly important to be successful with this client. I was also aware this would be a priceless learning experience for Brandon. Some leaders—maybe most—wouldn't be willing to take a raw employee low on the totem pole to a meeting as important as this one, where if the employee did or said something stupid it could ruin everything. But for me the value of having Brandon take precise notes and hear every word made logical sense. This meeting was very high stakes.

So we flew all the guns in, kind of like they did.

The morning of the meeting Travis, Brandon, and I rode together to the Jacksonville airport. Brandon was still living on the budget of a "poor student," so I gave him one of my suits to wear. Brandon's about six feet tall, and I'm several inches shorter. He showed up in my blue suit, with the short pant legs revealing black socks and brown shoes. His white wrists dangled below the cuffs of the sleeves. But it didn't matter. We were all so excited about how huge this opportunity was. I knew that if we landed this client, it would be a turning point for Transportation Impact.

Steve Huntley picked us up at Ft. Lauderdale airport. As the intermediary he was joining us in the meeting. This was a big deal for him, too. As his car neared 6600 N Military Trail, Boca Raton, Travis, Brandon, and I stared at the giant white building that was coming into view. The scale of it was hard to fathom. It looked the size of an Amazon fulfilment center. Most of the other places we'd been were in an office suite or maybe a floor in a commercial building, or a nondescript standalone building with two loading docks on the back. This building was so big it was divided in three parts, with two massive entrances that were identical except one had a palm-tree-lined drive leading to it. And out the back there weren't loading docks; there was a golf course. This massive place symbolized how massive the company was, and for us, that symbolized how massive the opportunity was.

Steve pulled into a spot in the acres of parking lot and we made our way to reception. Through my excitement and nervousness I admired how tastefully the reception area was decorated. We announced ourselves and the receptionist took us down a long hall to a conference room, which she opened via a digital access pad. Those are common now, but in 2010 that was a really novel idea. That one small detail drove home that we had stepped into the big leagues.

After depositing us in the conference room, the receptionist went to get Brent Beabout. We settled ourselves into the red leather executive chairs and quickly went over our strategy.

The door opened and Brent entered along with his number two and four other people from fulfilment, logistics, shipping, and finance. We rose, shook hands, and exchanged business cards. I'd had Brian make business cards for Brandon, giving him the title of national account manager. With the formalities out of the way, everybody sat down. Brent seated himself at the center of the table, directly across from me.

I started my pitch, the same way I always did. As I explained the savings that we could provide, how the negotiation worked, and what Office Depot's part would be, Brent interrupted frequently with hard-hitting questions. For every question, I had an answer that satisfied him. Travis explained the calculation of the savings and the billing. He was well prepared too.

After some time, Brent looked directly at Brandon. "Where do you come in?" he said.

Brandon started to open his mouth but I didn't give him a chance to speak. "Brandon is a promising national account manager that I'm mentoring, and this is a training experience for him." Brent nodded.

We continued to discuss how it all worked and to haggle over terms until after a couple of hours, Brent gave us a verbal agreement. We would send the contract once we got back to Emerald Isle. We had to concede to doing the negotiation for a flat fee of around sixty thousand dollars, which was pennies compared to how much Office Depot was going to save, but it didn't matter. Thanks to our experience with Reynolds Wrap, we knew the immense value of taking on big accounts like this and not looking at the immediate hard-dollar payoff. This was the first major Fortune 500 type opportunity that proved to the world that very big, important, smart people saw the value in what we did. Travis and I knew this was going to be a game changer in our destiny. That was the pinnacle. If we could get that logo on a piece of collateral, the sky was the limit.

Back out in the Florida fall sunshine, we danced and high-fived, and then Steve suggested we go to dinner. It was only around four o'clock, but the day was over for us. None of us felt like doing any more work in the couple of hours left. We were too excited and wanted to celebrate. So we piled back into Steve's car and he drove down North Military Trail for five minutes, and then swung into a parking lot dotted with Lamborghinis and Bentleys. Between two clusters of palms, a long brown awning led to glass entrance doors beside a sign that said "New York Prime." Inside were palm trees in pots and waiters in white jackets. The maître d' seated us at a table for four, and over the next hours of daylight we proceeded to eat and drink like kings. Steak, lobster, Opus One—food and wine that were so good they'd make you take back shit you didn't steal (to use another Keithism). The expense didn't matter.

We were so happy because we had reached such a big milestone. We were going to get sixty thousand dollars, we were going to get the Office Depot logo to put on our marketing collateral, and we had sold them on the audit. We knew how many packages a week they shipped and that we would get about thirty-five percent of what we recovered on the audit. We'd done the math, and we knew how big a windfall this was. We thought Reynolds Wrap was big. That company had only about a three-million-dollar small parcel spend, but it had a great brand. Office Depot had around two hundred U.S. locations and a fifty-million-dollar small parcel spend. There are not many companies in the U.S. that spend that much on parcel shipping.

Steve was happy because not only was he getting his cut of the sixty thousand, but for the next five or six years he was going to get his percentage of what we made on the audit. We were still blind labelling it through Veriship, and Office Depot immediately became the biggest of their two thousand clients. We figured we'd be billing

Office Depot six to seven thousand dollars *a week* just for the audit, and Steve would get his twenty percent of that. We also had to pay Veriship their cut, but that still left Transportation Impact a nice chunk of weekly income. Office Depot would be saving twenty grand a week, minus what they were paying us.

Eventually we were ready to leave New York Prime. Steve and I stood up and grasped each other in a celebratory hug, and next thing I knew we were on the floor and the table was on top of us. Eastern North Carolina goes to Manhattan. Another story for Transportation Impact lore.

We went somewhere else and celebrated further, and late that night retired to our hotel. The next morning, it was business as usual. Steve had lined up a nine o'clock meeting with another prospective client. Brandon emerged dressed in my suit again. I rubbed his face. "You didn't have time to shave this morning?" Another lesson learned. Appearance is important. Attention to detail. No detail is too small.

Over the next weeks we flew down to Boca Raton several more times. Like Debbie and her team at Reynolds Wrap, Brent and his team wanted a lot of face-to-face time. But we loved it because we were building that relationship. And when we met with them, it was not like we met with one person. Every time they involved the decision maker down to six people deep below him. It was amazing. They were just a team-type company. Brent believed in getting buy-in from his team, and they drilled us, just like Reynolds Wrap, because they were smarter than the usual type of clients we had dealt with. They asked us questions that helped us learn. It is great dealing with those bigger accounts, because usually they're more on top of their game. They analyze everything—which is good, because it makes our own game stronger.

One thing Travis and I were adamant about in the negotiation with UPS was keeping the guaranteed service language in the agreement. That meant that if UPS did not attempt to deliver a package by the guaranteed date or time, we could file for a refund via the audit. But then one of Brent's team asked, "Can we ask UPS for better discounts if we give up the guaranteed service refund?" Travis and I managed our response well at the time, but that freaked us out bad. If they took away our ability to audit, there went hundreds of thousands of dollars a year.

I explained that the discount UPS was offering was really an "elegant negotiable." The carrier brainwashes shippers. An elegant negotiable is when the carrier makes it seem like a big deal to the client, but it's nothing to the carrier. At the twelfth hour of the negotiation UPS and FedEx are famous for saying, for example, "I'm going to give you a sixty-eight percent discount. But if you give up your right to secure refunds, I will give you a seventy percent discount." The customer thinks, "Two percent means a lot to me. I need to do that."

Then we coach them: "First of all, go back and say you've got to have the seventy percent, but there's no way that you cannot hold the carrier accountable to do their job." In the end, the client would always get the seventy percent and keep the language in there, thanks to our coaching. We put it back on the carrier: "You're telling me you're going to give me two percent if I allow you not to do your job correctly? My customers would never let me do that."

As an extra challenge, the negotiation got political. UPS was the incumbent, and we had to tiptoe around our strategy and tone down our verbiage in the emails because the CEO of Office Depot was friends with the CEO of FedEx and they had a really strong relationship. Dangling too big a carrot in front of FedEx when Office Depot had no intention of switching carriers would have generated ill will and could have damaged their friendship.

But we managed it all successfully. That was the first one that we could always hang our hat on. "If Office Depot trusts these rednecks out of the middle of nowhere, we can too." It also gave us that confidence. When you're small and someone tries to squeeze you, you tend to get squeezed. When you have a feather in your hat like that, you have a stronger presence in those conversations. That served Transportation Impact extraordinarily well over time. We were able to sell value that our competitors couldn't, and we were able to maximize revenue potential. It was the first experience that really gave us the confidence that when there was price pressure from competitors, we could stand our ground.

We saved Office Depot millions of dollars and got paid sixty thousand. But having that name on our collateral earned us millions over the years. We immediately put the Office Depot logo on our one-pager, and forever afterwards, when people would say, "Office Depot's your client?" I'd stick my chest out and reply, "Yes, ma'am. Office Depot. I have a contact. We're saving them millions a year. Call 'em right now."

# 14

## GROWING THE TI FAMILY

By late 2010 we had been in Suite B six months and we had already grown out of it. Suite C, next door to us, was available and we arranged to lease that as well. We didn't want to have to walk outside to get between our two sets of offices, so I had a connecting door installed. The door was glass with our logo etched on it, and it looked really classy. I was so proud of that door! It cost fifteen hundred dollars, and Travis only stopped crying about the expense when we moved into our new headquarters in 2016. I loved that door so much, I took it with us. It now connects a hallway between our IT and freight departments.

As Christmas approached, Travis and I wanted to do something to celebrate our first good year and to thank everyone who had helped us, so we decided to have a Christmas party.

We met at my house and piled into a limousine for the drive down to Beaufort Grocery in Morehead. I don't remember what the food and alcohol bill was for that night, but it must have been high. This was one night that we spared no expense. Our TI family had grown by seven people since January, and that first Christmas party was the icing on the cake. It was a time to show our people that we appreciated them, that we were family, that their efforts didn't go unnoticed. We were saying, "We appreciate you and we wouldn't be here without you."

As we turned the calendar into 2011, Travis and I faced the fact that we needed more help. Erin and Brandon were working really hard, Travis and I were working seventy to eighty hours a week, and still there was more to be done. We used to joke that when UPS was in hiring mode, they couldn't find able bodies fast enough. One of Travis's managers would say, "I'm going to give you a three-minute interview. If you can fog a mirror, you're hired." It was tongue in cheek, but that was how we were starting to feel.

Erin gave us a rave recommendation of a friend of hers called Olivia Yankosky. Travis and I had a lot of respect for Erin, so a rec-ommendation from her was almost enough for us. I was out of town, and Erin arranged for Olivia to come in and interview with Travis. Olivia's story of her hiring interview and first day on the job have become another part of Transportation Impact lore:

> I walked into Travis's office, which became Brandon's at some point. There was only one little lamp on his desk; it was dark in there. He had a cold, and there was cough med-icine on the desk.
>
> I think the interview lasted five minutes. I had my re-sume, which didn't have a lot on it. I think Travis took a look at it and asked me if I was organized and a couple other things. Then he said, "Okay," and I said, "Okay," and that was the interview. He told me it wasn't guaranteed that I would stay on board longer than three weeks.
>
> There was a finance lady, Jenny. Somebody brought me to her and said, "Here you go. Here's Jenny. She's going to tell you what to do."
>
> I remember going in that back closet with the huge filing

cabinet which I think we still have and it was just a disaster of files. That closet was where our little server was. That's where you had to push "send" on the invoices. I remember looking at this paperwork and thinking, "I don't even know what this is." I think I got one-second guidance on the files, and then I had to get to work.

You can read the contract, what it says, and everything else, but to me it was a foreign language and it didn't help me in trying to organize the files. But I think even then—that's when we were with Veriship on the audit—I realized what the scalability of the company was going to be, because I remember seeing Jelly Belly as a client and the folder was about Jelly Belly. There were some other recognizable ones, but that one stood out to me in those initial minutes.

Olivia was probably the first employee we hired temporarily, because we were worried about how we were going to pay her. Erin and Brandon we had hired pretty much full time, and they had their roles. We didn't know what Olivia was going to do for us, but we knew we needed the help. She had gone to school for marketing, but Brian was our marketing whizz, so we had to find some other role for her. Her main work experience had been as a clerk in procurement for the Department of Defense, so helping with filing and finance seemed like the most logical place to start. We were a wreck in our record keeping. We were growing so fast we were just letting stuff go. Under Travis's direction, Olivia came in and cleaned it up.

Later that year she transitioned from her "three-week" temporary position into a full-time role as finance supervisor. She had never seen herself as working in finance, but Olivia gave that role the same hundred percent professional effort and became invaluable to Travis in helping with the weekly billing. More than that, she believed in us at a time when we still weren't doing a lot.

From the beginning, when we were developing the business model in my vacation rental house, Travis and I thought we had to hire a lot of people with experience working at the carriers. On one of the whiteboards that was one of the to-dos: Hire former UPS and FedEx people. But thanks to Erin, Brandon, and Olivia we learned very quickly that we had it all wrong. We needed creative twenty-five-year-olds with drive and commitment who we could develop. We didn't need a twenty-year veteran who was set in their ways. We learned that when you come from those huge corporations, you still can have blinders on. Your thought processes are in so many ways molded by how the carriers did it. By definition we were doing it differently. Just because you were in sales at UPS or FedEx did not mean you were going to be successful at Transportation Impact. One has nothing to do with the other. It's a whole different sales pitch. It's a whole different skill set.

It's a different breed of cat, when it comes to our salespeople. There are so many angles to what's necessary. You've got to be able to tell the story, you've got to be able to sell the service, and then once you sell the service, you've got to be able to ask the right questions, listen well, actually take in what the customer is telling you, and then come up with a strategy for the negotiation, sell the customer on the process without straying into questionable ethics scenarios, have them get the strategy into their gut during the negotiation, and manage their emotions and coach them through carrying out the strategy perfectly.

If you can sell TI, you can sell anything in this world, in my opinion. It's not just about closing the deal; it's about being the customer's coach, walking them through the entire process. The sales cycle on the front end is key, but then being able to successfully complete the negotiation from behind the scenes and have that trust from the customer to say what you want them to say and do what you want them to do, that's a whole 'nother skill set. It takes a special person to be successful across the board.

Erin was so impressive that from day one, I could already see she had that full skill set. And more. She was tenacious, not taking no for an answer, had great follow-up and attention to detail, and she was creative in thinking outside the box. She would do whatever it took to win the customer. She was especially creative in getting to the C-level. It became a kind of joke in the office that Erin would "stalk" a potential customer. It was a small office with thin walls, so we could all hear each other on the phone, and we would wait to hear what she said next. I was impressed by how she would make the customer feel like wanting to take the meeting. She also did a lot of handwritten campaigns, taking pictures—like we used to do—of certain products and writing: "I'm a customer of yours. Be a customer of mine." She was the best, as far as securing a meeting.

I started grooming her in sales, taking her along with me on all the calls, including the big ones. With her creativity, tenacity, follow-up, and attention to detail, I could see she was going to be a great salesperson. I saw her eventually taking over from me and being the sales lead. She was so young, she had the potential for big success at an early age. On the sales calls we made, she was knowledgeable, energetic, and positive. The customer saw it, and they saw her confidence. She was very effective in helping us win many accounts.

One of the more memorable calls I took Erin on was to a sneaker company in California. She had set the whole thing up, securing an initial meeting and gaining agreement for us to go out there. In midsummer we flew to Los Angeles, where the company's headquarters was. The meeting went really well, with Erin showing all her positive qualities, and we walked out of it with a signed contract. This was going to be a big deal. A million dollars in revenue—for us. I was so happy, I went out and bought everybody—Erin, Brandon, Olivia, and also Travis and myself—a pair of shoes with the company's sperm logo on them. They've changed the logo now, but that's what it looked like then.

We flew back to Emerald Isle and celebrated with the whole team, and then started preparing for the external strategy session with the client, when we would get the information we needed to create the negotiation strategy. But every time we tried to set up a meeting with them, they would always make some excuse. Before the first meeting, the company had given us access to their billing files so we could do the initial analysis to determine the savings we could get them, and we still had that access. Four or five weeks after they signed with us, we started noticing that they suddenly were getting better discounts.

When Erin and I met with the company in California, after they signed our agreement we basically told them the secret sauce, our whole strategy for the negotiation. Now we had evidence that they had violated the agreement and gone out and negotiated with the carrier behind our back.

That experience and the experience with finding a big chunk of retroactive savings for Reynolds Wrap and not getting a cent of it made us modify our contract. We started out with a simple one-page agreement, but after Reynolds Wrap, we inserted language stating that if ever we uncovered retroactive savings, we would get half of it. Now, after being burned by the shoe company, we went back to our legal team and got them to insert language protecting us in this sort of situation.

At the start, we made it simple by design. We wanted somebody to sign that agreement. We didn't want it to get hung up at legal and give people a chance to change their minds. But as we became a more formidable business and confident in the value that we could bring, we were more certain of ourselves. We could put that contract in front of somebody, and if it had to go through legal for a couple of weeks, then so be it.

As we grew, it became like the Notorious B.I.G. rapped: "Mo money, mo problems." People would sue us to try to get out of honoring their agreement. We got taken to the bank a few times. One company screwed us out of millions of dollars. They had good law-yers. But I can count on one hand how many times that's happened. We've been very blessed and fortunate.

Every time we did have obstacles with customers paying us, we strengthened the language in our contract. It went back to our legal when UPS and FedEx came up with different language on certain things like NDAs and we had to reflect the carriers' changes so we didn't violate the NDA. Over time it's also got more challenging to keep our terms at a fifty-fifty split and three years. Fine-tuning our contract was a big learning curve that went on for years. We've gone through lots of changes. It's now several pages long.

Maybe early on we were a little naive about business and the business world. We definitely were trusting. When somebody said they were going to do something, we trusted they would do it. Especially if they had signed an agreement with us. But through time, we learned that not everybody in the business world operates with scruples. We spent a lot on legal fees to learn those lessons and ultimately profit from them.

It was a big challenge in the early days to educate our attorneys on our business model. When we started TI, there was another guy that started doing something like this a little sooner than we did, so I called him. I said, "The only thing I want from you—is there any way I can hire your attorney?" He said, "Fuck you. You're going to have to pay for it, just like I had to." So we did. Now our attorneys know our business model as well as we do.

With each change, there was give and take with the legal team. They would advise on what they thought we needed to do, which was usually more than we wanted to do. In the end, we probably reached a happy medium.

Our biggest expense has always been our people, and the sec-ond has always been travel and trade shows, together (except in the Covid-19 years). For a long time, our third biggest expense was le-gal. It's not anymore, but it took years and hundreds of thousands of dollars to teach our attorneys so that they can respond on our behalf without a lot of consultation with us. Now, after over a decade, Lee Hodge knows our business as well as we do. And as well as being an awesome attorney, he is also a great friend!

One day not long before that California trip with Erin, my phone rang. The caller ID showed "Neal Newhouse." I tapped "answer."

"Hey, buddy. What's up?"

"Hey, man. I'm miserable. I got my twenty years. I'm out of here."

I grinned. This was the phone call I'd been waiting for. Neal was finally ready to join our team. In 1992, not long after I'd been promoted to sales at UPS, I got a phone call from a guy who introduced himself as Neal Newhouse and told me he'd just been promoted from loss prevention security to sales. I knew who Neal was, and I was suspicious that he was being sent for some other purpose. I told him to be in Jacksonville Center at eight o'clock. That day as I showed him the ropes of sales I conducted myself in a very professional manner and didn't say much. Next day, we continued the same and then went to lunch in Jacksonville mall.

I couldn't stand it any longer. "Buddy," I said, "I just got to say something to you. Are you here to fucking fire me?"

He stared at me. "What are you talking about?"

"I know you're in LP."

"No, no, no! I just got promoted, man. I'm happy as shit."

"Are you sure?"

Right then an attractive girl walked past us. Neal looked at me and said, "God, she's pretty hot."

I was so relieved. "I think I love you," I told him. "She's beautiful."

From that instant we were best friends.

Neal quickly became one of the top salespeople, and I arranged for him to be put on my team. When I left UPS to start TI I couldn't persuade him to come with me, partly because he didn't understand our business model and so he didn't believe in it, and also because he wanted to get his twenty years of service at UPS. That's when retirement kicked in.

"I'd love to have you," I said now. "We're turning the corner. We're starting to make some money. I can't pay you a salary, but you know you've got my word. I'll take care of y'all." I asked how much he was making a month. "You've got to be a hundred percent commission," I told him, "but we'll maybe give you an allowance the first couple months."

"I trust you."

"Okay, come on down. But I want your wife to come down with you."

I knew he was ready to say, "All right! Where do I sign?" but if his wife, Star, wasn't on board, it wasn't going to work.

When I left UPS, I was making between ninety thousand and a hundred thousand dollars a year. One year I think I made a hundred and ten thousand when I made a big bonus. When you leave that UPS culture and the salary, bonuses, benefits, retirement, it's a big step. I had the vision back then to know that we had to get the spouse's buy-in, because this was going to be a long road, especially for salespeople, until they started producing. Our sales contractors—Chris, Tim, Bob, and now Neal—were leaving secure, well-paying jobs to make a leap of faith with no guaranteed salary. We had to make sure their families understood and supported that decision.

Neal and Star came to Emerald Isle and we went out to dinner, all the couples. When we were sitting back relaxing after enjoying a nice meal, I said, "Syndie, tell us the good, the bad, and the ugly."

"Neal," she said, "You probably aren't going to make that much the first couple years. Keith didn't make shit. There might be a little stress. But there's light at the end of the tunnel. The good is you can work your own hours, and you can travel."

The remainder of the evening went really well. We all bonded. I felt good about Neal joining us, but he didn't make the final decision right then. He and Star went home, and the next day he called me.

"She's on board," he said. "She prayed about it, we talked about it, and then she said, 'Man, you're miserable at UPS. You got your twenty years. I give you the blessing.'"

Neal's boss at UPS was Jan McVeigh, who had been my equal and was still a good friend. Neal met with her to give her the news. "You're leaving to go work for Keith, aren't you?" she said. He neither confirmed nor denied, but Jan knew. I had also tried to get her to join us, but for Jan the uncertainty was too great, especially in the early years when we were really struggling. At UPS she had financial stability.

To Neal, she said, "Give your two weeks. Just think about it." Somehow Neal managed to be the rare exception to UPS shutting the door on employees the day they turned in their notice.

Neal started work the first week of June. I was thrilled to have him on board. As training, I took him on most of my calls with me, which is what we did with all the new sales contractors. We wanted to give them a jump start, so we also handed them a big deal that was close to being signed, and if they closed it they got the commission at a reduced percentage. I gave Neal a deal with a company that Erin had been instrumental in getting to this point. Neal worked it, and about a month and a half into his TI career he got his first win.

After we'd completed the negotiation and saved the company around nine hundred thousand dollars, we flew to Vegas to meet with the VP of logistics, who had been our main contact, and the CFO, who we hadn't dealt with much. They were exhibiting at a trade show there. Along with Neal, I took Olivia and Erin as training for them. Olivia was interested in moving from finance into sales, and I knew she had promise.

We met at the Red Rock for dinner. We were all in a celebratory mood. At the table, the CFO sat himself directly opposite me, and Neal sat down next to him. Olivia sat next to me. She was quiet and reserved, and this was her first experience of wining and dining a client. We got drinks and then placed our orders for food. As we were sitting relaxed and chatting, the CFO suddenly looked hard at me and started to question our billing and how we measured it.

I stared at him. "You're shitting me!"

I couldn't believe it. This was supposed to be a great dinner, because what a treat it is to share with the customer what we ended up doing as a team, but after we'd already saved them hundreds of thousands of dollars, this guy was suddenly questioning our integrity.

The discussion became heated and the tone started getting degrading. I glanced at Olivia sitting next to me, looking shocked and offended, and decided to turn it into a life lesson right there in front of her. First of all, if you're doing the right thing, you never have anything to worry about. The customer's always right ninety-nine point nine percent of the time, but sometimes you have to stand up to the customer.

I explained to the CFO clearly and in detail what we did on the billing and how we did it.

Just as suddenly as he had turned on me, his expression relaxed. "All right," he said. "You're right. Fine. You just have to pay for dinner."

Everybody exhaled and sat back in their chairs. After that we were all good friends and had a great time. The VP of logistics was quiet and had never gambled in his life, but by the end of the night he was throwing money at roulette. To this day, they have remained a happy customer and a great relationship, which proves another Keithism that my son Tyler calls true and valuable: "Most deals are secured over the dinner table."

Afterwards, as we were wishing each other good night outside our rooms, Olivia said to me, "You turned that around beautifully."

When you're right and you have somebody question you, especially in front of people, you have to stand up for what you believe in.

\*

# 15

## RING THE BELL

Travis was still living in Greenville and it was getting really hard not having him in the office full time. I was gone so much. By now I was going to ten to fifteen trade shows a year, on top of all the travelling I was doing for sales calls. I really needed him around full time. I needed his energy and assistance in the office. The problem was his wife was still working and didn't want to move. But he also was frustrated with not being here full time. At last, around fall 2011, when it was obvious the business was going to be successful, he told his wife to quit her job and the Burt family moved to Emerald Isle.

In late November, I got a message from a contact at one of my former UPS accounts. Many years ago, Paula Sutton had worked at a company here on the island that was using Airborne for its shipping. Back then, Airborne was a carrier, before it was bought out by DHL, and Paula gave me a chance to win that business for UPS. I loved dealing with her because she was really smart, she always asked really good questions, and she did what she said she was going to do. I did everything she asked, and she awarded UPS the account.

I was also impressed by her leadership. She was like the boss in that small office of five or six people. Plus she had good computer skills and knew the shipping software. So when she reached out to me on LinkedIn asking me to let her know if I heard of any job opportunities, I right away thought what a great executive assistant she would be for us. I wrote back asking if she was good with Excel, and she replied, "I can do anything."

"Come on in to the office!" I told her.

Paula came in and interviewed, and at the end of November started work as a full employee of Transportation Impact. I was excited to get her, because she had already demonstrated capability back when I was a UPS rep. At first her official role was in finance, mainly helping with the billing. We had a guy who would come in at midnight on Sunday to download the FedEx and UPS billing files, and then on Monday it was Paula's job to import the files into TidBit so it could extract the information to prepare the invoices. Paula printed the invoices and checked them to make sure they were accurate, modified any that needed to be adjusted per the client's request, and then mailed them. It was a two-day process back then when our client list was still short. In addition to the billing, Paula was also doing our travel arrangements and a few other things, and around mid-2012 she transitioned to being a full-time executive assistant. We needed one.

Our two connecting suites in the strip mall were getting full. Brian Dobler had the large front area of suite B, our original suite, so he could have his giant printer there and attract walk-in traffic for his printing and design business. Next to that was our tiny conference room, where we held our internal strategy sessions. The sales contractors also used it as their workspace when they came in. Then down the hall were individual offices. At the back of suite B was the closet that housed our server and a small kitchenette/break area. When we got suite C, Travis and I moved to larger offices in there.

Our name, Transportation Impact, was on the front of the

building, and there was hardly a day that somebody wouldn't come in and ask us to ship something for them. It was hard to understand what we did. It was even hard for our employees at first to understand what we did.

Olivia eventually became one of our best salespeople, and she told me she learned what we did from listening to me do my presentations. When she was in her office, which shared a wall with the conference room, she would hear me over and over and over giving my pitch, and she would mouth along with me, memorizing what I said. In her sales pitch today, ten years later, she still says things that I used to say in my presentations in 2011. "I can tell you 'til I'm blue in the face how great we are, but call one of them. Office Depot is a customer of ours. Call them."

We were growing and there was a lot of opportunity for every one of our employees to grow professionally and personally. But they had to be resilient and motivated. I wasn't easy on them or on our sales contractors. I was known for being short and asking for updates, and then I would follow up until whatever I was asking about was closed.

I was on the road a lot, so whenever I was on a plane, I would craft emails to everyone—employees and sales contractors—to find out the status of what they were working on. The joke in the office was that they could tell when I had got off the plane, because the phone would connect to the airport WiFi and everybody's inbox would ping with an email from me. The thing was, I didn't actually write to them. I would just send an email with the subject line: "Status?" Or sometimes it only had a question mark, with no words at all. Then all their emails updating me would hit my inbox. If someone was behind on something, I often would simply reply: "Wow."

They learned to be proactive, because, Brandon told me once, of the "sheer terror" of getting an email that said, "Wow."

He and Olivia found a way to escape the stress for a short time each day. Brandon was commissioned based on the NPoD revenue, so he used to bug Olivia asking if anybody had paid their NPoD invoice. They started walking to the post office together every day to see if any checks had come in. The post office was directly across the street from our office. Fifty yards away. At first they walked straight across and back. But then Brandon would say, "Hey, 'Liv, we should walk down to the intersection and across the crosswalk. We'd hate to get hit by a car." As the stress got higher, the walk got a bit longer, and a bit longer, to the point where they were worried they would get in trouble for walking too long to the post office.

I was hard on Brandon, but I did it for his good, because I believed in him. For me, business is business and personal is personal. When it's time to work, it's time to work. When it's time to have fun, you're going to have a lot of fun. At first, Brandon didn't understand that. He was more emotional, and sometimes there was friction between us.

Every year I took my two sons, Brian and Tyler, and their friends on a surfing trip to Puerto Rico. Brandon was an old high school friend of theirs and it was a tradition that we'd invite him to come with us, along with my old high school buddy Dennis Rebert. This year's trip was coming up, and we were all excited thinking about it because it was winter time and we were going to the Caribbean.

Not long before the trip, Brandon walked into my office.

"Keith," he said, "I think I'm going to sit out this vacation."

I couldn't understand what he was talking about. Why didn't he want to go? I stared at him.

He shuffled his feet, looked at the wall, and then looked at me. "I feel like you just ride me. I just don't want to go."

"Man," I said, "that's business. You just have to learn to separate business from personal."

We went to Puerto Rico and had a fantastic vacation, and after we got back I was a little easier on Brandon. I understood he wasn't me. I would still lean into him, but not as hard.

Sometimes you've got to be an asshole to get the respect. The thing is, you've also always got to give the respect. I think we all did a good job of that. We had people in their mid-twenties and early thirties who were making big decisions, creating big things.

For this book, Brandon and Olivia talked about how formative those early years had been for them, both professionally and personally.

*Brandon:* We learned from you and Travis a lot of lessons. I've been to business school and a lot of these things are taught, but you and Travis, you know this in the right way. You didn't go to business school; you didn't have to learn these things. We would clean and you would be there cleaning. It was like a learning exercise of "You can't be too good for anything." That carries a lot of weight, not just in learning it for yourself, but when other people are doing it, too.

Where we really saw it was in the work that was getting done every day. Who was there early, who was there late. I wasn't an eight-year undergraduate student because I was disciplined, because I was a self-starter. I learned those things, and I became a different person because of the trial by fire that I got in those early days at TI. All that stuff has had a profound impact on my life.

*Olivia:* We had to figure out how we weren't going to get those "Wow"'s again. You guys had high expectations for us. I was fearful, but I respected you. That was great. It's set me up to who I am today. The fear was healthy for sure.

If TI hadn't become anything like what it has, I still would have benefited exponentially. Before our core values were ever written down on paper, you and Travis bled those. I learned a stronger work ethic, and I learned how to be professional in front of C-levels. That opportunity came from you and Travis and what you taught us. It is impactful that we had all those core values right there in front of us before we ever really wanted to call them that.

*Brandon:* This is important, because our first core value was "We do what we say we're going to do." It was raw. It was real. We did it. Every damn thing we did had to check that one box. We committed to our customers; we committed to timelines.

As I've branched off on my own, I always think back and I'm amazed by how many people don't adhere to timelines, they don't adhere to deadlines, they don't adhere to their promises. It's tough; it's not a perfect world. There are times when we fail, all of us. That was a guiding principle that I've never, in all my experience anywhere, seen followed more strictly than it was for a time there. That was really the catalyst for the growth of the company.

There were people with a lot of challenging things going on in their lives, or a lot of challenges posed by outside forces, by FedEx, UPS, the customer's expectations, yada, yada yada, but hell or high water, we were going to live up to that standard. We did. Time and time and time again.

We do what we say we're going to do. In my opinion, that one line in all its imperfection embodies how you guys made this happen.

All of us knew everything we did had to check two boxes. The attention to detail was everything, because our company didn't do but one thing. It was a very simple thing, what we did. It was simple, but one tiny mistake could have big consequences, and it was attention to detail that had got us to where we were now. Then there was doing what you say you're going to do. In meetings, there were many, many times I looked at Olivia and Brandon straight in the face to say, "So, let's recap. We're going to do this, this, and this." That trickles down to the company.

The whole beauty about building this culture is it got to where we didn't have to hold people accountable. Their peers would. As a company, we were very good at what we did. Everybody in our office was very good at what they did. We surrounded ourselves with really good people. We got better at hiring. We got better at uncovering who would fit in.

People either fit into the culture or they didn't, and they weren't going to fit in if they didn't work hard. In a broad sense, it was very effective. People were going to expose themselves if they didn't work hard, because everybody else knew how to keep the clocks running on time. You either figured it out, or you were probably going to be in a situation where you realized this wasn't a place for you. When you were working alongside an Olivia or Brandon or Erin, you saw how professional and how hard working they were, and you had to do it or leave, because your peers would not allow you to be a half-asser. What really started this company is that everybody believed in what we were doing, and they had the core values of work ethic, integrity, attention to detail, and always doing what we said we were going to do.

It was just funny how our whole mindset changed when we started hiring people. We had already weeded out some people we had worked with at UPS that we had a lot of respect for, because they weren't getting it. We were having to hold their hands going to make sales visits. And then we had these young people who we had to teach how to spell UPS and FedEx and they were the rock stars.

And we had found all these people in our small area a long way from any major city. Over the years, as we grew, most of our hires still came from eastern North Carolina. It was so cool to see how this local power could be. We weren't recruiting from New York and Los Angeles and Chicago, but I would put our team against any company in the world in terms of professionalism, the core values, and knowledge of the industry.

It has also been very rewarding to watch former employees go on to create their own businesses and contribute to us with their success. Former senior marketing coordinator Jillian Lister (née Farrington) left to start her own social media consultancy, Set Sail Marketing, which is doing really well. Carla Abee, who single-handedly won Carhartt for us, runs Buy the Beach Realty – Keller Williams Crystal Coast. And Jamie Vogel, our former EVP of sales and marketing, has also launched her own realty firm, Recoast Homes. When I see them talking on social media about how TI gave them their foundation and work ethic, I feel very proud. Each person's success is a rising tide that lifts all boats.

Even with the stress, though, the office environment was fun. We were growing, and the pride of the company was contagious. You knew that something great was happening and transforming in front of you, even though there were only four or five people in the office at the time.

In the reception area, we had a pin plaque on the wall, a map of the United States, and we had pins everywhere we had clients. I did that as a motivational tool for our employees, and also so that anybody who was waiting to see me would see that we had clients all over the country. It was really satisfying to look at it over time and see our growth. Whenever we made a sale, either Paula or the person that actually "sold" the contract would put a pin in the map. I was so proud of that board. It was a huge sin if a pin did not get placed. I would find myself "auditing" the board monthly. It was an obsession.

Once Travis moved to EI and joined us in the strip mall full time, the office really started humming. It was nothing for any one of us to just blurt in to somebody's office. It was a beehive. On a normal morning, everybody came in, got their coffee, and then hunkered down to work. Mondays we had a weekly conference call at eleven with all hands. That was a roundtable session to check in on what everybody was working on. I always had a list of questions for those Monday morning calls. Anybody who wasn't prepared with an answer when I asked them a question soon learned to be prepared the next time. Olivia and Brandon spent the first two hours of every Monday preparing for the call, to make sure they had an answer for anything I might ask them. They didn't even go to the post office until afterwards.

Our dress code, if you can call it that, was very casual, flip-flops and shorts. Obviously we dressed professionally if we had a meeting with a customer, but when it was just us, it was relaxed. Our work ethic, though, was not relaxed. The cool part was, you never knew from one day to the next exactly what you would be doing. We all had our core work, but if something else needed to be done, then whoever could do it, did it, from changing light bulbs to getting called into an impromptu meeting to writing emails to going to pick up something.

We were figuring it out as we went. We developed the company's culture during those early days. There never was a time clock. If you needed to get off work and go do something, you just did it.

For the first couple of summers, Brandon would come in an hour early and then at four o'clock, he would change into a penguin suit and go next door to work the evening shift at Kathryn's Bistro. At the beach, summer is primary tourist season, and you can make a lot of money waiting tables. Travis and I were his best customers. We would always leave him a great tip, but he had to earn it! He had to get that ribeye medium well and the Pinot Noir with a couple of ice cubes.

Cleanliness was very important to us. Every person in the building would take turns cleaning the commode, sweeping, vacuuming, because we were too tight to hire anybody to come in to clean.

Nowadays we'd call it the startup mentality that everybody chipped in. Plus it built teamwork. It was written on a whiteboard who did what. Almost everybody loved it. It really built a sense of camaraderie, that we were all in this together. But sometimes people would sneak around the schedule. Brandon liked to grab the vacuum right after lunch and stick it in his office because he didn't want to clean the bathrooms.

Brian Dobler was part of it too. Once we got into the office with Brian and his creativity, we became workaholics. We would leave that office at eight-thirty, nine o'clock at night. But it was so fun. We weren't tired, because when you left there you were just as excited as when you got there that morning at eight. It's a tremendous feeling to be able to go out, run an analysis, commit to somebody to do something, and then be able to do it—you got addicted to it. I was on the road at least three days a week, every week, and I just loved it. I was addicted. Once you get one, you've just got to get that next one.

In the office, Brian would burst in with a marketing idea, and then it would bloom into a conversation, and three hours later we were signed on. We would talk about the pros, cons, what are we missing, and then he would design it. As a leadership team we took a lot of time over our marketing. It was a big deal when we were going to pay three thousand dollars to have one page in *Business North Carolina* magazine. Brian would come to us with an idea and we would try to pick it apart, but then the ideas would start flowing. When we had all our creative minds together in one room, along with Travis's analytical mind, we would make some big shit happen. I can't describe the energy.

One day Brian showed up at the office with four big brass bells. Etched on each one was our name, Transportation Impact, and there was a mallet so you could strike the bell to make it ring. He handed them to Travis, Doug, Erin, and me and said, "Every time you sign a customer, ring this bell!"

We had to ring the bell as soon as the deal hit. You couldn't wait. Everybody loved it because it was so loud, and it became a pretty common noise that we heard around the office. You would be sitting in there in the middle of the day and hear somebody's bell ring, and everybody would rush out going nuts. "Congratulations! Tell me about it!" Everybody wanted to ring that bell. It was like a competition. Even when I was out of the office, I would call in so I could say, "Erin, I just signed ABC company. I want to hear the bell ring!" and she would bang the bell with the little mallet.

By the end of 2011 we were growing like crazy. Along with our full-time office crew, sales contractors would drop in and need a quiet space to work. Even though we had the two suites, we were bursting at the seams. At one point the landlord got kind of ill with us because our employee count was growing so fast we were taking up all the parking places. We could really have used Brian's large space at the front of suite B, but there was no way I wanted to ask him to leave. It was clear we had to do something, though. Travis and I came up with a plan that involved knocking a hole in the closet where we had our server. Shortly before we were ready to put the plan into action, Brian walked into my office.

"Buddy," he said, "I think I can give you more by not being here."

I filled with relief. That was a great moment.

It turned out he was really wanting to get back to working out of his own space so he could actually get some work done. With the constant movement of people in and out, he was finding it hard to concentrate, and our employees kept wanting to use his very large and very expensive printer as a photocopier. Plus the walk-ins were killing him. He would invest forty-five minutes in a thirty-nine-cent color copy because the little old lady was nice.

So we had both been wanting to separate, but we hadn't known how to tell each other because we were scared we were going to hurt each other's feelings. This didn't mean we were getting divorced, though. I made sure he understood that. Just because he was going home was not going to negatively impact the time that I had with him. And even though he moved home, he stayed in our office a lot of the time afterwards, because we still bled off each other.

# 16

## SNOWBALLING

We closed 2011 having brought in 2.65 million dollars in gross revenue. That was the year we really started snowballing in terms of money coming in. Travis and I were writing each other salary checks for thirty grand each, and soon it got up to fifty thousand a month that we were paying each other. Everywhere I went I would buy presents for my wife. When I flew out to California for the meeting with the shoe company, I went to Rodeo Drive and bought Syndie a pocketbook and a pair of shoes. We were rolling.

At the start of 2012, Olivia moved into inside sales as a national account manager. She didn't like finance, and we needed more people dialing for dollars, as it were. Somebody on the phone to try to get us in front of the customer. By this time Erin had transitioned fully from inside sales to outside sales, and I was taking her on a lot of calls with me as training.

Olivia's job now was to set up meetings with new prospects through cold calling, email campaigns, and trade shows. She would present our core service offerings in the meeting, and then hand off the prospect to our outside sales team. She was shy, and at first there was a learning curve—she had to learn to ask for the meeting. That was hard for her, and we all worked with her on asking for the business. But in the end she did great because she was very well-spoken. She ended up being one of our best in sales.

Not long after, Brandon also transitioned to a new role. He proposed to us that instead of continuing to do NPoD claims processing, he could help the company more by taking on advertising, public relations, and aspects of marketing that Brian wasn't doing, like social media. We barely even had a social media presence. Thanks to his journalism degree, he understood the key elements of marketing.

We weren't sure it was a good idea. But Brandon pointed out that NPoD was a loophole and the carriers were starting to notice what was going on. Claims that previously had been getting approved with no questions asked were now being stalled or outright denied by the carriers. We had a candid conversation, and he explained the bottom line was he really didn't want to do NPoD anymore. It wasn't working like we had intended. Reluctantly, Travis and I agreed to close our NPoD "division" and let Brandon transition to marketing and PR on salary. He had been helping us with this for a long time anyway by writing many of the personal letters we sent to potential clients—Brandon had impeccable handwriting that made a great first impression!

As he took on the task of getting our message out to a broader audience and trying to get us using Salesforce to manage our data more effectively for marketing and lead generation, I noticed that Brandon's natural skill set was strategic. I realized his strategic mind plus his journalism training would make him a great asset to me in the strategy sessions with the customers, so I started taking him with me. Brandon was very good at not only asking questions of the customer, but also taking precise notes. He would write down everything that was said.

At this point, I was still in charge of coming up with the strategy for the emails that the customer would send to the carriers.

This task is about much more than just each individual email. It's also about getting creative in telling a story that makes sense. It's about understanding and keeping track of the storyline. Where are we within the storyline of this particular negotiation versus that one, who is the rep, where are they located, what are the obstacles here, there, and everywhere? Does this email sound like the customer? After writing each email I would give it to Brandon to quality check and edit, then he'd give it back to me, I would sign off on it, and then we'd send it to the customer. This whole process would take two or three days for each strategic email chain.

I was doing all the trade shows, travelling to sales calls, all the strategy sessions with the customers, all the internal strategy sessions, writing all the emails, managing the sales team, handling phone calls with customers and prospects, and things were really getting busy. We had recently signed US Toy and I had to deliver the first email to them by a certain date. I had so much going on, I called Brandon in to my office and asked him to write the email.

Twenty minutes later he walked back in and handed me the email. I couldn't believe it. That first communication from the customer to the carrier sets the groundwork for our entire strategy as a team, between us and the customer. I was trusting him with the most important task of the whole negotiation, and he just tossed something together.

He saw the expression on my face. "Just read it," he said.

I read the email. It had everything it needed to have, and it sounded like the customer.

I looked at him with new respect. "This is good work. Let's roll with it."

The most amazing thing was that we sent the email to the customer, the customer sent the email to the carrier, and within a week, they had a new agreement that saved them well into six figures.

That was a light bulb moment. From then on, Brandon wrote all the emails.

In the strategy session with the stakeholders of the company, while we were asking questions and taking notes, Brandon also listened for the strategy. He was good at it. On the way out to the car, I would tell him what the strategy was going to be, we would discuss the details, and then I'd say, "You put it together," and he would craft first-rate emails. From working together like that, he got to understand my train of thought, and we got to where we could do it in no time because we'd mastered it. The asking of the questions, the bringing out of the *aha* moment from the customer, the customer buying into the strategy—all the pieces of it.

That took a huge load off my plate and out of my mind. It also removed a very important bottleneck in two ways. The first was that I was so busy with everything else, it had been getting harder and harder for me to make the time to write the emails. The second was that Brandon was a lot faster. He was a genius at taking what was in my head and putting it on paper. I know what I want. Sometimes I don't know how to say it. Brandon knew me so well, he could take my thoughts and put them into beautiful words and craft an email that got the customer what they wanted.

Now we were snowballing. We had a process that worked, and it worked very well.

We were starting to get structures and processes in place, creating some order out of the disorder, and then our finance person, Jenny, told us she was moving on. We quickly ran an ad in the paper and got a strong-looking application from a woman who had recently moved to Emerald Isle from Florida. We called her in for an interview.

Sharon Johnson arrived punctually. We greeted her and showed her into the conference room, where Travis, Jenny, Richard Brown, and I joined her, taking up almost all the chairs at our granite slab conference table. Sharon was dressed professionally, and I think she was a bit taken aback that Travis and I were in our usual office attire of shorts and flip-flops, but she stayed professional.

Our interview process at the time was a bit intimidating, especially for someone who wasn't really outgoing, like Sharon, but she did well at answering the questions we threw at her. Then Travis gave her a scenario of a normal day in our office, with one thing and then another and then another coming at you. "How would you prioritize?" he asked. "How would you handle this?"

"Well," she said, "I would do this and then this, and do what I needed to get done. And then I would go home and have a beer."

On April third, she started work.

Seriously, though, we had fallen in love with her at the interview—her personality, her skill set, how experienced she was, and also how professional and cool she stayed in an intimidating situation. Sharon was the first true financial-minded employee that we had. We gave her free rein to get us in shape as far as our internal financial processes, and the first thing she did was lock up the checkbook that we used to keep in an unmarked drawer. Then she got us on online accounting software and ordered laser checks.

Right from the beginning, she would come to us with initiatives to make us better. She really straightened our stuff up, after Richard Brown had come in and got the basic structures in place. Sharon was very smart, and she became the quarterback that was the glue of the finance department. A couple of years after she started she wanted to move back to Florida, and we thought so much of her, we let her work remotely. That was not common in 2014. To this day, she's still the glue of our finance department and she still works remotely.

It was a big relief to know that we had a true finance person taking care of things in-house. We had Richard Brown as outside oversight and doing budgeting and financial planning, and we had a local CPA, Ken Banks, doing our taxes. We've always been big believers in the three-man rule when it comes to the financials.

A couple of months after Sharon came on board, our personal and professional relationship with the Petty family brought us an incredible opportunity. Richard Petty Motorsports was a client of TI, and we had saved them thirty-five percent on their shipping costs. Richard was so happy he made us a testimonial video, and he offered us a gift.

The 2012 Pocono 400 NASCAR Sprint Cup Series stock car race was due to be held on Saturday, June 10, at Pocono Raceway in Long Pond, Pennsylvania, and Richard Petty Motorsports didn't have a sponsor for that particular race for one of their cars. As a last minute deal, they offered us the sponsorship of the number 43 car, driven by Aric Almirola, at a generous discount. We would get a primary paint scheme and a yearlong associate with Richard Petty Motorsports. Of course, we jumped at the opportunity.

That weekend, we flew out to Pennsylvania and lived it up. We took at least eight employees—every employee that wanted to go— plus my two sons and Travis's daughter and son. Brian Dobler came along too and shot video of the whole experience.

When we arrived at the track and saw the number 43 car with our name and the TI green on it, standing right next to the FedEx car, we got chills. We walked down into the pits to watch the RPM crew prepare the car and found ourselves standing beside the FedEx Racing team in their purple and black fire suits. It was so, so cool. I was so proud. It was a feeling I can't even explain. That was a milestone of *Wow. We've made it.*

For the race, we had the best seats in the house, a booth right on the crash cart overlooking the pit. We could watch the crew chief and engineer as they managed the team and all the technical aspects of the race—when we weren't watching the Transportation Impact car scream around the track!

*When we arrived at the track and saw the number 43 car with our name and the TI green on it, standing right next to the FedEx car, we got chills.*

*Travis and I standing proudly next to the TI 43 car at Pocono. That was a milestone of Wow. We've made it.*

When you sponsor a NASCAR car, unless you're a major B2C (business to consumer) brand like Tide, you don't get business from the people in the stands. Where you get business from your sponsorship is through the other sponsors. It's about the relationships of being in that "in" group. The people that sponsor a particular car are very loyal to each other. The major sponsor for RPM that year was Smithfield Foods. Brian Moffitt, my old friend and the CEO of Richard Petty Motorsports, called the executive level at Smithfield and said, "Hey, will you allow an hour for another sponsor of ours?" Because we were in the same "club," the executive gave us that time. We ended up saving Smithfield about 1.2 million dollars a year, and at the end of the first three-year agreement, they signed on again for another three years. That race more than paid for itself.

This was another example of leveraging relationships to work smart instead of hard. Early on, we recognized very quickly that was the way to work, and we became masters at it. We worked very hard, but we got exponentially more out of our hard work because we were smart about it.

Way back in 2009 we understood the value of paying people who had their own set of relationships to make introductions for us. We could knock on doors all day long and not get in, but that person could make one phone call for us, and suddenly we were in the door, because that person had already established trust. For the last three-plus years we'd been developing a collection of affiliates who made introductions for us, and then we paid them a percentage of our earnings from the client. Steve Huntley, who got us in the door at Office Depot, was one of those people, and there were many others. By mid-2012 we were paying people regularly.

At that time we were paying our sales contractors twenty percent. We wanted to give the affiliate at least twenty percent to make it worthwhile, but it took a while to get up to that level because we were stingy in the early days. We didn't want to give affiliates but five or ten percent. But we found out pretty quickly that it's worth paying them almost as much as the salesperson for the life of the agreement to get us in the door.

Ultimately we formalized it as a partner and affiliate program. Affiliates are individual people, like Steve Huntley, and partners are companies. We created a department dedicated to developing and nurturing those relationships, and we promoted it on our website. It was an extensive amount of work, but we were springboarding off what we'd done with our relationships with individuals. We put a lot of thought and effort into creating a structured standard operating plan for the P&A program. What is the objective of the partnership? What does the partner want to get out of it? What do we want to get out of it? If that's what you want to get, and that's what we want to get, how do we get there? Then we flowcharted our processes around how many leads it would take per month for the partner to earn the amount of revenue they wanted out of the relationship.

To make sure both of us reach our targets, we've got partner development supervisors, who are basically account managers for the partners. They hold the partner accountable to giving us the number and quality of leads necessary to achieve the revenue targets they've set. The supervisor and the partner meet on an established cadence to discuss the opportunities they're going to send us and the status of ones they've already sent, as well as what's necessary to get them to the finish line. It has become very structured. There's also a partner development director, whose sole responsibility is to recruit new partners. In 2020, the big Covid-19 shutdown year, we brought twenty new partners on board.

Working to establish and formalize those relationships was one of the stepping stones that powered us to success rapidly, once we built up momentum. It is a very smart way to do business. After you bring a salesperson on board, it takes six to eight months to develop them to the point where both we and they feel confident they can go out on their own and bring in business. With partners and affiliates, the learning curve is very short. All they have to do is make the introduction; we do the rest. To understand how to position our services in the market takes a training session or two. Then there's what comes along with that partner. If I hire one salesperson, I get one salesperson. When I bring on board as a partner a company that has fifty salespeople, now I've got fifty salespeople that have been tasked by their own management team to go out and position our services. The velocity of sales, the opportunities that they bring in, everything becomes that much faster in every way.

Today, in the early 2020s, income generated via the partner and affiliate program represents around forty percent of our total revenue. That's a large percentage of revenue generated by working smart. We've got some partners we're writing a six-figure check to every month.

Another key aspect of the working smart strategy is our focus on customer retention. It's much cheaper and easier to keep a good customer than it is to find and sign a new one. Customer retention goes beyond providing outstanding and proactive customer service. It means treating that customer like a valued and appreciated guest.

Our business location was on the Carolina coast, with long sandy beaches, lots of outdoor activities, and a full infrastructure for vacationers who wanted sun, sand, and luxury too. It was the perfect setup for a special customer retention perk. We could offer our clients a beach vacation, free of charge.

Travis and I wanted to own the property we bought for this purpose, so we formed an LLC called "That Bothers Me" (all our LLCs had crazy names), and in mid-2011 we started looking for a suitable place. That October we bought the three-bedroom Ocean Keys Villa in North Myrtle Beach, South Carolina. It wasn't on the ocean, but we bought a golf cart so our guests could easily roll themselves and their towels, picnic lunch, beverages, and children down to the beach. It proved so successful that in August 2012 we bought Cinzia Cottage, also in North Myrtle Beach and with golf cart service.

One of the first people we invited was Scott Burger, the CFO of Pandora. He loved the idea, and brought his whole family down to Myrtle Beach. Scott has six children, and at the time they were all still small, so I showed up at the villa with donuts and Chick-fil-A minis for them. Scott and I had become good friends and I wanted to take him and his wife out for a fun night in Myrtle Beach. The kids thought that was a great idea. Munching on donuts and fried chicken they did their best to help me convince their parents to go out for the night, but all of us failed!

Regarding who we invited, we didn't want to get unethical, so we didn't offer the vacation to people who were on the fence or who we were trying to sign. This was a special touch that we offered once they had signed with us. At first, when we didn't have so many customers, we handwrote the invitations and mailed them out in early December every year. There was also a carefully thought-out strategy regarding which contact person at the client company we made this offer to.

Let's say that we dealt with the CFO to get the contract signed, but the manager under that CFO was the person we really kept in contact with and had the relationship with. That was the guy or woman that really made it happen, and they weren't used to having the perks of the C suite. Let's say that that guy or that woman didn't have a lot for Christmas for their family. Imagine receiving a Second Day Air letter with a handwritten invitation to bring your whole family for a summer vacation in a villa on the Carolina coast. Just pick the week of your choosing. What a great Christmas gift to say to their family: "Look! We're going to Myrtle Beach in the first week of June!"

At the condos, presentation was everything. The place would be immaculately clean. When they walked in, I made sure that we had a nice bottle of wine, a gift certificate to Greg Norman's restaurant, and a gift certificate to Cinzia Spa waiting for them. I worked out a deal with the manager at Greg Norman's restaurant, who became a good friend of mine. We committed to so many each year and he gave us a little discount. The gift certificate was enough for a nice meal for the family accompanied by a good bottle of wine.

This customer appreciation perk also gave us an opportunity to get in the car and go spend time with those people. We would plan a dinner, or go play golf—whatever they wanted to do. As well as strengthening the relationship, we got to say: "You've seen what we've done. Can you think of anybody else that can use our service?" Or, "Look at these new service offerings we've come out with. Would you entertain at least just listening and letting us pitch it?" How could they say no?

It worked. We formally closed the program in 2022, but over the decade we used them, those condos made us millions. There were customers who would go year after year. We had to keep buying more and ended up with three in Myrtle Beach and one in Emerald Isle. The retention rate on them was outstanding.

# 17

## IT COULD ALL BE GONE

We now had parts of the operational structure in place, but we were still missing the one person who would look at and manage the whole picture—we needed a head of operations who would create more structure and put in place foundational pieces for the next scale of growth. One of those pieces was taking some of the load off Travis in operations and billing. I knew the perfect person for this role. From the very beginning, my goal had been to get John Howard to join us as head of ops.

John is best defined as a strategic thinker, a problem solver. In 2010 and 2011 we begged John to join us. That's when we were losing it internally. But he was still with UPS and kind of skittish. In those early years, when UPS came after us, we were like the plague. Periodically, I would meet John up in Raleigh, but no matter how much I talked, he still didn't believe in it; he wasn't sold that what we were doing was a viable business that could take him where he wanted to go.

But now I was getting desperate and I had to do whatever it took to get him. The business was growing too quickly. We had to have John. If we had him, I knew that would take us to the next level. He was the key hire for us. One night I couldn't sleep for thinking about it and near midnight, I texted him. "I need you so bad. I want you to join us. Name your price."

The following day we talked, and I shared revenue numbers with him so he could see how rapidly we were growing and what the profit margin was. Next thing we knew, his wife was leading the negotiation for him to come on board. She was a contract negotiator for Glaxo SmithKline. Plus it was our policy in those early days to always get the buy-in from the spouse.

We completed the negotiation to the satisfaction of all involved, and John joined us in Emerald Isle as EVP of operations. I was so happy.

I gave him free rein to see whatever he needed to see and do whatever he felt needed to be done. He was in charge. I wanted him in charge! His first move was to get all the financials as far back as we had at that time—which was really only 2011—and start digging in to figure out what the cash flow situation was: which customers were bringing in the revenue, how much money was going out the door, and where was it going. His primary concern was to keep on top of my vision for growing the business and make sure we had money to make payroll, commissions, rent, and other essential regular payments, and that we didn't get out ahead of our skis on any given decision. At that time, we wanted to maintain a very high margin, at least forty-five percent. So John spent a few months just becoming very intimate with the financials.

Then he sat with every single employee and spent a whole week learning their job and what they did. He wanted to understand how they were doing it so he could find simple ways that technology could help to make us more efficient and accurate without a big financial or time investment. John is a masterful leader and probably the smartest person I know, and getting him on board proved to be crucial to our incredible success.

Except for TidBit, our first-generation FedEx and UPS invoice analysis software, all of our investments to that point had been in people. We really had not started in technology at all, so John was looking to create better processes and use the tools we had in a more efficient manner, and at the same time understand how he could contribute to sales. He was not at all a salesperson, but he enjoyed contributing from his experience at UPS in revenue management. He would sit in on my sales calls and write on the whiteboard tidbits of information that I might be able to use. Or when it came time to negotiate a gain share, he would get onto Excel and calculate what it would take and what the cost impact would be. He found some room for improvement in the discounts we were able to obtain for our clients on accessorials, but overall he was very impressed with the discounts we'd been achieving. Especially given that our sales staff weren't experienced in the industry. He told me we had done a great job of finding smart people who were hard workers.

One of the findings of John's study of our processes was that we needed more operational support. To relieve Travis's load, we needed an analyst who would gather the customers' parcel data, run it through TidBit, and then build out the Excel templates that we used to qualify an opportunity. We needed someone to do the meat and potato grinding of dialing in on the exact savings that we could qualify for that shipper.

John and I had the same person in mind: my oldest son, Brian.

After graduating in 2007 with a Bachelor's of Science in Business Administration from UNC Chapel Hill—Kenan-Flagler Business School, which accepts only around three hundred and forty applicants a year, Brian wanted to go into finance. He had always been an analytical person at heart. He loved looking through data and identifying pullback, doing trend analysis, and reasoning out from there. It was 2007, and the sexy jobs coming out of business school were investment banking, working on Wall Street, trading, anything financial related. That was before the 2008 crash. Stock markets were really healthy and there was a lot of activity in private equity.

I had always hoped both my boys would join me in the company someday—as Travis hoped his children, Branden and Kirsten, would too—but I never put pressure on them to do so. I wanted them to do their own thing, go out and make their own mark, and get experience in the "real" world. Then, if the time came when they wanted to join us, it would be because they were ready and they would make a valuable contribution to the company. We wanted them to work in a different industry, for a different boss, for a different company, and then take that experience and contribute it to Transportation Impact. They would come in with a different perspective—a healthy perspective that would allow them to potentially challenge things. Hiring our children just because they were the "co-founders' kids" was never an option that Travis and I considered. If they came on board, they had to contribute genuine value.

After five years working at a hedge fund, Brian was ready to join us. We brought him in for an interview, to say we had done it, but it was really just a formality. John, Travis, and I had been friends for twenty years, and they both knew Brian's skill set and strengths as well as I did. In December 2012 he started work as director of operations, transferring his core analytical skill set from the stock market to parcel shipping data. We gave him an office in suite B and he dove into the data, getting very familiar with the UPS and FedEx billing websites and helping bring scalability and process improvement so that we were turning around the baselines and savings opportunities quicker—so that sales could keep pushing through the leads and qualifying opportunities. However, like the rest of us, he wore whatever hat was necessary at any particular moment.

Brian's official boss and mentor was John, obviously because John was head of ops, but also because I wanted to keep a level of separation in the accountability chart. In fact, the whole time we were both at the company, I was never his direct supervisor. That didn't prevent growing pains as we learned how to work together in a business relationship, though. A few times over the years we had a difference of opinion or one of us would say something that would pull an emotional trigger in our relationship, and then we would stop talking for a week. Eventually we would apologize and make up and move on with our relationship. Perhaps because we're so alike, we needed a week's buffer to let cooler heads prevail. But we had always been close, and those instances of friction were rare.

Standing in the doorway of his office one day and watching Brian work, I felt immensely proud. Both my boys had turned out so much smarter than I could ever have imagined, and nothing could have pleased me more than to have both of them working at Transportation Impact. I knew both would contribute a lot, and I hoped that Tyler would eventually join Brian and me.

We were now in pretty good shape in both operations and finance. Transportation Impact was beginning to feel like a real company, and Travis and I started thinking about getting company cars. We went to Richard Brown to ask his advice.

"Do you think we could have cars paid for by the company?" we asked him.

Transportation Impact was now pulling down a few million dollars a year. Richard thought for a moment, and then said, "You guys are doing so well, you could have any car you want."

He advised that we lease rather than buy. That suited me perfectly, because I wanted to get something new every few years. I'm a big car guy, and this was the first time I'd ever had the money to do anything with cars.

Travis and I went shopping.

We started modestly. Travis chose a Porsche and I got a BMW 640i. As the years went by, we became less concerned about being conservative and indulged our love for cars with iconic makes like Maserati Gran Turismo, Bentley, Aston Martin, Ferrari. I also bought myself a '69 Camaro Z/28—the same car I had when I was a kid. I still have it.

Travis didn't always lease, so to make it fair to him, whatever payment he was getting for the monthly car allowance, if I had to pay some at the beginning of my lease to get the payment down to where it was equitable, I would do that.

We were starting to enjoy the fruits of our labors, but the atmosphere in the office was still like a startup, and we were still dependent on Veriship for our audit platform. An advantage of that partnership, though, was the leads they kept feeding us. Around August they sent me a lead on a company in Minneapolis that was spending about half a million dollars annually with UPS. The contact at the company was the president, Mike Bothof. I called Mike. We had a conversation about the company and their needs, and then I explained how we could guide them through a renegotiation of their UPS agreement to generate long-term savings. He was interested and got the go-ahead from the owner to give us access to their billing data. We ran the analysis and found we could save them around fifteen percent. "Let's do it," Mike said.

After a few more phone calls, in early fall we kicked off the negotiation. He was doing it in person, rather than by email, so I coached him on what to say and the angle to take. Before the first meeting with his UPS rep we had a call to review his talking points and the strategy. "This is what your rep's going to say, and this is how you respond," I told him. I made sure he was clear on everything and told him to call me when he was done.

A while later, he called me. "Dude," he said. "That was crazy. It's like you were in the room with me telling me what to say."

I laughed. "Buddy, I trained these people. I told them what to say."

Mike's negotiation went so perfectly, it was like an orchestrated . . . orchestra—a Keithism that John and Berkley love to kid me about.

It took a few weeks, we achieved the savings, and all was well. Then I got a phone call from Mike. "I have to tell you something," he said. "I just had a meeting with my rep, and she asked me if I had anybody working with me on the negotiation. She said she has million-dollar shippers that don't have the deals that I have. I told her, 'No, we figured something out. We're a little more educated than we were three months ago.'"

That was how it worked. That was where the relentless focus on attention to detail and perfection paid off. And we didn't have to say it. Our customers said it.

Mike and I had hit it off, and over the next few months we had many more conversations. As our relationship blossomed, he introduced me to a few companies and I had some success with one or two of them. It was nice to build the relationship in that respect. I offered a few times to fly up to meet with him, but he always told me not to burn money on the airfare. We'd established enough trust over the phone that it wasn't necessary to meet in person. But right at the end of the year I had to go up to Minnesota, so on New Year's Day, 2013, we got together for a quick dinner in Minneapolis and cemented the relationship.

A few days later, around four o'clock on Friday, January fourth, I was in the suite B conference room with Sharon and John going over some year-end things, when Travis appeared in the doorway. He was sweating and didn't look very good. "I've got something going on," he said. "I'm going to go see some doctors. They'll keep you guys informed."

A minute later we heard his car start and drive off.

I'm going to let Travis tell the whole story.

I was in my office in suite C and had a funny taste come in my mouth. A taste that was unique to anything I've ever had. I've been sick before, had the flu, had the metallic taste in the mouth, but this was a very unique taste. The outside of my arm hurt for about forty-five minutes. I broke out in a sweat. After telling the others I was leaving, I went home, took some Aspirin, and got my wife. We went to a doctor in Greenville. I'd had a heart attack. I ended up seeing five doctors over nine business days.

Got to the best of the best when it comes to cardiac surgery. I'm adopted. That's important for this story. Every time I'd ever been to a doctor, family history was always N/A, N/A, N/A. You simply don't know. This guy met me pretty quickly. At this point in time, he'd done over six thousand open heart surgeries. That's all the man had ever done for the last thirty years. He was just brilliant at what he did. He sat down with me and my wife.

"Look," he said, "I could put some stents in you. One, it's going to take nine stents to fix what's wrong with your heart. Two, you'll just be back in here in ten years."

So I said, "Go ahead and fix me, as young as I am." I was forty-nine years old.

The surgery was right around February first, because I remember it was Superbowl Sunday. They let me out on a Monday. They cut me on a Thursday. Six or seven days after going in I drove back to where our house was. Within a week.

This is a smiley face at the end of a tough week. We stopped by the local elementary school in our neighborhood. They were doing their "Jump Rope for Heart" kickoff that week with their third grade class. I went into the class for ten or fifteen minutes and actually started jumping rope to kick off the Jump Rope for Heart. There was a girl who lives in our neighborhood that I didn't know at the time.

About six months later, her parents came over and introduced themselves. The girl was with them. I looked at her and said, "How are you doing?"

She said, "I remember you."

"Where do I know you from?"

"You came to my school and did the jump rope to help us with our Jump Rope for Heart."

"I don't remember seeing you."

"I remember seeing you," she said. "You didn't look too good."

Out of the mouth of a third grader. She said I looked like a ghost. Of course, I didn't know it. I was just trying to prove a point to myself or my family or whoever. But it was kind of a cool moment.

Ever since then, we've been involved with the American Heart Association. I support it personally, and every year as a company we do a fundraiser. Travis is a huge supporter, and he and Cass have even chaired the Down East Heart Ball, one of the biggest annual fundraisers for the Eastern North Carolina branch of the association.

Those weeks when Travis was doing the round of doctors and then was in the hospital—that was a hard time. Being face to face with the possibility of Travis not coming back made me realize how much I didn't want to lose him. It made both of us realize we should appreciate each other more. We were going a hundred miles an hour at that point. We were gangbusters. Making millions. But that put it in perspective. It shocked us into an awareness to be more giving, because it's rolling in right now, but it could all be gone.

# 18

## THE A TEAM

In the very back of suite B, where we had our office printer, taped to the wall was a five-page foldout section from *Inc.* magazine. It was the 2010 list of Inc. 500 winners. Every year, *Inc.* publishes a list of the nation's 5000 fastest-growing private companies, and the Inc. 500 is the top ten percent of those companies. It's the ultimate list of American entrepreneurial success. I always loved *Inc.* magazine and always admired the list. Right from day one of TI, I would think, *Man, if we could just make that list, one year.* It became an obsession. I told everyone in the company, "We're going to make that list one day." I put the foldout on the wall to inspire and motivate them, to show them what we were working towards. Every day, when they went to collect something from the printer, they would see that list and be reminded.

When we hired Richard Brown to work with us on the accounting and budgeting, I told him that as soon as we were eligible, I wanted to apply for the Inc. 5000. That was Richard's job. He had to do whatever was necessary to get our financials in order for that application. I wanted to have TI recognized for credibility in the industry as being one of the fastest-growing companies in America.

Richard had to do a lot of work to understand what could go in and how to make our numbers conform with the requirements. He was often on the phone with the Inc. 5000 people clarifying what we could include and what we couldn't include. Since we were a cash basis business, we had to convert all financial statements to accrual basis. Almost every day I would ask him, "How are we doing on that? What do you think we're going to come in at?"

Finally, he was done. Richard submitted the application, showing that we had increased our revenues 833 percent from 2009 to 2012. With that big an increase, I was optimistic we would make the top five hundred of the Inc.

The deadline for submission was April 30, 2013, and then we had to wait until August for the results to be announced.

In early August, a Next Day Air letter was delivered to the office. I opened it. It was from the editor-in-chief of *Inc.* magazine, Eric Shurenberg. "Congratulations," it began. I sat at my desk and cried. I couldn't believe it. We had made the Inc. And we had made it with two companies. Transportation Impact's ranking was 547. Our 2012 revenue was $7.15 million, and we had missed being in the top ten percent of fastest-growing companies in America, the Inc. 500, by only forty-seven places. But our sister company, First Flight Solutions, actually did make the top five hundred, coming in at 183, because their revenues went up 1,609 percent.

We got everybody together in the office and announced it. Everybody went crazy. They all knew how important that was to me. It was one of those moments that you never forget, because it's something that you work towards for three years. And to see the type of growth that we had to have to have one company make the actual Inc. 500 and the other company just miss it was phenomenal. That was one of my proudest moments. In my mind, that was the first time that we had accomplished something. When we started the company, my first goal was to make the Inc. 5000. It was a huge, huge win for us to do that because I knew it opened up doors. I knew it spoke for itself.

The Inc. 500/5000 conference was held that October at the JW Marriott at National Harbor, right outside of Washington, D.C. It was a three-day event, and of course we went. I was on cloud nine just to be in that room with all those successful entrepreneurs.

Those three days were very rewarding. That event validated all of our efforts. Throughout each day we listened to educational speakers, most of them very successful entrepreneurs sharing their stories: the pitfalls, the struggles, and also the successes. Each evening included social activities, drinks, dinner. The dinners always had a theme. And then to wrap it up, there was a black tie gala on the last night. It was a fantastic experience.

It was also superb networking. For three days we were handing out cards and hearing people's stories. Standing in the elevator with people, at the bar, by the pool, you would see on their name tag the number of their company's ranking in the Inc. Because we had two companies in those low numbers, that got people's attention. If you were in the top five hundred, that was incredible. That was a special group of entrepreneurs. People want to be surrounded with other successful people, and at the Inc. celebration, they listen to your story because they care, because you're in that unique club. It's a lot different from a trade show. At that event, people want to hear your story. People want to listen. People want to talk. The camaraderie is remarkable.

It was awesome to listen to other people's stories and make those connections, and then go back to the room and look them up on LinkedIn and connect with them there. After the conference was over, I started reaching out with a deeper dive into what we do. We got a lot of business from that event.

To celebrate the win with our employees, we gave everybody a twenty-five-hundred-dollar bonus and took them all out to a really nice dinner. But it wasn't a one and done. We continued celebrating that accomplishment for months, because it was such a super goal that I'd had personally from the time we started the company.

Making the Inc. 5000—and with not only one, but *two* companies—was a major accomplishment, a validation of Transportation Impact as a successful entrepreneurial business, and we wanted to show it off. We put the Inc. 500/5000 logo on our business cards, our website, everywhere we could. We had plaques on everybody's desk. We bought all the memorabilia. We squeezed every bit out of that accomplishment.

We particularly wanted to capitalize on it in our marketing, so we hired a local PR guy, John Nelson, who had worked with politicians. We gave him a six-month assignment to promote the heck out of TI making the Inc. 5000. This was the first time we ever did a press release. John did a great job getting Transportation Impact exposure and recognition.

After the six months were up, he wanted to stay with the company. We really liked him, but we couldn't justify hiring him as an employee. So we offered for him to continue on as an affiliate, and he has turned out to be one of our best and most consistent affiliates. He makes three touches a day. When he gets up in the morning, he'll spend half an hour reaching out to three people on LinkedIn or via email. If his wife ordered something, he'll take a picture of it and handwrite a letter to the C-level person at that company: "Hey, I'm a customer of yours. Here's what my wife ordered. Let my company help you out." Three touches a day. Every day. Ninety-nine times he'll get told no. The one time it's yes will be a home run. He is model of persistence. He's got us so much business. There's no telling what we pay him. We offered him double what normal affiliates get because I liked him so much and because of what he did for us during those six months of getting us recognition and credibility. I didn't really think that he would take off with it like he has, but that guy is a beast when it comes to securing meetings for us. That's all that affiliates do. They secure meetings, and then it's up to us to sell it.

Around this time I got a break on a huge account that I had been working for a long time. Thanks to a former client taking a leadership position at SodaStream USA, we got in the door there.

John and I, and I think Brandon too, flew out to New Jersey and met with our contact along with three other people. We showed them the savings we could generate for them, and our contact gave us a verbal commitment to sign the contract. He said he had to get through the company bureaucracy first, but it was a done deal, and he wanted to know how the negotiation with the carrier would be done.

We knew this guy. He had been the decision maker who had hired us before, so we violated our own policy and gave the customer the secret sauce before getting a signed contract. We trusted him when he told us the contract was being inked, so we revealed to him the strategy, the emails, the psychological approach—everything. The savings we had identified was well over a million dollars; 1.6 million if I remember correctly. We were so excited. Even though they had beat us down to around thirty-five percent on the gain share, this was going to be a big one.

Sure enough, they never signed the contract. They did the negotiation behind our back. That taught us not to rely on trust anymore. We were really banking on that revenue. That betrayal was an eye opener as to how cruel business can be.

A few months later I got more bad news. Erin told us she was leaving to pursue other opportunities. She was such a bright talent with the perfect skill set and tenacity. We wished her well, but it was a blow to lose her.

With Erin gone, more of the sales load fell back on me. I wasn't complaining. On the contrary, I loved it. I ate it up. Every time I got a client signed, it was like crack—you want to keep going. The problem was I couldn't keep up with the supply and demand. We had got John to support Travis on the operations side; now we needed to get someone to support me. I had to have a right hand. John could recognize that my nerves were getting shot. I wasn't burned out, but I needed help.

I also had lost some of my reinforcement at home, because in July 2011 my wife and I had separated for good. Syndie believed in me and always supported me, but there had long been stresses on our marriage. I was not the perfect husband by any means. Syndie had also become resentful that I called it the TI family and the business took up all of my time. Our separation during the time Travis and I were whiteboarding the business model was just one of several. Syndie and I had been together since high school. We had grown up together, we had worked together to get through the difficult early years when we had no money, and together we had raised two smart, responsible, hardworking young men we were immensely proud of. She was the mother of my children, and I would always have a special love for her, but our relationship as a married couple was over.

Although I knew it was the right decision for both of us, the end of my marriage lay heavy on my heart. When I face a personal or professional challenge, I do something to get out of my comfort zone and prove to myself that I can overcome. So I signed up for the Emerald Isle sprint triathlon and started training. Towards the end of the year I competed in the race and successfully surmounted that challenge. It was such a satisfying experience that I repeated it a few years later, when I found myself again struggling with a heaviness on my heart.

When he started work at TI, John and his family weren't ready to move to Emerald Isle because his wife still had a full-time job at Research Triangle Park and their kids were still in school. Rather than get him a hotel room and expense it back to the company, he lived with me Monday to Thursday and went home to Raleigh on weekends. Brian, my son, was doing the same Tuesday through

Thursday, because he also wasn't ready to move from Raleigh. This became a phenomenally productive time for us. So many nights we would congregate in the kitchen talking about the company for hours. We came up with many great ideas that we wrote on paper towels so we would remember them in the morning.

One of the topics we kept coming back to was who we could hire to take over from me in leading sales. We wanted a person who could also be my replacement in leading the company. Not true succession planning, but someone to take over if anything happened to me. I had so much invested and I still had my family to look out for. I was travelling all the time, and if I were to die in a plane crash or a car wreck, the business needed to continue. John and I sat up at night talking about this and brainstorming who would be the perfect person. We landed on Berkley Stafford. Berkley was the shining star I had trained at UPS in the late 1990s. About a year before Travis and I quit, Berkley left to take a key sales role at a Swedish company called Envirotainer, and he eventually moved up to be Head of Healthcare Sales for the whole of the Americas.

John and I started strategically planning how we could get Berkley.

Since he left UPS, Berkley and I had stayed loosely in touch. Every once in a blue moon we would pass notes to each other via email. Our relationship stayed intact just from me letting him know how we were doing. Then I started flying a lot and he was traveling all the time too, so we started running into each other at airports. Our paths would commonly cross at the airport in Charlotte, North Carolina.

The first time it happened, we caught up in a casual way with a hug and "Hey, man, how you doing?" The next time I told him we were starting to build momentum and he needed to come join us, but it was more just a comment than a serious attempt to recruit him. We were both busy and I didn't greatly need him at that point. But in 2012 and early 2013 I started putting the pressure on. One flight we were sitting near each other and I said to him, "I'm serious. We're really growing. It's getting big now. Why don't you consider coming on over?" He said no, he really enjoyed the job he had. The next time, I asked him to come down to Emerald Isle to meet with us. Again he said no.

Now it was time to do whatever it took to get him, like I had with John.

I called Berkley.

"Look, we're really growing. I know you like your job," I said. "I know you do. I respect that. Just come talk to me. That's all I'm asking."

At UPS I was Berkley's mentor, and there was a deep bond of love, trust, and respect between us. Berkley didn't want to come to Emerald Isle because he knew that if he sat in our company offices with me, he wouldn't be able to walk away without helping, and that would be the end of his career at Envirotainer, a job he loved. But this time, he said okay, he would come down and meet with us.

He sat with Travis, John, and me in the conference room and we gave him the full picture of our growth and our success. As the conversation came to an end, I said to Berkley, "Go home. Talk with your family. Call John. Ask him anything, the good and the bad. And then call me with your decision."

As he was driving home, Berkley called John. "Look, am I going to make it?" he asked.

"We're doing big things over here. It's the best career move I've ever made in my entire life," John told him.

Berkley joined us in October 2013 as vice president of sales. I was very happy. I knew I had the A team.

It was as if he'd never left my leadership at UPS. I told him first, "Don't get on the road. Don't sell anything for three months. Get your department in order. Get your people squared away, learn the product, and then we'll start hustling." So for three months, he dug into things and got a lot of information from John. Then he set up a sales training program and got us properly using a CRM.

At that time we had ten to twelve sales contractors, and Brandon had got us on Salesforce but we weren't doing anything with it. We were paying money to use it like a glorified Rolodex. Berkley got the CRM organized and started holding our salespeople accountable.

The first training trip he made with me, we flew to a CFO conference in Phoenix, Arizona. Berkley listened to me do our presentation sixteen times, the same presentation every time, in a speed dating–type conference, where you got a chance to speak to sixteen decision makers in a day and a half. Berkley got a crash course in the operational execution and the science behind my sales delivery. It was a PowerPoint, and all the content was well thought out. It was methodical, it flowed, it made sense. It showed the mathematical benefit to the client. When we left there he was ninety-five percent squared away on how to deliver our presentation. He also got a first-hand demonstration of how effective my presentation was, because it impressed the COO of Ping so much that they ultimately signed with us.

Then we started dividing and conquering.

Berkley and I were out beating the street. I was on a plane every week. Travis and John were keeping up on the back side. We still didn't have a whole lot of processes, but they were improving. And we had big dreams and big plans.

The Stafford family weren't ready to move from Wilmington to Emerald Isle, so Berkley joined John, Brian, and me living in the house during the week. Work didn't stop at five o'clock. Most of the time, we would eat lunch together, work until seven o'clock, and then walk next door to Kathryn's or go to Portofinos or RuckerJohn's and eat dinner. Even at dinner, we were talking about work.

Then we'd come home, go sit on the back screen porch with a few cocktails, and continue to talk about work. It just consumed us. We talked about the company, our contractor model for sales, about affiliates, about prospects and opportunities and challenges. Sometimes one or two of the sales contractors, like Neal Newhouse or Tim Brock, would join us, and my younger son, Tyler, would often be there too. From eight-thirty to eleven at night, we came up with some of the best ideas for the company and wrote them down on napkins or paper towels. Then the next morning, we grabbed that napkin off the back porch and went into work and tried to implement some of the ideas that we'd hashed out. There was so much passion, so much investment in the business in those days, because that's all we did. Because we had to. John and Berkley lived with me during the week for over a year, and those nights in my house, with the A team, we had some of our best thought sessions. Those ideas we wrote on napkins and paper towels, we implemented probably eighty percent of them. We had that trust with each other. It was unique, special.

By the end of 2013, we were in good shape.

Then in late December, my phone lit up with Mike Bothof's number.

"Are you planning to open an office in Minnesota?" He was walking to his car in the parking lot after finishing his last day of work as president of the plumbing supplies company, and he wanted to join our team as a salesperson. He believed in our business model so much, he wanted to sell it. Being an operations guy at heart, the hard dollar savings was very appealing to him, and as a business manager, the idea of using a consulting company and looking at things from a different angle was invaluable. He knew he could use those two aspects to sell our business model to decision makers.

"Buddy, just get to work," I said. "We'll figure something out."

✳

# 19

## IT'S THE GOVERNOR, Y'ALL

Mike wasn't ready to make the leap to being full-time commission, so he signed a deal to start working with us as an affiliate. Over the next months he sent in a couple of referrals while he figured out whether he wanted to make the leap to being a contractor—to "eat what you kill" as he put it.

Finally, one summer Tuesday, he came down to meet with us. As he walked into our little conference room in Suite B that was eighty percent filled with our giant granite-slab table, I could see on Mike's face that he was thinking, *This is it? Really?* That was a common reaction from the few clients who actually came to Emerald Isle. We were so good at presenting ourselves as a professional, well-established company that it was a shock for them to see our set of offices in two suites in a strip mall.

In early fall our former client became the newest member of our team of sales contractors. The day Mike talked to us about coming down to Emerald Isle, he also got an offer from a company in Dallas Fort Worth—and that company is now a client of TI. It's funny how things come full circle.

Travis's son Branden was also interested in coming on board. After graduating from Campbell University with an MBA, Branden had worked as a trust administrative officer for US Bank/Bank of America Private Wealth Management in Seattle. But I think he saw Brian's success and that we were a legitimate company, and he wanted to be part of it too. Branden's a smart guy.

We put him through the hiring process because we didn't want to treat any of our kids any different than we did anybody else, but it was a shoo-in. In July 2014 Branden Burt joined his dad, John, and my son Brian in operations as a finance analyst. Over the years he has added a lot of value and worked his way up, and in 2019, he became director of operations, reporting to Brian. Branden came on board just in time for two wonderful pieces of news.

The last Monday in July, I was in my office with Berkley and John when a call came through on my cell phone.

"Keith Byrd?" said the person on the other end. "This is Governor Pat McCrory."

My palms started sweating. I had to take a brief pause. Muting the phone, I turned to the others.

"Oh, my God, y'all, it's the governor! I'm so nervous."

They looked as stunned as I felt.

I unmuted the phone and managed to talk normally.

North Carolina Governor Pat McCrory had called me to congratulate Transportation Impact on being chosen for the Governor's Award for Excellence in Workforce Development as an "Outstanding Employer."

After I hung up, I told John and Berkley the news. We whooped and high-fived. We could hardly believe we'd been honored like that. That call put us on cloud nine.

The governor also sent us a letter, which for us was an award in itself. He wrote:

> Your company was selected from many deserving companies from across the state because you embody the true spirit of our new message, NCWorks. You are indeed a positive role model for North Carolina's employers.

Pat McCrory himself came out to present us with the award. Each year it's given to a North Carolina company that demonstrates involvement and commitment to the workforce development community in the state. We also got a separate visit from the lieutenant governor, Dan Forest. We were incredibly honored by their personal recognition. There are only fifty governors out there, one per state, and they live and work in metro areas. To be recognized as a small and upcoming company that contributes to the state's workforce development—you can get drowned out quickly when you're in a sleepy beach town at the edge of eastern North Carolina. We didn't, thanks to Dr. Kerry Youngblood, president of Carteret Community College.

Early the previous year Dr. Youngblood had come to our office looking for funding. We saw this as a great opportunity to support local education and local business, so we made a commitment of fifty thousand dollars. Over the next months we worked closely with Dr. Youngblood and his staff to create the Transportation Impact Small Business Forum in conjunction with "Small Business Week" in Carteret County. It was a great success, and we hosted it again in May 2014. Dr. Youngblood and his staff were wonderful to work with, and apparently he appreciated our efforts so much he nominated us for the Governor's Award.

A fundamental part of our culture has always been our support of our community. That was important to Travis and me from the beginning. We always said that when we turned the corner we were going to start giving back. We just knew that if we were that fortunate, we needed to do something to help somebody else. The first year we really made any money was 2010, and it was a real pleasure to sit down together and talk about ideas for what we could do—and then to make those ideas a reality.

We began that year with a scholarship for the local senior school, Croatan High School, awarding twenty-five hundred dollars to one student to use towards their college tuition. The next year, we gave scholarships to two high schools. We kept increasing the number of scholarships, and now we offer four for Carteret and Onslow counties.

The scholarships have become well known, and each year the quality of the applicants blows us away. These young women and men are awe-inspiring in their achievements, their dedication, their determination, and their character. Every one of them embodies our core values and has incredible plans for the future. It absolutely amazes me how resilient some kids are. They are so driven—in many cases they have very few or no financial options or opportunities to go to college.

Eventually we formed a committee specifically for the purpose of selecting the awardees because we were getting so many applications from deserving students. They first submit a written application. The committee then selects the top three from each school for thirty-minute interviews. It's very high pressure for them. But to see those young people thrive in that environment, as they're sitting in front of business professionals knowing that they may not have an opportunity to go to college—it's inspiring to see them step up. It's often not easy to choose only four! To make it equitable, we rank them numerically on a number of factors, and in 2020 we had two students tie for the last available scholarship, so we went back into the budget and pulled out more money so we could give a scholarship to both of them as well as the other three students.

It's inspiring to read about the achievements of these students and hear them speak about their dreams and goals, and it's rewarding to know that we are helping them to move towards that future.

A year or so after we started offering scholarships to all four high schools, we added one specifically for a Campbell University student. Campbell is a four-year, private university in Buies Creek, North Carolina. Although we provide the scholarship directly to the school, we are also involved in the selection process.

The other traditions we began in 2010 and that still continue today are the Christmas Family and Christmas Grocery Shopping. These two are special favorites with all of us. As we approached the end of the year, we thought about all the children and families in our area who might not have such a happy Christmas because they couldn't afford all the nice food and presents and decorations and all the other things that their friends and neighbors were enjoying, so we wanted to give one deserving family that kind of Christmas.

We got help from the local schools to find a family that was a good fit, and made sure they had all the things that would make it a very special Christmas for them.

This was such a wonderful experience for everyone that we made it an annual tradition, and like we did with the scholarships, we kept increasing the number of families. Now it's up to four or five each year. To identify the families, every year around Thanksgiving we have lunch with five local school counselors who understand what we're looking for, and we understand what they're looking for. They identify kids within elementary, middle, and high school that have a significant need for attention. For example, one year there was a young lady who lost one parent early on through suicide, and then when she was only seventeen years old, she lost the second one to cancer. She was a straight-A student, and she had been working since she was sixteen. She bought her own car and paid her own car insurance, but she didn't have enough money to go to school. The only thing she wanted for Christmas was to continue the dance lessons that she used to have before her parents passed away. Every year, we hear stories like that and ten times worse.

The descriptions the counsellors bring us of the families in need are detailed—here are the members within the family that we need to help; here's the grandma that's taking care of the kids because the parents were drug addicts; here's what the grandma needs. She needs a washer and dryer. She can't even wash clothes; she does it by hand. There are three kids that the grandma's taking care of. The kids need coats, socks and shoes, and underwear. They want Barbie dolls, they want PlayStation—stuff they'll never get. A pair of Air Jordans they could never afford.

We are able to give these families a dream-come-true Christmas. When they're forty years old and have their own family, they'll remember that Christmas. If there are multiple kids in a family, we make sure they each get the same number of presents—some kids get fifteen presents under that Christmas tree, moderate to big ones. We spend two thousand dollars per family. It's a dream Christmas they'll never forget, one that can inspire them that there's hope in the world.

As an organization, I believe we have a social responsibility to society. We want to share what we have, because we have more than enough, and we want our employees to be able to join in as well. The Christmas Family is wonderful for that, because the employees get to go shopping for the kids, and they love it. They love thinking of the joy that will be on the child's face when they open that present.

The other piece of exciting news came the month after we got the Governor's Award. We learned we had made the Inc. 5000 list again! Our ranking this time was 728. After that first achievement in 2013 we had no idea we would keep making the list, because they go by the last three years of growth, so once you make it, it's that much harder to continue to make it.

We again gave everyone a "true-up" twenty-five-hundred-dollar bonus, and to this day we've kept that up. I used to hate getting bonuses at UPS that had the taxes taken out. If you're going to give twenty-five hundred, give twenty-five hundred! Everyone was excited and proud to make the list again, and we went crazy again buying all the memorabilia and getting everyone a plaque for their desk. As the years went by for quite a while we kept doing that, but then you start to have the problem of where to put all the stuff. So we stopped. But we still got very proud and excited.

Making the list a second year in a row gave TI even more credibility, and it allowed us to show potential clients that we were a force to be reckoned with in the industry.

As if those two achievements weren't enough, the Carteret County Chamber of Commerce also awarded us the honor of 2014 "Employer of the Year," and the University of North Carolina School of Government ranked TI at number five in their listing of the top eight corporate citizens.

But although we were starting to win awards and our revenue and number of employees and contractors were steadily increasing, the attitude and atmosphere throughout the company were still entrepreneurial and family-oriented. We still had no technology skill set to speak of. We were working out of a strip mall. We were very small. People's roles were becoming more defined, but it was still much like any other startup where a lot of the business and ideas came from after hours just as much as during hours, there weren't many rules or regulations or protocols or titles, and everyone was wearing multiple hats and doing whatever they needed to do to be productive and successful.

We had set up shop next to a nightclub, and in the Emerald Club Thursday night was the deal. On Thursdays, we'd shut the office early so people could get their game face on and hit Kathryn's to warm up for the E Club. Come Thursday night, we were going to have a good time, and on Friday whoever showed up, it was all right.

In those years, we were building our core values and we didn't know it. It was a work hard, play hard mentality. We didn't punch a clock—it was all about come in, do your job, get it done, make sure it's done right. It was like it was with the UPS drivers. If it's measured as a 9.2 day and you did it in eight, you got paid for 9.2. The same way, at TI, if you needed to go to Walmart or your kid's baseball game, then you went and we didn't track the time you were gone. We didn't want to micromanage. Of course, eventually we started getting so big we had to create structure so that one person was not doing less work than their colleagues. But for a long time, there were no time clocks. Every person knew that their teammates were working hard. That attitude bled into the dress, the flexibility with our people, the half-day Fridays.

The culture was very important to us. An open-door policy. Time off. Being good to our employees. Rewarding them for milestones. Getting their car washed. We'd have somebody come in and give massages. It was very important to us that our people be relaxed. We wanted them to be sharp and work hard, but play hard too and have fun. The atmosphere was casual, but we knew when to turn it on, and we were always prepared.

In late fall, out of the blue I got another awesome phone call. The man on the other end introduced himself as Jeff Collins, president and co-founder of Cascade Orthopedic Supply. He was renegotiating his UPS agreement and had a proposal from the carrier sitting on his desk, but it fell far below his expectations.

In October, Jeff had completed an acquisition of another company, and one of the items in the investment thesis he had presented to his bank to secure the funding was that the acquisition would enable him to negotiate with UPS for greater discounts based on the greater anticipated collective volume. But the discounts offered by UPS did not meet his investment thesis. Jeff had a board meeting coming up in a few days and he was hoping to have some good news to present, like: "We did this acquisition and UPS is now going to reduce the rates."

After having a challenge negotiating on his own and being

disappointed that UPS wasn't handing him the volume discounts he thought they should, given the amount of collective volume Cascade had, Jeff understood he could use some help and searched online for third-party freight negotiation. It was still an early concept, and TI was one of the handful that existed in the space.

It was a Thursday or Friday when we spoke. Jeff's board meeting was the next Tuesday, with one of the members flying in from Hawaii, so Travis and I worked over the weekend—which we were very comfortable doing—to calculate the estimated savings based on the volumes that Cascade was anticipating. Jeff had calculated that the new agreement offered by UPS would result in savings of around a hundred and fifty thousand dollars. We verified it as being one hundred and thirty thousand. I called Jeff.

"What can you do?" he asked.

"We can save you a little over a million dollars."

"That's very enticing," he said, "but I don't know. I need board approval to move forward with you, so I would like you to come and present to my board the savings that you found."

"We'll be there!"

We quickly put together a proposal and flew out to California. Cascade Orthopedic was headquartered in Chico, a small college town at the northwestern edge of the agricultural Sacramento Valley. The office was out by Chico airport in a leased facility of about six thousand square feet. At that time, Cascade was doing a little less than fifty million dollars in revenue, but they were quickly growing, as the recent acquisition proved.

As we walked into the small conference room, I was both excited and nervous. This would be a really big deal for us if we could convince the board it was worth hiring us. In the middle of the room a few long, narrow tables had been pushed together to create a conference table. I was surprised to see only three people sitting at the table: Jeff, who was minority partner, the majority partner, and their attorney. Jeff and the majority partner were the entire board of directors of Cascade Orthopedic.

Everybody turned to face the flat screen on the back wall. I had Scott Jordan's fabulous video voicemail testimonial cued up, and without saying a word, without even introducing ourselves, I hit "play."

Scott of SCOTTeVEST came on that big screen and told his story that hit every pain point about giving us the data, how efficient we were, how little time he spent on it, how successful the negotiation was, and how we saved him thousands of dollars in one week.

Then, once Scott had done our selling for us, we presented that we could save Cascade almost one and a half million dollars a year and explained how the gain share worked. They asked us to leave the room so they could discuss it. We went out into the lobby. We were nervous. This was such a huge deal. While we waited, we placed bets on what they were going to come back at us with. How much they would try to beat us on the gain share—or how quick they'd throw us out the door.

At last they called us back in. The business case was really strong, so the board was fine accepting the proposal if we could achieve what appeared to them to be an almost unrealistic amount of savings. They were prepared to sign on, but told us they wanted more of the savings up front and less towards the end of the three-year agreement. Our share would be thirty percent the first year, forty the second year, and then fifty the third year, so they could achieve the cost savings sooner. They had really ramped up their debt levels for the acquisition and needed to have the cash flow for the business. After some discussion, we agreed to those terms.

Cascade guarantees overnight delivery anywhere in the U.S. at published ground rates, so maintaining a good relationship with the carrier was crucial. That was Jeff's biggest concern. He definitely did not want UPS to know that he was using TI to support the negotiation. Jeff had already been negotiating with UPS, and he was obviously smart enough to be the point person in our behind-the-scenes "coach and counsel" strategy, so we set it up that way.

In our analysis of their shipping data, we pinpointed where Cascade was significantly off market in the areas that caused a significant portion of their freight spend and brought those insights to Jeff along with a range of where their discount levels or pricing should be. Then he used that information to craft emails to the UPS and FedEx account representatives.

Near the end of the negotiations, he had an important in-person meeting coming up with UPS, so we sent one of our best people out to Chico to be a Cascade employee for a day or two, to help them through the final rounds. Wearing a Cascade shirt and with the title of logistics officer, our guy jumped in to the discussion every time a question came up that needed a more granular answer than Jeff could provide.

When it was all over and we had achieved the savings for Cascade that we had promised, Jeff told me in a follow-up call that once he was able to start talking about specific areas and specific accessorials, the negotiation changed radically. In his experience, prior to using a third party negotiator, UPS would hand him a proposal and expect him to sign it without much review or pushback, but the game changed once he was able to bring in the level of detail and the ask that we helped him prepare. At the same time, he brought in the FedEx Healthcare group to offer proposals, to show UPS that they had competition for his business.

After the new agreement went into effect, Cascade's relationship with UPS actually improved. They got more attention, and really the attention they should have, given the volumes they were moving at the time. UPS treated them with more respect.

On our side, this negotiation showed us how we could get creative on the gain share. We also saw how the carrier used "smoke and mirrors," the old magician's tricks, to fool the customer into thinking they were getting a much better deal than they really were. From then on, Brian Dobler took that phrase, "smoke and mirrors," and used it effectively in our marketing.

# 20

## TEENAGE TROUBLES

Our gross revenue in 2014 was 18.7 million dollars, which earned us a third consecutive placement on the Inc. 5000. To this point we had experienced unbelievable growth at a high velocity. We were riding high. Year-over-year revenue growth was between thirty and forty percent. One year, I think it was even sixty percent. It was extraordinary growth—double digit for a long time.

But we were about to get a big wake-up call.

There was one significant problem with our business model, and it was exactly the problem Travis's dad had pinpointed seven years ago, when we stood in his kitchen after months of hashing out every detail of our plan and told him all about it, and he had only one comment: "What are you going to do at the end of three years?"

We started signing clients in big numbers around 2011–2012. Now those three-year agreements were expiring and a large amount of revenue was disappearing from our books.

We realized for the first time that we were an entrepreneurial company that was growing into a small business, and we had reached a gap where clients fall off. If we saved somebody a million dollars and they were a client for three years, after that time they would fall off because we had saved them so much upfront and we still didn't have many other services to provide them. There was not another opportunity to really save them a bunch of money. Everybody's happy that first year. "Oh, we just saved half a million dollars. This is great." Well, guess what, that's what your budget gets anchored to, and in a year or two, you're cutting a check to some company called Transportation Impact and the CFO doesn't know who the hell that is. Yes, they're bound by a contract. But there are a lot of clients where the revenue generated from their contract wouldn't be worth suing them for if they decided to stop paying, because we would spend more on the legal costs than we would ever recoup, and companies know that. It's an unfortunate reality that not every corporate citizen is an upstanding corporate citizen.

So, even if our direct contacts were really pleased with the savings and happy with our service, their attitude was "If you can't save me a moderate to significant amount of money again, I've got to part ways with TI." Many promised to send us more business through referrals, but that didn't help us right now.

We hadn't been completely blind. We had known that after three years, because we had done such a good job, we would likely lose that customer, but our expectation was that because we had done such a good job, that customer was going to go out there and promote us to half a dozen other people. That was how we were going to scale the business. And the reality was they were giving us more leads. That's why we had the double-digit growth over the past several years. Those clients were very satisfied and they wanted to help us. But we recognized that we had reached the size where the model was going to create a scale issue going forward.

During 2011 to 2014 we were so entrenched in generating the business, supporting the growth, and fighting the internal operational issues that we really weren't seeing any detrimental impacts to the organization from client falloff. It was just all growth, and we were loving it. When you're young and you're constantly falling into opportunities, you're not paying as much attention to that fall-off in revenue. But now we had hit a certain size and the revenue loss was pretty significant—and now it hurt. When we looked at the numbers, we were like *Holy cow. Maybe the model is not sustainable the way that it is today, or at least not scalable at the rate that we want to grow at.*

"Do we have a problem and don't know it's a problem?" is a Keithism that Berkley used to kid me about, but the point of it was to make us look at our processes and see if there was a problem hiding in plain sight. Well, this problem was now obvious and looming larger every week. As my dad used to say (and which became another Keithism), "Ray Charles can see that." Berkley, John, and I spent hours and hours discussing it. We knew we had to come up with additional streams of revenue to support our company, its growth strategy, and the things we wanted to accomplish. We knew that it couldn't come from just one stream. That's a very dangerous place to be. We recognized it was time to start branching out. Many, many times we had said no to clients who had said to us, "Damn, you helped me so much on my small parcel. Can you help me in freight?" (freight being less than truckload and truckload). Could we help them reduce costs in some capacity in those arenas? We didn't grow up in that industry, so we always said no, because we just didn't know enough and we weren't prepared to do anything halfway. If we put our word behind a contract, it's going to be nothing less than excellence. And we knew that we couldn't provide excellence in freight.

But we were sitting on four or five hundred customers that we had demonstrated capability to and that trusted us. We knew we were sitting on a goldmine. How could we tap into that market? I challenged Berkley to find out the best way for us to do this. Did we need to partner with somebody? Did we need to buy somebody? Did we need to start it in house?

Berkley did his due diligence, reported to the rest of us, and as a team we decided we needed to hire the expertise. We could not gain the competence necessary to be effective, so we were going to have to hire people who were born and raised in that industry, and have them come in and provide that service within TI.

We first found one person to lead the new department, and then went out and hired the entire rest of the staff, one hundred percent, to build and launch our first-ever freight offering. That's the soil our freight department was born out of: *We've got to have another stream of revenue, and this makes sense.*

It was the right way to do it, but having to hire the confidence level that we did not have for the first time in our company's history drove us crazy, because all of us on the leadership team are type A's. We want to know everything that's going on, but we didn't know anything about freight, and we had to rely on this one individual we had chosen to lead it. Because it was such a big decision for our company, I did get involved in the high-level decision making, like selecting the partners we would work with. And I was very involved in making sales calls to get customers, starting with the people we already had relationships with. Here's the power of relationships and proven value: We signed our first freight client in December 2015, and it was The Hammock Source, the fourth TI client that we signed, all the way back in September 2008.

But it was clear the new freight service was going to take a while to get off the ground, let alone make an impact on the bottom line, so we turned our attention to things we could do right now. We decided to start sending out a newsletter as a way to communicate what we were doing, so Berkley asked Brian Dobler to put one together. He came back with a simple HTML email. That wasn't what we had in mind. We called him in for a meeting to better communicate our vision.

"We don't think you understand, buddy. We want to blow this thing up to look the best in the industry," Berkley told him.

Brian went away, and a week or two later he called us into the conference room to present what he'd come up with. We filed in, and there sitting on the granite slab was a full-color glossy magazine.

Once again, Brian had exceeded our expectations. We flipped through page after page of well-written articles on topics relevant to small parcel shippers illustrated in full glossy color with photos and charts. The table of contents listed a Partner Spotlight—a profile of one of the companies in our partner program; a four-page feature story on the recent increase in the FedEx fuel surcharge; and an article explaining how shippers can use cheaper Ground service instead of Air to get their packages to the destination in the same time frame for much less cost—a simple and effective shipping optimization strategy. And on page two, there was my headshot next to a welcome letter with my signature at the bottom! Brian had titled the twelve-page magazine *QReview: Transportation Impact Quarterly Review,* and he'd given it an awesome tagline: *Parcel news you can use.* Brian came up with the concept and design, and Brandon Staton wrote the articles.

We immediately fell in love with it.

The best thing about the magazine was that there was no advertising, no plug of TI, no call to action, nothing promotional. The company name and logo were discretely placed, so that if you weren't looking for them, you wouldn't really notice them. The magazine was purely informational and showed us off as experts in the industry. Brian told us that when he went back to the drawing board after Berkley's challenge, he asked himself: *What would UPS or FedEx put out there?*

We mailed a copy to every existing client and anybody we had on the fence, and got a very positive response. Everybody thought the content was relevant and on point. So we continued the way we had begun. Each quarter, we produced content that was relevant. Ecommerce, fuel price hikes, carrier efficiency—whatever the buzz in the industry was, Brian Dobler and Brandon would feature that in *QReview.*

Right after they produced the third issue, Q3 2015, we were headed to PARCEL Forum. It's the biggest trade show in the industry, and of course we were going to take copies of the latest edition of *QReview* to hand out. It was a no-brainer, because we had that beautiful piece of collateral that gave us instant credibility and professionalism. Why not take that to an event where you're trying to gain people's trust and establish your identity? Then someone—it might have been Berkley—had the brilliant idea to do a door drop.

Through my contacts at PARCEL I was able to get the room numbers of all the attendees staying at the Hyatt Regency Chicago, where the convention was being held. The first night around midnight, four TI people ran the floors of the Hyatt Regency, silently sliding a copy of *QReview* under each room door marked on our map. In the morning, instead of *USA Today,* everybody would wake up and find the slickest new magazine in the parcel industry waiting for them.

The next day we saw *QReview* everywhere. At the restaurants, the bar, in the reception areas, when people gathered for breakout sessions—everybody was looking at *QReview*. It was so cool. Instantly we had credibility for our professionalism. We'd hit a home run. And then it got better.

That night at the bar before dinner I felt a tap on my shoulder. I turned and saw Rob Martinez standing beside my chair. Rob was the king of PARCEL. He was founder and CEO of Shipware, one of our biggest competitors, and he was a regular presenter at all the leading industry conferences, including PARCEL Forum. In his hand was a copy of *QReview*.

"I got to hand it to you guys," he said, holding up our glossy magazine. "Nobody else thought of this. You did it first, and you nailed it." He was sincere, and it meant a lot.

That was a huge moment. It was proof that we had raised the bar again.

My proudest moment that year, though, came in March, when

my younger son, Tyler, joined his brother and me in the business. Like Brian, Tyler had graduated from UNC Kenan-Flagler Business School with a degree in Business Administration. After a short stint in finance, he'd gained a few years' experience in the logistics industry with Magellan Transport, so he brought a valuable combination of skills and experience to his work with John as a business analyst.

He also had the full recommendation of the first person to hire him. Bob Gipp was a VP at a hedge fund when he had hired Brian out of college, and when Tyler graduated, he hired him too. Unfortunately, after nine months or so he had to let him go because the fund went from human to automated strategies. Bob also eventually left and became a financial advisor with Wells Fargo, but he and my sons stayed in touch. Around 2013, as TI started to take off, Brian thought I might benefit from the services of a financial advisor, so he introduced me to Bob, and I engaged him.

What started as a professional relationship soon became a good friendship, and it's now a running joke between us that I'm Bob's biggest client and he almost fired my two sons at one time. (Tyler because of the layoffs, and Brian for playing fantasy football during a training session. After Brian demonstrated sincere remorse and how much he loved the work and wanted to prove himself, Bob took him back, and he went on to become one of the best traders out of the group of twenty-four hired that year.) Over the years, I've developed a lot of respect for Bob's business acumen, his polish, his strategic thinking, his collaboration. He's not scared to reach out to people within his organization if he doesn't know the answer to something. He's also a visionary. He's a good, honest person that I trust with my assets, and his guidance over the years has been invaluable.

Early on in the relationship, we made a business trip to St. Louis. As we checked in to the Four Seasons, I saw that the hotel had a casino. I looked accusingly at Bob. "You didn't tell me there was a casino!"

"Yeah, that's because Paula said I can't tell you there's a casino."

As well as being the executive assistant for TI, Paula Sutton took care of all my personal stuff, paying my bills, organizing my travel, and so forth. I loved casinos and I often called her to send me more money. She was always telling me, "Stop spending money in a casino." Bob and I laughed at Paula's attempt to prevent me from gambling on this trip and went up to our rooms, and then that night after dinner we hit the blackjack table.

We weren't doing very well. We should have won easily, but every time the dealer would pull out four or five cards to beat us. I was getting mad. I'd bet a hundred dollars, and I'd lose. I'd bet two hundred, and I'd lose. I maxed out my credit cards and had to call Paula to send me more money. I kept doubling my bet, until Bob said, "No, no, Keith. Wait. We got to play small now and wait for the momentum to switch and let the tide turn in our direction, and then we send it in." We backed off, and then it started going our way. As we pulled in our winnings, I told him, "That's why you're my financial advisor."

Bob's guidance didn't stop with me. One day we were out playing golf with a couple of other members of the Transportation Impact leadership team, and Bob was doing what he should be doing on the golf course—he was probing. We told him our revenue and some other numbers, and we mentioned that our margins were around fifty percent—back then we were making fifty cents on the dollar.

Bob stopped and looked at us. "Uh, guys," he said. "You may have an estate tax problem here."

He explained how estate tax worked, and we were like, "Wow, really?" We had no idea. We knew we were onto something with the way we were making money. We had a great team, we were determined, we were workaholics, and every time we signed a client—I couldn't get enough of it. You want to keep going! Also, we didn't do anything on credit; everything was always paid for. But we weren't thinking about tax exemptions, the strategic thinking of what to do with the money we were making.

I only ever cared about one number. John looked at hundreds of numbers, but the number that I always wanted him to report to me on was if we closed the doors today, if UPS or FedEx shut us down today, how much money did we have coming in based on the existing contracts, with the time that was left on those contracts, with the projected demonstrated amounts that we'd collected? John always knew that number, because he knew that was a very important number. He always said, "Keith, if we close the doors today, we've got eighty-eight million," or whatever. We always knew that number, and we thought that was the value of the company.

"No, no, no," Bob said. "You guys get a multiple on your earnings. Because your profit margin's so high, your multiple's massive. This thing is worth a lot more than you think."

After that we started thinking both personally and in terms of the business about what roads we were going to take.

Around this time I got a call from my old friend Brian Moffitt's brother, Stephen, telling me about a guy he thought could be a good sales resource for TI. Stephen was director of national sales for Richard Petty Motorsports and I trusted his judgment, so when he recommended that Travis and I talk to the guy, I said, "Sure." Harper Lee knew the Moffitts from his work with the marketing agency that RPM used. He'd never been in sales, but he told us he had good contacts. We agreed he'd start as an affiliate and see how that went.

I hooked him up with Chris Burns, one of our best sales contractors. Harper sent Chris any opportunities he identified where we might be able to help one of his clients, and Chris took it from there. After about six months, Harper called me. "This may surprise you, but I'd love to put a hundred percent at this and see if I can do it."

"Come see us in Emerald Isle," I said, "and we'll talk."

Wearing a suit and tie, Harper walked into our conference room. Travis and I were in our usual shorts and flip-flops and I probably had my hat on backwards. John and Berkley were more professionally dressed, but still casual.

We had asked Harper to prepare a list of all of the companies that he felt he could open the door to out of the gate starting in sales. He handed out copies of the list and then sat down across from John and Berkley, who started firing the usual interview questions at him. Travis and I were at the ends of the table, which seated eight people. Travis usually didn't say much in interviews. Relaxed back in my seat, I was studying Harper's list.

After John and Berkley had asked all their questions, I looked at Harper. "You've got a good list here, and you've had some success in sports, but I can tell you right now, as good as you think you are, it's going to take you nine months to close any of these prospects you have on this list." I looked him straight in the eyes to make sure he understood. "It'll take you nine months. Now, we've got to talk. But if you can hang in there and wait nine months to close a deal, maybe we can do something."

Harper's expression told me he didn't believe me. I said what I did to prepare him. He had a good list of contacts, and I believed he could be an asset to TI as a full-time sales contractor, but I wanted him to know what he was getting into. Then I had another meeting to go to, so I left.

Harper worked through our process and got started, and then early the next year he made the move to hundred percent commission. It was a huge adjustment from a being a salary guy, but he was willing to take the risk. He was also smart. While working with Chris, he'd seen first-hand how partners and affiliates opened doors, so he started right away on connecting to as many people as he could inside his network who had any kind of supply chain background, who he felt could open doors, and started building his own personal network of paid affiliates.

His strategy paid off. After hearing about our business model, a contact Harper had reached out to told him he'd just finished a project with the COO of David Yurman jewelry company and offered to give her a call to see if she'd be interested in our negotiation service.

We had been trying for a long time to get David Yurman. We'd even tried our guerilla marketing tactic of taking a photo of us with the product and sending it with a handwritten letter. That was one of our more memorable ones. We roped in everybody, even my wife at the time and my dad. The photo has all of us standing on Emerald Isle Beach on a cloudy day smiling and glittering with David Yurman jewelry. That didn't work. All our emails didn't work. But now we had an inside line to the COO.

One phone call from someone who already had the client's trust. That's all it took.

We got the data, identified savings in the realm of 1.4 million annually, and set up a meeting at the David Yurman offices in New York City. Harper had closed a couple of small accounts, but this was his first big one, so Berkley and I flew up to New York with him. Ruth Sommers, the COO, sat in for the majority of the session. Also in the meeting were Stefanie Russo, non-merchandise procurement manager, who was going to be our point person working directly with FedEx, and a couple of operations people. Four or five folks from Yurman and the three of us.

The meeting went well, and nine months after he officially came on board as a sales contractor, Harper closed his first big account.

In the car on the way back to the airport, "The next priority for you," I told him, "is to get me a deal on some of that David Yurman jewelry."

We did the negotiation and over-delivered on what we'd promised. When the three-year term was up, the new CFO, Maria DeMatos, renewed with us for another three years. For Harper as well as for Transportation Impact, working smart has paid off, big time.

That wasn't the only great connection Harper brought us. Through his contacts in sports, he had a relationship with Pete Merkel, a marketing consultant for Elite Motorsports. Pete was responsible for finding sponsors for Elite. Harper and Pete got talking about the companies Elite and TI were in relationships with and decided it made good sense for Elite Motorsports to become a partner of Transportation Impact. After meeting with the owner, Richard Freeman, and his top driver, Erica Enders, and determining they were definitely interested, Harper called me.

"You need to meet Richard and Erica. They're really doing well in NHRA," he said. "If we can get into that industry we can get potential clients, like you did with NASCAR, getting Smithfield through Richard Petty. Let's go get some of these customers."

Saying that Erica Enders was doing really well in NHRA was like saying the Atlantic Ocean is quite big. In 2005, she achieved more round wins than all other female drivers in NHRA Pro Stock history combined, and she was a finalist for the "Road to the Future" award for the season's top rookie. Six years later, she broke the National Speed record in Pro Stock. The following year, 2012, she became the first woman to win in NHRA Pro Stock, beating four-time champion Greg Anderson, and then two years later Erica was the first woman to win the NHRA Pro Stock World Championship, winning six races for the year. In NHRA Erica is like a god, being a woman in a heavily male-dominated industry, and she's the most feared Pro Stock driver around. To this day, she's considered the best—and as of late 2022 she has five Pro Stock World Championships to prove it! She also has a Disney movie about her. In *Right on Track*, Disney shows how hard Erica and her sister, Courtney, had to work to make it to the top of a sport dominated by boys and men.

We agreed to talk, and Richard and Erica flew down to meet with us in Emerald Isle. We soon came to an agreement on a one-year sponsorship deal that put Transportation Impact on the hood of Erica's car.

It became a wonderful relationship. Erica is a great person with a great work ethic. She's a great partner, a great communicator, and does really well at putting her sponsor's name out there. Richard and Erica became good friends of ours, and from time to time they came to visit us in Emerald Isle. At TI, we hadn't really followed NHRA before, but after we engaged with Elite, we became big fans—and still are. We would often take people to Erica's races. One of the elegant negotiables in our agreement was that we could use Richard's plane to fly six or eight people once a year to a race. He would fly down and get us. That was pretty cool. We'd treat customers or employees to the Charlotte race, and Richard would fly to Beaufort right outside of Emerald Isle to come get us and make a day of it, and then fly us back home. No matter how many times we went, every time it was such a thrill to see *Transportation Impact* flashing past us as Erica roared down the track!

Richard and Erica were instrumental in getting us engaged with car part manufacturers and other sponsors of Elite. That was part of the deal—they had to get us a certain number of customers. For each customer they brought us, we gave them an additional gain share over and above the sponsorship deal. We would go to SEMA, a big automotive trade show, in Vegas, and Richard and Erica would walk the floors with me. Everybody knew them, especially at that venue—they were like superstars—so having Richard and Erica walk me up to a booth and introduce me got us a lot of business.

Overall, with our negotiation service, we delivered 43.3 percent savings to the Elite race team and engine company and an average of 32 percent savings to six of their partners. Erica personally made us a testimonial video, which has helped get us I don't know how much business. In every way, the sponsorship was a good move, and in 2019 we renewed our relationship with another one-year deal.

*The Transportation Impact sponsorships of Richard Petty's race team and Erica Enders have been rewarding both financially and personally. L-R: Richard Petty, Ginger Byrd, Erica Enders, me*

One thing that differentiated us from other small parcel audit providers was that we had a great relationship with our clients. In the beginning, when we first started blind labelling the Veriship audit in 2010, it was a challenge market for us. The audit served as a gateway to our negotiation service. We would sign companies on the audit and then once we had access to their data, we could sell them on the negotiation. But as we grew, the balance shifted, and by 2015 at least half the time we started out with a negotiation and then signed them on the audit. So our relationship was stronger, because they had already engaged us on another service.

Veriship had been a good partner in many ways, but as TI grew, the differences in our perspectives became more and more of an issue, to the point that in 2013 we started building our own audit. The differences with Veriship weren't the only motivator, of course. The main reason was that having our own audit would give us the capability to modify and scale it. Thanks to our good relationship with our clients, we had a long wish list of suggestions and requests that would serve as the foundation for us to build a much better audit.

As with freight, we didn't have the expertise to do it in house, so we had to either hire or partner with someone with the expertise to lead the project. A web systems engineer who Travis and I had known at UPS told us he could build it. He insisted on part ownership, so it was established as a separate company, he came on as a co-founder, and Travis and I put up the initial investment as majority owners. Like most tech projects, this one took a long time, but finally in mid-2015 it was ready to launch.

We hadn't told Veriship what we were doing, so it was funny that right as we were getting ready to launch, they backed down on our biggest point of disagreement. "Too late," we said. "We're getting ready to leave." The timing ended up being perfect, because not long afterwards Veriship also entered the negotiation space and became a direct competitor.

But we still had to migrate four hundred–plus customers to a new platform. That took a lot of strategic planning, not only on the tech side, but also on how we framed it. We didn't go tell our clients, "We've been blind labelling somebody else's audit and now we've built our own." Instead we positioned it as an upgrade.

That part was easy, though. The actual migration was another story. I lost sleep over that; there was so much that could go wrong. We did it slowly, migrating clients in waves over a period of months, and each person in the company was assigned a group of clients to make sure the transition went smoothly. We also brought Brian Byrd over from small parcel ops to help stand it up from a client success standpoint. We told him to hire two client service representatives and train them how to do demos and how to handle the client journey from onboarding to possible cancellation—how can we create stickiness with that client, keep them engaged, keep them logged into this web-based portal that we've built with a brand-new dashboard? The audit was our first client-facing web-based product.

It all went well, thank God, and our clients loved the new audit, although there were some glitches in the beginning. It's not uncommon when you throw four or five hundred customers at something that is brand new; there are tweaks you have to make. One of the problems was the downloads every week. We had to download all the carrier data and load it into the software, which we did over the weekend, but the volume was so great and our server was so slow that on Mondays and Tuesdays it was still loading. That meant the system was really slow for several days for end users, such as sales demonstrations. We told the team not to do any demonstrations of the product on Mondays and Tuesdays, so that customers could get their audit reports and operate.

Eventually that all got worked out, and Brian spent the next couple of years helping improve the product from a user experience and user interface standpoint, building reports to create what we call a Client Services Snapshot. If a client called us or we had a meeting with them, we could immediately know at the touch of our fingertips what custom reports they had built, if they had any GL coding within the software, how many times they had logged in, what their audit point recovery was, and so forth.

Travis's daughter Kirsten—the last of the four siblings—also joined us at TI during this time after graduating from Campbell with an MBA. As part of the MBA program she had to create a mock-up strategic business plan for a Fortune 500 company, so we assigned her to eAudit as operations manager to make sure everything stayed on track.

As we were getting the audit up and rolling, I was approached by a guy who'd been on my sales team at UPS, Mike Mays. Many times over the past years I'd told Mike to come talk to me if ever he thought about leaving UPS. Well, now he was so miserable that his wife was about to kill him if he didn't make the leap from Big Brown. I would have loved to have Mike working for us, but he said that he had watched us bring on friends and family as we built up TI, and that was something he had always wanted to do. He wanted to start his own company helping customers save money on their shipping costs. There was plenty of market out there for both of us, so I said I'd help him in any way I could.

We were offering our audit as a standalone product called eAudit, and a few companies were white-labelling it, the way we had white-labelled the Veriship audit. I asked Mike if he wanted to sell the audit as a channel to market to help him grow the negotiation side of his business. Even though he was a competitor, if he sold our audit service, first and foremost that was going to create revenue for us. Plus I had to put on my eAudit hat to try to grow that side of the business. He accepted the offer and came to Emerald Isle for training. Every now and then he still calls me with a question, and over the years it has been a pleasure to watch his business, Mindful Logistics, grow and succeed.

Between John and Sharon, along with a local CPA and BDO, we were now in such good shape with our accounting that Richard Brown said his work was done and it was time for him to leave. He had brought financial and administrative discipline to the organization in the early years, with the ability to project, budget, and control expenses. He also helped us with our first moving on to a real, top-ten-type CPA firm, BDO, which he had worked for in public accounting. We were at the point where we needed the type of sophisticated tax planning and tax return preparation that an internationally renowned firm like BDO provided. It also added that next level of credibility when we could speak to a client and say BDO was our accounting firm.

From the beginning Richard had made it clear that he was

retired and didn't want to go back to work full time. He loved our company and wanted to help us out, but only on a temporary basis. As much as we would have loved to keep him, we knew that wasn't an option. In any case, he had work that was a much greater calling than our accounting. For many years he had been going on trips to Nicaragua with Global Health Outreach, a Christian medical and dental mission. The first year he was working for us, we found out he was doing that and offered to pay for his trip as an end-of-year bonus. It was about twenty-five hundred dollars. Richard said that in all his years working for universities and in public accounting, bonuses "just weren't things that happened." Transportation Impact was the first company to give him a bonus at the end of the year. Supporting Richard in his mission trips was another way for us to give back, so over the years we continued to do so, even after he left TI.

One year the Baptist children's home on Emerald Isle lost their dock after a hurricane, and they weren't going to be able to host any children for that summer. They needed around fifty thousand dollars to rebuild their entire dock and bulkhead. Richard asked if we would support part of that project. He said the Baptist Association could manage to put up ten thousand. He asked if we would consider putting up twenty thousand, and they would find at least twenty other people who would put up a thousand apiece. We agreed to that, and inside of a month they had the fifty thousand. TI gave ten thousand and Travis and I together gave ten thousand, and other donations made up the rest.

As we entered 2016, the year-end revenue numbers for 2015 told us it was as bad as we had feared it would be, maybe worse. Total gross revenue was 17.94 million. We had suffered −4.06 percent revenue growth over 2014. This was the first year we had dismal—negative!—growth. We couldn't believe it. We were crushed.

But even though the numbers don't reflect it, 2015 was really good for us as a team, because it forced us to learn. It taught us we had to start growing up as a company, and we had to identify another stream of revenue to start alleviating the dependence solely on one. If we hadn't done that in 2015 by starting our freight service, we would not be where we are today. In the midst of not-so-good news, we were wise enough to know that.

As amazing as it was when we were experiencing it, the exceptional pace of growth was actually a big obstacle. It blinds you. The shock of a setback taught us something. Fortunately, we're quick learners. We were quick to discover the problem and quick to take action. In our time together as a leadership team—first Travis and me, and then with John and Berkley too—most of the time any action we took was based on good judgment and good direction. We didn't deliberate for long. Once we got the facts on the table we made a decision quickly, and nine times out of ten it was the right one.

It had been a hell of a ride.

# 21

## A HOME OF OUR OWN

It was late 2014 when Berkley arrived back from a sales trip to Wisconsin full of excitement about something called Entrepreneurial Operating System. He had been impressed by how precise and organized the prospect company was, so he asked them about their process. On the way to the airport to fly back to North Carolina, he stopped at a bookstore and bought the book they'd told him about, read half of it on the plane, and now he was trying to sell us on the idea.

"We're growing so fast that we're in danger of outgrowing our infrastructure and disappointing our clients. We can grow ourselves right out of business. I know this from experience. We need structure and we need someone to help us," he said. "We all have experience in specific areas, but we need outside counsel for the big picture. This is what's going to help us grow into the next phase of our company's evolution. We've got to listen to this implementer. The first ninety minutes are free. All we have to do is listen to him."

I wasn't convinced, but I thought there was no harm in listening, so Berkley found an EOS implementer in our area and set up a meeting. By the end of the ninety minutes with Ben Goetz, our skeptical leadership team was asking, "When do we start?"

As a leadership team, we were ultra-focused on growing the business. We knew what we were doing in the area of competence that we were experienced in. But putting it all together to where we would be a fluid company and every employee would be in the same boat—that was the part we were missing. Ben showed us that the Entrepreneurial Operating System (EOS) could provide us with structure and processes that would get everyone rowing in the same direction and enable the company to gain traction. That was the name of the book that Berkley read: *Traction*. As you kept using the system year after year, you gained traction and momentum to keep moving forward, to keep growing, but with control, vision, and unity.

In May 2015 we signed up.

Getting going on EOS required some major changes to the way we operated. One of the biggest and most tense arguments we had early on in the implementation was about our weekly leadership team meeting. Every Monday our LT would meet from ten o'clock to five o'clock. It was an all-day Monday meeting. We got things done, but a lot of the time we would discuss and discuss and discuss and not arrive at a decision. Then we would get into the meeting the following week, and we would often circle back to the same type of conversation without arriving at a crystal clear decision that everybody could be bought in to. We would meet all day, and probably it wasn't necessary. In fact, after implementing EOS, it became crystal clear it wasn't necessary.

Then, in the meeting, we had what we considered our scorecard (the scorecard is one of the key features of EOS to keep the team on track). Our scorecard was an extensive spreadsheet that John Howard spent an exceptional amount of time on putting together. Berkley and I would skim read about two pages, and John would dive into every page, because that's his nature. He's very analytical with an operational mindset.

We had tense fighting around that scorecard. "You don't need to look at six pages. You need to identify the seven to ten most important things that represent the temperature or health of your company," Ben told us. "If those seven to ten things are going well, then stop right there. If they are on track, you don't have to get into the details. Stop spending so much time on it." On top of that, he also wanted us to cram our all-day meeting into a ninety-minute weekly session. We were starting to think that maybe EOS wasn't for us. Maybe it wasn't going to work.

"Just trust me," Ben said.

We spent all day fighting about it. "There's no way in the world we can do without looking at these twenty metrics," we told him. We fought and fought and fought.

Finally Ben said, "Okay, look. I'm going to let you have your twenty metrics for the first quarter. But when we come back in the next quarter, you have to be honest and tell me that you looked at and analyzed all twenty metrics."

Damn, if he wasn't right. We came in the next quarter, and he was all over it. We only really looked at ten metrics that represented the holistic health of our company. If they were off track, then we dove in. Ben accomplished a miracle, getting six type A's out of a report into ten simple KPI metrics. It took us two quarters to get there, but he did it. Then taking an all-day meeting to ninety minutes—he did that, too.

From Ben and EOS we learned that if we are prepared with a list of issues when we walk in the door, we prioritize the top three issues, and then we truly identify the issue, discuss the issue, and solve the root cause of the issue, then solving those two to three most important issues in the ninety-minute meeting actually knocks off seven to ten underlying issues that we don't have to solve any longer.

Those two things—the structured meeting and the streamlined scorecard—were paramount in our confidence in moving forward with EOS. It's been so fluid and welcome. Our meetings are so productive now.

It also gave us clarity, structure, and confidence around goal-setting and personnel management. One of the underlying philosophies within EOS is open and honest conversations. Our leadership team didn't necessarily have a problem with that. We would get in there and fuss and fight and call each other out. But our young managers and leaders were inexperienced when it came to having a difficult or uncomfortable conversation. If you don't get to a root cause by facilitating open and honest discussion, you're not gaining traction, as EOS teaches. You don't get anywhere. All you're doing is perpetuating an underlying problem that everybody knows but nobody's surfacing. It's not going to serve anybody any good.

Up to that point in time, it wasn't in our DNA to let people go; we always just tried to fix the problem. Ben cured us of that. "Some people can't fire themselves," he said. "If they don't have the five core values which you guys established, and they're not a believer in your core focus, and they don't GWC—they don't *get it*, they don't *want* their job, they don't have the *capacity* to do their job—then it doesn't matter how much you try to fix them; they're not going to work out."

Under EOS, if you're not having a quarterly head-to-head, discussing with that individual why they don't have the one or two of the five core values, and why they don't either G it or W it or C it, then you're not having an open and honest conversation. At some point, either they've got to change their behavior, or you've got to let them go. That's when we started having good and beneficial conversations with our employees. Previously, we would let things linger versus letting someone go.

These conversations bubbled to the surface not only whether that person was good for our company. The other part of EOS in terms of employee management is "right person, right seat." We might learn that this person has our five core values, but they don't get their job, they need more training, or they don't want the job they're in because they're bored to death. They've got so much potential that we need to offer them advancement somewhere. The quarterly conversation shows us that we've got the right person in the right seat, we've got the right person in the wrong seat, or we've got the wrong person for the company.

Those two fundamental things allowed us to shuffle our team to put them in the appropriate position for what they were born to do in this world, while the focus on core values and goals helped to give purpose and meaning to their work and their connection with the company. From the beginning, we had done everything according to our core values, but we had never written them down. EOS made us formalize them and incorporate them as an integral part of our ethos. We distilled them to five: perfection, passion, professionalism, integrity, and work ethic. Those five values guide everything we do, both as a company and as individual members of the company. They also have personal meaning for me. My Papaw exemplified those core values. He was the model for a lot of them, especially integrity and work ethic.

The scorecard, the meeting structure, the core values, and the personnel management were the pieces that you put together to reach your goals. Until EOS, we didn't really have an annual plan or a three-year plan. Once EOS was introduced, for the first time we had something that enabled us to build and reverse engineer all of our plans to set and accomplish a three-year plan. EOS says: "What does the one-year plan have to look like in order to track towards the three-year? What does this quarter have to look like in order to track to your one-year? Now, what does this weekly meeting have to look like in order to track to your quarter?"

It also encourages you to set a ten-year target. You can't plan around ten years. But you can throw a dart at a ten-year target. It is supposed to be an improbable target, not an impossible one. One that you think is unbelievably challenging to meet. In 2015 we threw out there that we wanted to be a hundred-million-dollar company. Now, in early 2023, with a couple more acquisitions, we'll be there.

Would we be here without the EOS system? Maybe, but almost certainly it would have taken longer, maybe a lot longer. We would not have set those three-year, annual, quarterly, and weekly goals. We wouldn't have tried, because you get too caught up in the daily grind, if you aren't focused on stated goals. EOS allows us to set big goals, chart a path towards achieving them, and stay accountable and deal with problems along the way.

Ben lives less than three hours away in Fayetteville, North Carolina, and after seven years he is still our business coach. Once a quarter he comes to Emerald Isle to meet with us and keep us on track. That is very unusual in EOS. Usually the implementer stays on for a year to get you going, and then you're on your own. Ben is a good, Christian guy, and an excellent, smart business person. If I could, I'd hire him to come to work at TI. We can run this on our own. But we don't want to because Ben's such an integral part of our success. He keeps us focused, and that's a necessary thing.

Not long before that first meeting with Ben Goetz, we acquired a third suite in the strip mall, suite D, to go along with our existing suites B and C. But the pressure of our growing company on the available space was still too much, and it was clear we had to find another solution.

Our landlord at the strip mall was a guy called Larry Watson. We hired my brother, Billy Ray, to do a few things, and one day Larry came by and saw him out back washing the leadership team's cars. Larry got on my brother about using the water to wash the cars. When my brother told me what had happened, I couldn't believe it. Here we've got three of Larry's units, we pay our rent on time every month, and he's bitching about two dollars' worth of water. That put me over the top. Because of that damn water bill, we ended up building an eight-million-dollar building.

That's the joke among our leadership team, and maybe Larry's tightfisted comment was the last push I needed. We knew it was time because of our growth. We wanted our people in a nice place, a place that they would take pride in, a place where they would enjoy coming to work. We found a great design firm in Morehead City called Coastal Architecture, and the owner, Lee Dixon, took on our project. Over the next months, we met often with Lee and his team in our conference room to go over the design.

We wanted our building to be best in class; modern looking, but still with that coastal flair. I was really involved, down to picking out the design of the shutters. It was hands-on, because we were so proud to be creating this building for our people and our company. There was nothing like it in Emerald Isle. I wanted that thing to look just beautiful, with meticulous attention to detail, from the colors to the horseshoe pits, the cornhole, the benches with plaques bearing the names of my and Travis's grandparents, to the veterans parking, because I was in the Marine Corps. We stayed up a lot of nights thinking about the details in that building.

One of the TV shows I used to watch was called *Billions,* about a very successful stock market guy. In his office he had a hole in the floor so he could look at his people. I thought that was a great idea to support our transparency and open-door policy. So we designed our building with a big hole in it, where we can see our people and communicate with them.

In the early planning stages of the building, we thought it'd be nice to include a place for us and our people to go after work to get a bite to eat and a drink. At first we joked that we wanted somewhere to get a beer and a hot dog, but as the money kept coming in and the success grew, it transformed into a five-star restaurant.

We wanted a way to tie the name of the restaurant to the

company. The waters off North Carolina are a shipping graveyard, so we did some research and found a wreck that was a transportation ship and had a cool story, so we named the restaurant after her.

Early in the morning of Wednesday, March 11, 1942, the *Caribsea* was steaming up the North Carolina coast on her way to Norfolk, Virginia, from Santiago, Cuba, with a full cargo of highly combustible manganese ore. Suddenly, about eleven miles east of the Cape Lookout Lighthouse, *Caribsea* was struck on the starboard side by a torpedo fired from a U-boat. Three minutes later, only the masts were still visible. The twenty-eight men on board had no time to send distress signals or launch lifeboats, and only the seven men on deck or in the wheelhouse managed to climb onto two rafts that had floated free. Later, they watched the U-boat that had sunk their ship passing within a hundred yards. After ten hours in the water, the survivors managed to attract the attention of a passing freighter, the *Norlindo,* which picked up the two officers and five crew and took them to safety at Cape Henry.

That's the story of the *Caribsea*. Our Caribsea occupies the third floor of our building. It has a theater-style kitchen where patrons can watch head chef and his staff hard at work, a rooftop bar called the Torpedo Lounge, and panoramic views out over Bogue Sound. We are also turning the restaurant into a commemoration of its namesake. On plaques around the walls we tell the stories of *Caribsea* and *Norlindo* and of the U-boats that sank those two ships. We even have some artifacts from the wrecks.

On August 11, 2015, we had a groundbreaking ceremony for our new headquarters building. We had food and drinks and champagne, and lots of people from the community came to celebrate the big event with us. Even the State Secretary of Commerce, John E. Skvarla, III, came. He made a few remarks, and so did county and local government officials, as well as key stakeholders from local and regional economic development committees. That ceremony was a big deal. For us, it was a very proud moment, because nobody in Emerald Isle had ever seen a building like that.

At the same time we were constructing our very own building, we were looking for a VP of IT. As we had known with the building, it was time. Transportation Impact started out as two guys offering a negotiation service, but we could see that technology was going to play an increasingly bigger part in what we would be able to offer companies, not just for parcel, but also on the freight side. Being strong in IT was going to be crucial for us to continue to be successful and to keep growing.

I had someone in mind who I thought would be a great asset to us, but I didn't think we could get him. Very early on in my UPS days, one of my accounts was Big Rock Sports in Morehead City. The UPS contract was managed by the director of IT, Norm Pollock, but I didn't have much contact with him.

One thing Big Rock liked to do was take their vendors offshore fishing, which is when you go out thirty or forty miles and try to catch the larger fish, like mahi mahi, blue marlin, or tuna. A couple of years after I took over the account—Norm will tell you the date exactly: April 29, 1998—Big Rock invited me and the national account manager for Big Rock, Mike Fross, to go offshore fishing, and Norm came on the trip too.

Norm's wife was pregnant. It was two weeks till her due date, but she'd told him to go enjoy himself, because it was the first time the company had invited him to go on one of these fishing trips and she was feeling fine. We left at 4:30 in the morning and it took us almost four hours to get out to the deep water where we were going to fish. We set up our rods and lines and were reeling them in like crazy—all of us except Norm, who was in the cabin, seasick—when a call came through on the radio. Norm's wife's water had broken and she was headed to the hospital. Thirty minutes after we started fishing we headed back inshore, arriving about one in the afternoon. Norm made it to the hospital in time.

Norm and I developed a good working relationship, and I always thought a lot of him. He was a no-nonsense type of guy. When I requested time with him, he made sure it was productive. He was smart, had great attention to detail, and was very precise. He was not your normal kind of IT guy. He was more like a good operator and a good IT guy combined, and those are hard to find. He had an operations mind and a skill set in IT.

For probably six months we interviewed for our VP of IT opening, but I didn't have a good feeling about anyone we talked to. Then in February or March of 2016, I was driving to the airport with Travis when my phone rang. It was Norm. He said he had heard about our opening and he was interested. I was thrilled! We needed an IT leader so bad. He came in for an initial interview, and when we got through with him, we knew he was our guy.

He came on board in April and immediately took a tour of our new facility, which was taking shape and already looking beautiful, but Norm had hardly walked in the door when he found a problem. And then he found a few more problems.

Norm had noticed that the hole in the floor to bring up the wiring for the conference room table was way behind where the table would probably be. He talked to the contractor and told us it would cost a thousand dollars to recut the hole. But if we didn't do it, everyone would be tripping over wires behind the table, because the hole would be right where everybody had to walk.

So we had to spend an extra thousand dollars to move a hole in the floor because we had built our conference room without choosing the table first. Lesson one.

Lesson two came with Norm's next question. "Where's the computer closet?" he asked. We told him we hadn't planned a computer closet in the new building because we were cloud-based.

Norm sighed, and patiently explained that we still needed to have a computer closet. We ended up giving him a tiny room, and we had to run an air conditioner in it to deal with the heat from all the electronics. We filled the racks, with everything packed in very tight, and then we had to cut out five feet off the back of the gym and build a wall to have somewhere to put all the restaurant electronics. Lesson two.

Lesson three saved us a lot of money. On the island, everything was coaxial cable, which is normal for a home, but it's not reliable for high-volume internet use, especially with the high humidity on the coast. Spectrum, the provider for our area, had convinced us to run T1 fiber into the new building, but Norm said that the pricing we had agreed to was way too high. He and Travis met with the Spectrum rep, and Norm ended up getting the price reduced by around twenty-five percent per month.

We did two other major electronic upgrades in the new facility. One was the phone system. In the suites, whenever the phone rang it would ring on all the phones simultaneously, and sometimes someone would answer it, and sometimes somebody wouldn't. Norm got us on a more sophisticated system that allowed for call queuing and all the other features that we really needed.

Our other big upgrade was to install an enterprise network system—a massive upgrade from where we were. Norm also created a local server that mirrors the one in the cloud, so we no longer needed to send everything to the cloud before we could use it. The local server kept everything in sync, so we could work in the building on files as fast as we could in the cloud. That saved a lot of time each day.

WIMCO Corporation of Washington, North Carolina, did the construction, and they did a fantastic job, finishing on time and without overruns. Before they installed the sheetrock, we had a steel-signing ceremony. We handed out black Sharpies, and our employees could write whatever they wanted on the steel. That day, Darrell Mays came to visit us in his private jet. Darrell is chairman and founder of the nsoro Foundation. Through TI's charity work, he and I had become good friends, and I loved that he got to see what our culture was like, as well as the design of our building.

In August 2016, after only fourteen months, our building was complete. Our new HQ was 13,299 square feet, had a five-star restaurant, and cost a little over four million dollars—which would ultimately double to eight million dollars when we later doubled the size of the building.

When we moved in, it was just awesome. From the carpet to the towels to the hand dryers in the bathrooms, to the soap dispensers—I played a big part in choosing all those items, making sure they were attractive and good quality. Our people could see the attention to detail, and they were very proud.

We also put in some features to make a powerful first impression. One of my favorites is the glass-walled main conference room, right in the lobby. When a visitor walks in the front door and turns to the left to get on the elevator, they're looking straight at a best-in-class conference room and can actually see the people meeting in there. But if the people in the meeting want privacy, they simply hit a button and gas fills the glass and fogs it up.

I also wanted a waterfall with our logo behind it, so the first thing you see when you walk in the front door is water cascading past a backdrop of our logo. I wanted to create the wow factor, and we accomplished that.

It was very important to me that when we could, we used our customers' products. For example, Sony was a client of ours, so all the TVs were Sonys. Edward Don was a big client, so the restaurant was equipped with Ed Don. Elkay makes sinks and water coolers, so all our sinks and water coolers were Elkay. Any product of our customers that we could use, we did. Then I went through the building taking photos of all the products we had used, and I sent them with a handwritten letter to the C-level person who was our contact at that company. "Proud to be a partner of yours, as we remain loyal

*The friends, colleagues, and community leaders we had invited stood on the immaculate tarmac of the parking lot and applauded as Travis and I snipped a giant green ribbon with a pair of giant scissors to celebrate the opening of our very own building.*

just as you have." That was part of the story, to show our people and our customers and even the local people how important loyalty was to our relationships. Our customers loved it. It created just a little bit more stickiness, and it was good to throw out the word *loyalty* so they didn't forget about it.

The day of our ribbon cutting ceremony, August 23, the weather was perfect, sunny and warm with a light ocean breeze. The friends, colleagues, and community leaders we had invited stood on the immaculate tarmac of the parking lot and applauded as Travis and I snipped a giant green ribbon with a pair of giant scissors. In only nine years we had progressed from no fixed office to a four-million-dollar building of our own. On top of that, we had also recently learned TI had been named to the Inc. 5000 for the fourth straight year, had been designated in the N.C. Fast 40 list, which celebrates privately owned business growth, and had made the list of the top one hundred privately owned companies in the state based on revenue. I was both immensely proud and immensely humbled. We thought we'd have to work fifteen or twenty more years to get to this point, but we set a goal and focused on execution, and we had made it.

*Our new HQ was 13,299 square feet, had a five-star restaurant, and cost a little over four million dollars–which would ultimately double to eight million dollars when we later doubled the size of the building. Here, Phase 2 is under construction.*

I watched people's reactions as they walked into our building and saw the waterfall flowing over our name and the glass-walled conference room. They were in awe. Local leaders told me they were proud to have this one-of-a-kind, best-in-class building in Emerald Isle, and they were also impressed by the loyalty we showed in using our customers' products. I saw the light bulb come on in their minds as to how successful this little local company had become.

We gave our guests a guided tour, and then they enjoyed hors d'oeuvres and the fantastic view from Caribsea. Our new home was the tallest non-residential building in Emerald Isle, and the panoramic vistas out over the Atlantic from Caribsea and the Torpedo Lounge are stunning, especially at sunset.

That day was a special one for another, very personal reason. At my side was my fiancée, Ginger Lambeth. Ginger and I had been dating only a couple of years, but in an ironic twist of fate, our lives had crossed decades earlier. In school, Ginger was my sister Candace's best friend. There's a seven-year age gap between Candace and me, and by then I was already in the Marine Corps. When I came home on leave to get married, Ginger came to my wedding as Candace's guest, and after Syndie and I moved to my Mamaw's old trailer, to make extra money, Ginger would babysit Brian.

In October 2016, thirty-two years after she attended my first wedding and in the middle of a hurricane, Ginger and I committed to a life together. This was truly a year of new beginnings. To commemorate our own new beginning, in the morning before our wedding, we went through a baptism ceremony with Pastor Brad Smith.

Ginger had shared my excitement in planning the new building, and she shared the joy of our moving-in day. There was only one problem with moving into our new building. It wasn't big enough. Because it took a year and a half to build, and in that year and a half we grew a lot more than we thought we were going to, as soon as we moved in we were already maxed out. We actually had to keep the suites in the strip mall, and in addition we ended up getting a place at the pier and fixing it up. At one time we had three locations, not even counting eAudit in Greenville. Realizing we would need to expand sooner rather than later, we purchased a lot next to the one we had just built on. I was regretting putting the restaurant in, because we could have really used that space, and Caribsea is not making the money that TI makes. But over the long term it has worked out to be a good decision. The restaurant has been good for the community, and it's definitely one of the local favorites. It is one of the nicest on the Crystal Coast. And it has been good for TI. We have entertained many clients and prospects and signed many deals in Caribsea.

To go with our new home, we also unveiled a new logo. Our old logo (our second one) was a package car driving towards a capital *T*, and cutting through the package car at a slant, right behind where the driver would sit, was a lowercase *i*. That logo was great, but it no longer represented what Transportation Impact offered. We were already diversifying into freight, and we knew we would start getting into other things as well. So we challenged Brian Dobler to come up with a new logo that would better represent what we did. Again, he knocked it out of the ballpark.

In the design he presented to us, he ingeniously combined a package—to represent parcel—and a pallet—to represent freight—with the initials TI. It was brilliant. It was simple, clean, compact, and represented all the services and products we currently offered, but without limiting us. What I loved about it most was the attention to detail. None of the elements jumped out at you. At a glance it looked like an ordinary logo, but if you looked carefully, you could see that the shape of it was a package, and in the background it was like a pallet. It was a 3D best-in-class logo. And of course it was TI green.

As we settled into our new facility Norm got down to work. He had a big job ahead of him. At this point he was our only IT person, and there was a lot to do, beginning with upgrading our equipment.

While we were building the business, we saved pennies everywhere we could and bought things only as we needed them, which meant that our setup was a patchwork of various things and we were using consumer-grade products. Norm fixed that problem with the enterprise-level setup in the new building, but he also discovered that we were using a bunch of different operating systems. If someone needed a new computer, we would go down to Best Buy and get the cheapest one that we thought would do the job. We had some people with HP computers, some with Samsung, some with Vaio, and we had machines that were on Windows 7 Home, Windows 7 Pro, Windows 8.1 Home, Windows 10 Home, and Windows 10 Pro. He couldn't believe that we were managing to operate this really successful and profitable business that relied so heavily on the internet with such a mixture of consumer grade electronics.

The other thing he didn't like was that our analysts had two machines. In the office, they had a desktop because we thought that would be faster than a laptop, and then they also had a laptop that they took to work at home. Norm said it made no sense for each person to have multiple machines and to have keep them all in sync, so he bought new computers for everybody. We all got new Lenovos—another customer of ours!—and everybody had only a laptop, with an external monitor and keyboard on their desk. Then he bought licensing for Windows 10 Pro for every computer. For a whole month he took a different machine home each night and converted it. One advantage we discovered of everybody having a single laptop as their work machine was that when we got hit with a hurricane, everybody could go to somewhere they would be safe and continue working. That meant we could offer uninterrupted service to the companies that relied on us. For security, Norm set up a central location for authentication that also tracks when people are using their laptops and who's logged into that laptop. If the laptop's lost, we can remote wipe it. Just like UPS wiped our computers when Travis and I left.

We wanted Norm to start hiring people so we could have a full IT department, because we had a list of things we wanted done in the next six months, but he put the brakes on us. "I can't hire four inexperienced people at one time," he said. "I'll pull my hair out. I don't have any hair, but I'd pull it out if I had it." He explained that to build an IT department, it's an evolutionary process. You hire a few people, you train them, the next few people come in, and you can train them, and slowly it snowballs. As we grew, we could bring

people on quicker. But when you start with a lot of really inexperienced people, like we were hiring, you have to build slowly. That
made sense, so we took the pressure off and let Norm lead what we
had hired him to lead. In a leadership team the biggest thing is trust.
You have to have trust in each other, and we did.

# 22

## MOVING INTO THE FUTURE VIA TECHNOLOGY

It took Norm all the way until November to sort out all the tech issues related to the new building and employee equipment. Then he turned his attention to WebBit. WebBit was the cloud-based software that Travis and a freelance programmer had developed to replace the underpowered TidBit 2.0. Since the new software was going to be web-based, we called it WebBit.

First TidBit, and now WebBit, did two critical jobs. One: It did the initial analysis of the savings that we could generate for a potential customer. Two: It did the weekly calculation of the savings that we had in reality generated for a customer so we could bill them for our percentage of it. At this point, most of our business model and almost all of our revenue relied on this software.

The main motivation for developing WebBit was the need to measure more of the discounts we had managed to get from the carriers, and to do it much faster. In our weekly billing, instead of analyzing three hundred records on the client's carrier invoice as we had been several years ago, we were now analyzing thirteen hundred—or more. Multiplied by hundreds of clients. It was a massive amount of computing to do every week, and TidBit, which was built in Access, just couldn't handle it. Plus it was so slow that if one person was running billing files, the company was its own hostage until all bills had been generated for the week. Only after that was done could we move on with any analysis for the week. So the other urgent motivation was to get the software off our in-house server and make it into a set of rules visible to our employees that could be accessed from anywhere—in other words, to put it in the cloud.

At first, Travis thought it would take us one to two years to develop and launch the successor to TidBit 2.0. It ended up taking five years.

By the time Norm came on board in April 2016 we had managed to move WebBit to the cloud on Amazon Web Services, roll it out properly, and sunset TidBit 2.0. However, for the analysis piece of its job, WebBit had two big limitations. One was that really large clients wouldn't load into it for analysis. For billing it worked, but for some reason for analysis, they wouldn't load in. The other problem was that it still tied us to using spreadsheets. Once WebBit did its basic slicing and dicing of analytics, it dumped everything into a spreadsheet. From that point forward, everything was done in a spreadsheet. If you wanted to go back to put in new discounts or anything else, in some cases you had to go back and reload. It was very, very, very inefficient.

There was another problem that was about to make WebBit obsolete for the analysis even if we could live with the spreadsheets and other limitations. For as long as we had been in business, UPS and FedEx had always had the exact same pricing. But in September 2016 both carriers announced changes for 2017 that were going to make their pricing models different from each other. Before, if you sent a two-pound package to a certain zone, the base prices were the same, but shippers' individual discounts would be different. Beginning January 2017, that would no longer be the case. This meant that WebBit wasn't going to work any longer for the analysis at all, because that's not how it was designed. It was designed to work as though the pricing was the same. Our analytics team asked Norm how we were going to do the analysis. He said we needed to start from scratch on a new platform.

"Can you have the new application done by December fifteenth?" they asked him. "Because we're going to need to test it before January."

"There's no way," he said. "Maybe we can have it done by March."

Building a new application from scratch allowed us to make some major improvements, including incorporating a rating engine, which was something Norm brought to our attention. We needed to be able to run packages through with parameters: What service do you want? What's the weight? What's the origin? What's the destination? Being able to do that would give us the ability to accurately compare rates of a package between two carriers, including all the correct accessorials and everything else. Among other things, this would allow us to accurately calculate the advantage or disadvantage to a shipper of switching carriers.

We decided that the new software would be strictly for the analysis and we would continue to use WebBit for the billing. In November Norm and a couple of people he had hired started building the analytics application in QlikView, a business intelligence tool.

While it was being built, they looked around for a name. Brandon Staton, our marketing director, came up with the winning suggestion: Titan. In an email to Norm, he made his case for the name:

> The first two letters of Titan are TI, which gives us a lot of leeway relative to marketing promoting the strength of our backend analytics.

Titan also gives a number of storylines to help prospects relate to our technology.

In Greek mythology, Titans were gods with immense strength who ruled during the Golden Age. The name inherently describes the power of the analytics technology, and subliminally is suggestive of its organic nature (Titans were children of Mother Earth and Father Sky).

The most famous Titan probably was Helios, the god of the sun, which obviously invokes the concept of shining light upon the data we're are looking at.

Titan is also the name of Saturn's largest moon, which is the only other object with clear evidence of water. That suggests life, which translates, again, into the organic nature of the function of our analytics.

If this were my technology, I would want to portray speed and power, in addition to light, to make an overall assertion that there is no better technology. More literally, I would want something godlike. The word evokes all those things.

A 40-watt light bulb in the lamp by your bed contains 450 lumens. One Titan was as bright as the sun.

A year after FedEx and UPS announced their pricing differences, Titan was ready, and we launched it immediately. Suddenly, we leaped light years forward in terms of what we could do with the analysis and how we could impress clients and prospects.

For starters, the built-in rating engine allows us to tweak percentages and other factors and see exactly what the impact would be. For example, we can input an offer from UPS and rewrite it with a particular set of discounts to show the client what that UPS offer is actually worth. And then we can take an offer from FedEx and do the same thing to see which offer is better. It also enables us to look at the impact of dimensional changes, a capability WebBit didn't have. This has allowed us to increase revenue quite a bit, because dimensional billing is one of those things you can really tweak. WebBit was accurate, but the rating engine has made us that much more accurate. We can offer a finer analysis, right down to the package level. And we can do it much—much!—faster.

Visually, Titan is light years ahead of WebBit. The output we can give a client is unbelievable. Because it's built on a true business intelligence platform, we have a tremendous number of drilling and analysis capabilities, not to mention graphs and charts, and the visibility is on steroids compared to what it was. Occasionally we'll show a client a screenshot of some of our tools, and they always respond as though they're thinking, *Wow. These guys are way smarter and better at this than I am. I know they're doing a better job.*

To keep it accurate and up to date, every time the carriers make a change, we put those numbers into Titan. That gives us huge capabilities, including the ability to look into the past or the future. For example, to do a proper analysis, our team wants to look at thirteen weeks of data to get a good feel for a client's spend profile, because it's seasonal. Because the carriers change their pricing at the start of every year, at the end of January, for example, our analysts could only look at four weeks of data. They couldn't look at packages prior to the last rate change because the rates weren't correct. Now we can load in thirteen weeks of data and rerate the prior year's data to the new rates, so we can always look at thirteen weeks of data no matter the time of year.

Titan also enables us to predict the future. Every year in late summer or early fall, FedEx and UPS announce the pricing changes they're going to implement the next year—they call it the general rate increase, or GRI. With Titan, we can take a client's or prospect's data and tell them in which specific ways their shipping costs will change under the GRI—which is almost always an increase. This is incredible value we can offer. A CFO sees the GRI announced and wants to know the answer to a critical question: "Under these new rates, what am I going to spend next year?" We can take the company's current spend, rerate it according to the GRI, and tell that CFO: "Your spend is going to go up by this much in these areas." Titan creates a very detailed report, showing every service, every week, every zone. It breaks it down every which way. We can then use this precise knowledge to assist the shipper to renegotiate their carrier agreement to mitigate the increase.

Titan is fantastic, but no application is perfect in its first iteration, so we're working on Titan 2, which is being built in a combination of QlikView and a database backend. Norm, who's already looking ahead to Titan 3, thinks that the third version will possibly be one hundred percent built in other programming languages, like Python.

The parcel side was now in great shape, but we couldn't say the same about freight. We were having a challenge getting that side up and running profitably, so in mid-2017 we asked Tyler to move over there from parcel operations. We thought that his analytical expertise, attention to detail, and obsession with finding the root cause of problems and fixing them would be a good fit. Tyler is very good at dissecting something to process map it, making sure every step is covered to decrease the number of possible disconnects.

A big part of the problem was that freight is much more complex, much more hands on, and much more integrated than parcel. With parcel, we hit a goldmine in terms of how black and white it is, how simple the business model is, and how quick the sell cycle is—and freight is the opposite in almost all respects. We didn't know anything about less-than-truckload (LTL). We were all parcel guys. The pricing agreements, the discount structure, the way the industry operated were all very different from parcel. Tyler describes freight and parcel as being in the same solar system, but on completely different planets. It was a totally different industry that was much more backwards—ten to twenty years behind parcel in terms of technology. Some carriers were still sending paper invoices, and there were no electronic bills of lading, like there were in parcel. In LTL and truckload, change happened very slowly.

For a freight client, not only were we negotiating their rates, but we were often negotiating with eight or twelve carriers instead of two. Also, in many cases we needed to sell the client a transportation management system (TMS), a piece of software that we had to maintain on the client's behalf. A TMS is very expensive to build and maintain in house, so we partnered with another company. That was another challenge, because, as we had found with Veriship's audit, we were selling this product to other companies but we didn't control it. We weren't responsible for its quality. But we couldn't tell the client that, because we were white labelling it, so the client thought it was our product. We also had to white-label a freight audit. Again we were selling a service that we couldn't control and we couldn't vouch for the quality of.

In freight we were basically just partnering with other companies to sell our business model. The only thing we were doing in house at that time was negotiating the rates through a longtime industry expert we had hired. When Tyler moved over, it was still disorganized and the team was small. In addition to Tyler and the old industry expert, there was the guy we had hired to lead the department and a young woman who had been working upstairs at Caribsea, Giovanna Rossi. We hired her to key in invoices. Giovanna ended up staying on and helped us turn freight into a profitable business unit, eventually working her way up to account supervisor.

Early on, we were fortunate to have a strong base of parcel clients that we were able to sell on freight. We didn't have to go sell freight to clients that we didn't know. That was a blessing because, obviously, it sped up the sales cycle. The relationship was already developed, and we had demonstrated our capability on the parcel side. Some of those early clients are still with us on the freight side.

For Tyler, Giovanna, and the rest of that small team it was a wild time. Like Travis and I when we were getting TI going, they were figuring things out as they went, flying by their coattails. The business model for freight was in a constant process of evolution. One thing we knew, though, was that technology was the way forward. In most ways the freight industry was stuck in the mid-twentieth century, but it had to change. From our perspective, the best, easiest, and most scalable way for us to offer value to clients was through technology.

Once Norm had Titan up and running, we asked him to build an application for freight. We wanted something similar to Titan, but it was very difficult because in freight there is no standard set of rates. Every shipper has a different base rate with each hauler. For example: Hauler A says, "I'm giving you a fifty percent discount. This load that I'm about to ship for you normally costs five hundred dollars, but it'll cost you two hundred fifty." Hauler B says, "I'm going to give you a twenty-five percent discount. My list price on this load is two hundred dollars, but it's going to cost you a hundred fifty." It's confusing for clients to know what they're really paying or whether they would get it cheaper somewhere else. It's like with sales in stores when they tell you, "We're giving you thirty-five percent off!" Well, thirty-five percent off what?

Some larger clients demand that every carrier they work with discount off a standard base rate. Those base rates are called Czar. The problem is the Czar rates have changed over the years, so you can get based off Czar in different years. All of this variability meant that when our freight team wanted to do an analysis like the parcel team, one single analysis would take them two weeks—sometimes six weeks. Here we were with Titan, able to do a parcel analysis in thirty to sixty minutes, and the freight team was taking on average two to four weeks.

The freight team walked Norm through what they needed. He then built them a Qlik application that took their analysis time down from weeks to around three days. The application gets everything to a standard rate, which they were having to do manually. They can use the standard rate to figure out where they need to or can apply discounts and everything else. It helps them analyze in a similar way to Titan, but without the sophistication. The software has also dramatically reduced mistakes. It doesn't generate anywhere near as much revenue as Titan, because there are a lot fewer clients on the freight side, but it's definitely a huge time saver for the freight pricing team.

A couple of months after Tyler moved over to freight, Brandon Staton told me he was leaving. From writing the emails that are the heart of our negotiation process to using his journalism skills to help put in place a true marketing and promotion strategy, Brandon had been a key part of our growth from 2010 until now. Seven years to the day, in fact. In that time we had grown from a few hundred thousand in revenue to tens of millions, and Brandon had played a big part in that. It was a blow that he was leaving. He had seen an opportunity to start his own business in this field and wanted to see what he could do. It was hard to see him go, but I understood and gave him my full support.

Personnel management was always an ongoing process, and we used EOS to help us make sure we had the right people in the right seats so that all our departments were operating as well as they could. One big change we made during this time was in our sales staff model. Up until now we solely had 1099 sales contractors (1099 is the name of the form the Internal Revenue Service uses), but the dip in revenue and the setback to our growth that we experienced in 2015 made us change our thinking.

In the beginning, because we didn't have the money to hire an in-house sales staff, the 1099 independent contractor model was the right structure to get the company going. The early ones we hired were mostly from our group at UPS back in the day, and they understood our vision for TI. They lived and breathed it with us, and they respected my leadership. But as we started to get bigger and to add people we had no prior relationship with, we started having difficulties. With 1099 contractors, there's only so much control you have. You can't do certain things or make them be certain places, otherwise you'll not comply with labor laws.

They were pulling in so much money with their commissions that we were worried about these 1099s getting fat and happy, and about how we would hold them accountable to go to the trade shows. We had this conundrum of *why?* In our heads, it's so simple. A plus B equals C. We expect this amount of revenue. We expect you to do your job. By the way, how come you're not doing your job? You've seen us do this a thousand times. How come you're not doing that? We just could not make them do it. They were making a lot of money. We couldn't make them call our customer. We couldn't make them follow up. We couldn't make them do anything.

There were other risks that came with the 1099 model. For example, sometimes sharing information is a risk. A big one. We were putting very sensitive information in the hands of people who weren't on our payroll. My philosophy has always been that we've got to be transparent. We have to give our people the tools to be the best they can be. We got burned a couple times because of that. From my perspective, being transparent was always the right thing to do, but just like we learned with some clients, sometimes people you consider part of your team aren't always honest and will take advantage of you. Our big wake-up call came when we discovered two contractors were taking our proprietary information and emailing it to a programmer to get them to duplicate it. Ironically, given our experience with UPS, we caught them with computer forensics. We sued them and the case was resolved in a way that was satisfactory.

It was a big risk to share a model that we had perfected. We might not have been first in this industry, but we pioneered it. It wouldn't be what it is, without us doing what we did in the way that we did it.

As we revised our business model in 2015 and 2016, Berkley made us recognize that we had hit the point in the company's lifespan and size where we needed to transition away from 1099s and put a more scalable pay structure in place for W2 salespeople. That was a risk because of the responsibility of ensuring a livelihood for those employees and also because of the burden of much higher overhead costs, but it was one we had to take.

We took the risk to make sure that the scalable issue would be solved and we wouldn't have the fat and happy issue anymore. Fat and happy equated to this: They didn't work as hard in the following years after they made big commissions, and our pipeline of prospects suffered. This ultimately meant that all the other people in the company who were supporting the business operations—finance, ops, marketing, IT; all the behind-the-scenes people—weren't getting the full benefit of their bonuses because of one group not being W2s and not working as hard as everybody else. That's why we changed it.

Going to the sales employee model meant that everyone would have the same incentive to work hard and to *keep* working hard, and it would give us full control of our sales strategy. It was the road forward for the company.

# 23

## MAKING AN IMPACT

I used to lie awake at night thinking about the ways the carriers could put us out of business. As a leadership team we talked about these issues, because we knew we had to get to where we weren't so vulnerable to action by the carriers. I had the idea of getting together with owners of companies like ours to share our thoughts. It would be a forum, a "more heads are better than one" type of thing, where we could talk about things that bothered us in the industry—things like NDAs. We were competitors, but we could do it without giving competitive intelligence to each other.

I decided to do a trial run with four or five of our biggest competitors: AFMS, Rob Martinez with Shipware (the guy who had praised us for *QReview*), and two or three others. I sent out an email introducing myself and outlining my idea at a high level, and got some good responses.

We got on an initial call. There were nice pleasantries, but it was clear everybody was being careful in what they said, aware they were talking to their competitors. My attitude was that there were enough customers for all of us, so let's talk about the things that keep us up at night. What would we do if this happened? Or this happened? What's our plan B? What's our plan C? We could dis-cuss those issues without divulging competitive or proprietary infor-mation, or anything about our customers. But even though every-body thought it was a great idea, in the end it never went anywhere because there wasn't the trust.

After this experience we decided not to worry about what we couldn't control, and we revived an idea Berkley had brought to us a while ago. "Let's not get with competitors," he said. "Let's get with people that we admire in the industry, that are smart, that are vi-sionary, that are forward thinking. People who can tell us what our customers' wish list is and if we're on the right track or not."

It was a concept used successfully by Envirotainer, the Swedish company Berkley had worked for. We had discussed the idea before, but it was just talk. Now, we considered it as something we would really do. I had always loved to get our best clients in the room to make us better—How can we be better to keep you on? What do you want more of?—but this would be a much more structured approach. We would create an advisory board, bringing together leaders at some of the top companies that used our products and services in a way that gave us guidance and got them engaged in our future path.

We needed advice and would benefit greatly from hearing their ideas. What do they want? What are we missing? What do we need to do next? Are we heading down the right road? We've got three or four initiatives going on—do we need to can two of them? We needed somebody other than ourselves to give us advice on the wish list in the market. Their thoughts on our vision. What to cancel out, what not. What to add.

We crafted a vision statement:

To build a Transportation Impact advisory board contain-ing customers and specialists from the parcel/supply chain technology industry in order to increase TI knowledge and understanding of the industry's needs and service-level expectations. The advisory board will have access to exclusive and proprietary information and a direct influence on service, product, and IT development. The advisory board is led by a chairman and contains a number of voluntary members from the supply chain and technology industry. The advisory board meets once per year upon the request of the chairman on behalf of TI. The chairman will create an agenda and introduce subjects in the form of presentation white papers, questionnaires, or documents.

We put a lot of time and effort into deciding who to invite, because we didn't want "yes" people. We wanted people who were smarter than we were, very well versed in the industry, and with great business acumen. We listed our fifteen best customers who were also the most challenging. They enjoyed the products and services that we offered them, but they were open with their feedback in a constructive but critical way of things that we fell short on. These were our smartest customers that we respected. We really thought through who would bring the most. We wanted ten, but we approached fifteen because we figured some would not accept.

For the invitation, we created a really nice brochure that explained what we were doing and why we were doing it. We emailed each person on our list, let them know the time commitment that would be involved, which wasn't much, and asked if they would like to participate. After answering in the affirmative, they agreed to a two-year commitment and signed a charter. They also signed a strict nondisclosure agreement, because we intended to really open up, revealing financials, our strategic roadmap, everything. There were employees in our organization who didn't know the things we would be telling them. But that kind of openness is the only way to get good, candid conversation going. And that's the only kind of conversation that's genuinely beneficial and useful.

We also asked former North Carolina governor Pat McCrory. When he presented us with the Governor's Award for Excellence in Workforce Development in 2014, we hit it off and subsequently stayed in touch. Pat has shrewd business sense and he had recently lost his re-election bid for the governorship, so I reached out and asked if he wanted to be on our advisory board. He said he would love to.

To lead the board, we wanted somebody neutral and independent who had no ties to our company or our offerings, so they could be objective. Berkley suggested a former colleague of his from Envirotainer, Gabriel Andersson, who was now the CEO of a Swedish supply chain technology company. We reached out to him and he agreed to take on the role.

As his vice chair we chose Norm, exactly because he is a good operator who knows a lot about IT. In business, that is like the key to success if you have somebody who's got the IT vision and knowledge and can marry that with understanding operations. Norm's a good visionary when it comes to the whole finished product of what we're trying to get to, and he's also grounded in reality. He's knowledgeable about what's going on in the industry, well read, and keeps up with what's coming down the road. He and Gabriel made a perfect team.

Our board as it was finally assembled was made up of eight clients, Pat McCrory, Gabriel, Norm, and Berkley. Everyone was appreciative of the invitation to participate and looked forward to adding value to our company, because all of them believed in Transportation Impact. We scheduled our first meeting for October 2017 and started preparing for it.

Berkley and I were hyper-focused on making it a black-tie type of event, because these executives were taking the time to fly in for a day and a half once a year, in addition to two hour-long virtual meetings. We wanted these polished professionals to feel this was an exceptional event that they would enjoy, that it was well worth their time, and that they were able to gain something from it.

For the venue we chose the Hyatt Regency Hill Country in San Antonio, Texas. To provide the true executive experience, we coordinated and booked first class flights and accommodation, arranged transportation to and from the airport, and planned the dinners at restaurants that promised the best in fine dining. We also arranged gifts. Everything was first class, because we wanted the board members to feel comfortable and appreciated and that we didn't take what they were giving us for granted.

The format was a day and a half plus a meet and greet. The evening before the full day we flew everybody in and then had dinner together. The next day we met from around eight until three in the afternoon, with a catered lunch brought in. We shut down that full day early so we could go do an extra-curricular activity and then enjoy a meal together. The agenda for the following half day was to cover any spillover from the full session along with one major topic, and then everybody would fly home after twelve.

We put a lot of effort into planning the agenda so it would be meaningful, because we only had the undivided attention of our board members for a day and a half, so we wanted to hit them with the most relevant target topics that could help grow the company. It was also important to make sure we had enough content but not too much.

We listed subjects we wanted the team's input on: business intelligence; regional carriers and U.S. Postal Service; international expansion; TI growth and development; sales and marketing. We put a tremendous amount of thought into making sure we would ask the right questions to get the information, feedback, and ideas that would be the most beneficial for us.

Even with our meticulous preparation, though, we really didn't know what to expect. We were very excited about the people who had agreed to be on our advisory board. We knew they would help accelerate a lot of our whiteboard projects and our technology path. With their talent and candor they would tell us what we needed to hear. We were looking forward to having open-ended discussions that would lead to more open-ended discussions that would lead to more open-ended discussions that would eventually benefit the company. That's why we put Norm over the board, rather than me or Berkley, because we didn't want it to be about us. We wanted it to be about the issues.

I went to the first meeting to explain what we were going after and what we wanted to get out of it. Berkley and I are very much alike in that before any meeting, we set our goals and document everything. Then afterwards, we recap: Did we get out of it what we wanted? What went wrong? What could we have done different?

On the flight out to Texas, we set our goals. For the first time, we felt like we were coming out of the skin of this small, maneuverable entrepreneurial company to a solidified corporate structure, where we had ten global executives coming in to talk about our company and how we could be better. It was very exciting that we had hit this milestone. We were also anxious to make sure it went off without any hiccups.

The dinner the first evening went well, and the next morning we convened for the all-day meeting.

I stood up and explained the mission. "We've hand-picked you because you're very intelligent. Everybody sitting in this room is someone that we've always admired in the industry, and we want you to be open and honest with us. Don't tell us what we want to hear. If our baby's ugly, we want you to tell us that. Tell us how we need to really be taking the company. What are the needs of the customer?"

Berkley said a few words, then we took a back seat and handed the reins to Gabriel, who would facilitate our agenda. But what happened to that agenda just went to show the meaningfulness of putting the group together. We made it clear that this was an open forum for a free flow of ideas and concepts, with nothing off limits, and it was very informative to hear the conversation. I'm not going to say feelings got hurt, but things that we thought we were doing right, we discovered we were not going down the right path. We presented our questions and then opened up the floor, and at the end of the conversation I found myself thinking, *Wow, I was really sold on our vision with regards to this element. Now, I don't even know if that's important.* They told us a few things that caused us to change the course of some of our major projects and goals.

At the dinner the final night, it was both amazing and humbling to see the change in how everyone related to each other. The first night, everyone took more of a business dinner approach. But during the skeet shooting extracurricular activity after the full-day meeting, we started poking fun at one another, and everybody connected. Looking around the table now, Berkley and I whispered to each other, "Man, this is effing awesome."

Afterwards we did an informal round table to get feedback on how it went. The responses were all very positive. Everybody more or less said they learned something themselves from the discussions, so it was informative and advantageous for both parties. They said they had learned things to take back and share with their own people. It was a great success, a true win-win.

Flying back, we recapped: "Did we accomplish what we went after?" The answer was a definite "yes."

We wrote up our notes to report back to the rest of the leadership team. Norm actually recorded this first advisory board meeting and then typed it up into a document that we used as guidance over the next months and years. The two annual virtual meetings we used to keep the momentum going and to show that we took the advisory team members' feedback and input very seriously. It's one thing to take somebody's time and solicit their feedback. It's a whole 'nother thing to put the feedback into action. So in the virtual meetings we tell them, "Here are all the things you asked us to do and that you thought were good ideas. Here are the ones you thought were bad. Here are the actions we've taken since the last meeting."

The advisory board meeting was such a great success because of the interpersonal relationships and because we deliberately fostered an atmosphere of creativity and openness, which allowed the team members to speak freely—and it allowed us to really hear what they were saying. Over the course of the two days, the trust and respect that we all had for each other strengthened and deepened. I think in the end, the advisory board and what everybody got out of it ended up being greater than the sum of its parts.

Relationships and creativity have always been at the heart of TI. From the start, Travis and I rewarded our employees' ideas and successes and did whatever we could to support them in their own development, and that continued as the company grew and the leadership team expanded. Then, when we implemented EOS, we set our core values of perfection, passion, professionalism, integrity, and work ethic. We hired and fired by those five things, and we as a leadership team tried to set the example on those five core values to our people.

As leaders, we have always surrounded ourselves with good peo-ple, and we have had unbelievable success in finding those people. We live in a community with four thousand residents that turns into fifty thousand in June and July, and most college graduates can't wait to get out of here and into the big city. I think part of our success is that we don't just say we work hard and play hard; we live it and breathe it. We work hard, and I believe we should enjoy the fruits of our labor. I already had that reputation back in my UPS days, so the people I recruited from there already knew that about me. They knew we were going to be successful, and we were going to have a good time doing it.

Emerald Isle is a beach town. There's no commerce here. There are ice cream shops, a supermarket, some bars. There's no industry, really. Which makes it incredible the amount of unbelievable talent and intelligent people that we've recruited right here in our backyard. It's a testament probably to young people who have gone away and then heard about an emerging company where you never think one would pop up. They hear about a great company culture and they want to come back. Or maybe they vacationed here as a kid, and now they've got a livelihood option they never had before. Work for a great company that provides real value to its customers, and go surfing at lunchtime.

By this time, we had built a reputation in the area that our culture was second to none. If you held to our core values, learned from your mistakes, and worked your butt off, we were going to buy Christmas presents, have ten-year anniversary parties, go to the beach together, do fishing trips together. Whatever we could come up with that was fun and we thought our employees would enjoy, we did it.

As a company we also lived by another value that wasn't on our list, but that has always been core to me, and that is generosity. I've been very blessed, and I like to see people happy. I believe in sharing the wealth. It's just the right thing to do. I've always tried to make the people around me happy, especially if I saw they did something without expecting any reward or they had a real need. If one of our people had a crisis in their family or a financial hardship, we would give money to that employee. We did that dozens of times. If we recognized somebody was having a hard time, we would instantly discuss it and take action. Family looks out for each other, and for us every employee was part of the TI family. We would say it when they came on board: "Welcome to TI. Glad to have you as part of the family." And we meant it.

Today the way we reward our employees is much more structured because we need to be equitable, but early on I used to drive John nuts, because he did the budgeting, and he was very regimented. Every time we got an important award, I'd give everyone a bonus, and sometimes I wanted to be generous just because we could be. One December I walked into John's office and said, "I think I'm going to buy everybody a piece of David Yurman jewelry."

"What?" He looked alarmed.

And then we bought everyone a piece of David Yurman jewelry.

But the one that really made him shit his pants was when I walked into his office in the middle of summer in 2016 and said, "Look, it's just been real good. I want to give our people a bonus."

"Okay. Fifteen hundred dollars?"

"Nah, I'm thinking ten thousand."

"Apiece!!"

John looked like he was about to have a heart attack. But I wanted to make a life-changing impact, to where somebody could pay off their credit cards or put down on a house.

Once John got over his shock, we did it. We gave everybody ten thousand dollars. And it wasn't gross ten K, where all the taxes were taken out. It was a true ten K, grossed up to net ten thousand. It wasn't because we felt good at Christmas. We just said we finally had a hell of a year.

We learned, though, that as much as people love bonuses, it's more important to them to have income they can count on throughout the year. When we started the company we were giving some people forty percent of their total annual pay as the annual bonus. Then we went down to twenty-five percent and stayed at that level for several years. As we got bigger we started getting more structured in our human resources management, and we surveyed our people to get feedback on our comp plan. They told us they'd rather have more discretionary money throughout the year and less bonus at the end of the year. So we restructured the bonuses to fifteen percent for non-management and twenty percent for management. We took part of the bonus that they would have gotten and put it in their pay throughout the year, and then reduced their bonus. Then we went down further to what we have today, which is ten percent for non-management and fifteen percent for management. That's on top of the celebration bonuses, like the twenty-five hundred for making the Inc. 5000 again.

It was great that we were growing so fast we could afford to be more generous, but the flip side brought challenges in human resources as in other parts of the business. In gradually implementing benefits for our people, from 401(K)s to health care to paid time off, there were so many ways to make mistakes in trying to make sure our employees were fairly rewarded, well taken care of, and happy. John had handled our HR since he came on board, but in 2017 we realized we needed a dedicated person, so we hired for that position and found a fantastic HR manager in Britt Vinson, who stayed with us for years.

Filling open positions was also getting harder. We started having to recruit out of Raleigh, Atlanta, New York, and other bigger places. As we became more sophisticated, it became more and more of a challenge to source local talent, and from a cultural perspective, we struggled with how to maintain the family atmosphere and keep people motivated.

One part of our culture that everyone loved and that brought everyone together was our generosity in giving back to the community. The Christmas Families, Thanksgiving Families, Christmas Grocery Shopping, the Scholarship Students—again and again our employees told us how much it meant to them to be able to give like that and see the effect on the people who received it. Transportation Impact was well respected in the area because of how we gave back. It was a huge attraction to our culture and really helped us in recruiting great people.

At UPS, Travis and I were groomed into giving back. We always said that when we made it, we were going to make sure that was a big part of who we were. As the company started growing, we recognized that we were very blessed and fortunate. We wanted to make sure that we gave back not only money, but also in time and common effort. Even when we only had a few employees, we would get out and volunteer. From the beginning that was a big part of the fabric of our company.

At the 2016 Inc. 5000 conference, Tony Robbins was the keynote speaker. Our whole leadership team was sitting listening to him when he started talking about how a company was giving back to the community by donating one percent in money, one percent in volunteering, and one percent in kind. We all looked at each other. That was what we had been doing for years! After we got back to Emerald Isle, Berkley reminded us of what Tony Robbins had talked about. "I know we've been doing all this—actually we've been doing more than just one percent of each thing. But let's put it on paper to where everybody in the company knows what it is, and the community knows what it is, and it's got organization to it. We'll give it a name and put it in writing, and we'll get everybody on the same page rowing in the same direction."

We decided to use the one-one-one framework that Tony described. Each year we would donate one percent of company profits, one percent in goodwill services, and one percent of our employees' time. The average full-time employee in the U.S. works around eighteen hundred hours. One percent of that is eighteen hours, but we rounded it up so each employee would have twenty paid volunteering hours each year, half to use for their choice, and half for a charity chosen by the company. Now, we just needed a good name for our program. A name that had meaning and would also be easy for people to remember.

We came up with the perfect name: IMPACT1, an acronym that stands for Improvements Made by People ACTing as 1.

IMPACT1 was officially launched in March 2017 with the enthusiastic support of everyone at Transportation Impact. At UPS, charity work was mandated. But under IMPACT1, the employees get out and volunteer because they're enrolled in the vision and it brings something into their lives they didn't have before. They learn how much they enjoy making positive change. They see the impact it has on people. In fact, Brandon got so much out of it that when he moved back to Raleigh to start his own business, one of the first things he did was find somewhere to volunteer. Our IMPACT1 initiative lives, breathes, and thrives because it's part of the fabric of working here, and because the IMPACT1 committee is made up entirely of employees—they choose what the one percent of profit gets donated to. We don't just get together once a year and donate to the United Way. Throughout the year, our team members are out shopping for individual families, they're getting sponsors and running marathons, they're serving lunch at the local homeless shelter, they're picking up litter on the beach, and much more. Almost every week we're doing something. We don't make them do any of it; they ask and volunteer. UPS planted the seed, but we do it our way.

Everybody that works for TI is proud, because the community knows. Locally, we have been the leader. Several other companies have asked me to help them come up with an organized plan, so they can model after us. Whether you're an entrepreneur or a solopreneur, I believe everybody has a social responsibility to society. We were the leaders in the community on that and still are. It's even funny because people know us more for our philanthropy than for what we do. They have a vague idea that we do something with shipping or transportation, but what they really know is that we're good people.

In the first year and a half of IMPACT1, we donated more than a million dollars' worth of money, time, and services. Our vision was that as we continue to grow, when we become that hundred-million-dollar-a-year company, the one-one-one is going to increase. Berkley's vision for IMPACT1 is that it will grow into its own company that requires its own staff, because at that point, the positive impact we have made as an organization will be at the front of everything we do. In February 2023 we took a big step towards this when we extended our philanthropy internationally with the sponsorship of an orphanage in India.

But our core value of giving doesn't start and stop at IMPACT1. Our people individually and collectively carry it into the whole of life in a spirit of supporting each other and our community in any time of need. One of the most moving examples for me was when the spouse of a TI employee was severely injured in a tragic accident. Watching our people pull together to support them was unbelievable. Our team organized a barbecue fundraiser with a goal of raising thirty thousand dollars. The community joined in, and altogether we collected $36,466.02 to help the couple cover their huge medical expenses and lost income. When one of our house cleaners for the condos in Myrtle Beach needed a kidney transplant, we raised forty or fifty thousand dollars for them. That's a testament to our people, being a true family, and working hard to help out a peer.

It's important to us as leaders to set the example. Travis and I and another member of our leadership team personally gave hundreds of thousands of dollars towards a new cancer wing on the local hospital, and there have been many other projects like that.

When a hurricane hits the isle, devastating buildings and flattening the landscape, we've all got each other's back. As the storm sweeps in we give employees money and say, "Here's some money. Whatever you need. If you need to go buy a chainsaw, go buy batteries, you need to stay in a hotel, you need food—just get yourself safe." Then after the damage is done, we show up to help cut trees, fix roofs, repair doors and windows—whatever has to be done for our people, everybody steps up to do it.

In 2018 we further developed the basic structure of IMPACT1 to provide a path for building employee engagement and take our charitable endeavors to the next level. Rather than simply taking external requests, we started planning monthly giving opportunities by creating employee events to coincide with specific awareness days or months, like World Health Day. Employees who have a special connection to a cause often submit ideas. Internally, this has promoted teamwork and community involvement, and externally it has promoted our IMPACT1 initiatives and the passion that all of us at TI have for giving back. Each year, a third or more of the IMPACT1 resources are now dedicated to scheduled initiatives chosen by our people, like the Walk to End Alzheimer's, reading to children at a local elementary school for Read Across America Day, a sponsored blood drive to support the Red Cross, and our now well-known annual Polar Bear Plunge to support the American Heart Association.

Since Travis's heart attack right after New Year's in 2013, we had personally been huge supporters of the AHA, and the company had also donated regularly. But it was a cause that had personal meaning for many people at TI, so the IMPACT1 committee wanted to do a special fundraiser to support research into heart disease, something different that would be fun and would also get a lot of attention to raise awareness that heart disease was the number two killer in North Carolina. Two members of our marketing team, Jillian Farrington and Lauren Edmondson, put their heads together with Leslie Sutton from our Partner team, and came to me with an idea. Lauren noticed that February 22 was National Polar Bear Day, so they said, "Let's do a Polar Plunge as a fundraiser! We'll have people vote with dollars for one person from TI to have to run into the freezing cold Atlantic ocean. Suddenly jumping into freezing cold water is a shock to the heart, so it ties together with the theme, and it's fun and attention-getting!"

I thought that was an awesome idea. We decided that our whole leadership team would be on the "hot seat," and whoever raised the most money in their name would have to go for a freezing swim. We set up a donation page through the AHA with a goal of five thousand dollars, and the idea of making one of the TI leadership run into frigid ocean water was so popular that we met our goal in only five days—and I raised the most!

For me, this cause was personal because of nearly losing Travis to heart disease. Everybody wanted to see the leader go in, and I fed off that—I was determined to win! As I ran into the ocean and the shock of the icy water hit my body, I really felt good about being the one to do it. It was exhilarating and rewarding.

Travis told our writer who did an article on the Polar Plunge for *QReview*: "I was impressed with the enthusiasm with which Keith tried to swim to England."

# 24

## RELATIONSHIPS

First impressions are important. I understood that early on, and it served me well in the Marine Corps and the Highway Patrol. Paying attention to detail is not just something I do in my business and then go home and be sloppy. It's something that's a part of me and part of my life. I spend time to build my wardrobe. I drive cars in which every detail of design and performance has been executed to perfection. I appreciate architectural details, and I like nice things in my homes. I even gave a future president architectural advice one time!

It was 2012. Travis and I had been pitching to CFOs at one of those conferences where you have ten meetings lined up head to head with a decision maker for fifteen minutes, but Travis had to leave early, so I was there on my own. We were at the Doral in Miami, and I heard Trump had just purchased the whole country club, the golf course and everything. Back then I was a big fan of *Celebrity Apprentice*, the TV show that he hosted. On the last day of the conference I was checking out of the hotel when I looked down the hall and saw Trump and his daughter and a guy following him around taking notes.

I went up to him. "Mr. Trump,"—except for his daughter and the guy taking notes, there was nobody around—"I'm a big fan of Celebrity Apprentice. Is there any way I can get my picture made with you?"

"Yeah, yeah, of course," he said. "Let me ask you something." He looked up toward the ceiling. "What do you think about this crown molding up here?

The question took me off guard. "Well, with all due respect, sir, I think it's a little dated."

"That's what I thought. That's what I thought," he said, and the guy behind him started making notes. It was funny.

Fast forward to his presidency and he was so into the details, but this showed his attention to detail even back then. Here he was a multibillionaire and he was going around everything, getting into the weeds, picking into details like that crown molding, making calls himself on the tiny stuff.

So then I had my picture made with him. You can see his daughter, Ivanka, in the background. I still have it.

Even earlier in the existence of TI, probably 2009 or 2010, I was at a trade show where I had been very unsuccessful. It was one of those where we'd spent a lot of money. It was the last day and I was at a bar, just sitting there, thinking about what we could have done different as far as research and presentation—because it was really unsuccessful.

I happened to look down past my left armpit and saw the most incredible, Italian-looking pair of shoes standing behind me. My gaze travelled up, past trousers creased to perfection, a belt that matched the shoes, and a coat that was off the chain. I swiveled on my barstool to face the guy and said, "Damn, buddy. I'm not gay or anything, but you look amazing."

We got to talking. His name was Dedrick Thomas. He was a supply chain engineer and he told me about his dream to start a bespoke tailoring business. I had just started TI, and I told him, this is my dream—here's what we do. Then I said, "One day I'll be able to afford you. One day you'll have your dream, and one day, TI's going to make it and I'll be able to support your business."

Over the years we stayed in touch. He quit his job as an engineer and started his business, Hideoki Bespoke. He was great about following up and would often send me an email or text. "Hey, brother, just wanted to check in with you. You made that million dollars yet? LOL We need to get you set up." It was marvelous, because TI and Hideoki Bespoke came up about the same time, and we exchanged notes and celebrated for each other as our two businesses grew to be very successful. We became good friends.

Eventually I was able to tell him, "I'm coming to Atlanta to get fitted by you!" That was a great day. A while later, I had the whole leadership team fly to Atlanta and get fitted. We allocated five thousand dollars per person. That included one suit, two trousers, two shirts, one sports coat, a pair of shoes and a belt, a pocket square, a tie, and a tie bar. It was a great experience for the LT to share, because when you go to Dedrick's salon it's all about the experience from the moment you walk in—the fine liquors, the good music, the atmosphere. *It's a lifestyle!* is his motto.

Now I get all my clothes from Dedrick. He keeps my measurements, preferences, and purchase history documented, so if I want three white shirts, I text him and he sends them to me. If you buy a lot of clothes from him, he'll sometimes deliver them personally. He likes that hands-on, building the relationship. When he comes out to Emerald Isle, he stays at my house. Dedrick graduated from Mississippi State with magna cum laude honors. He's very intelligent, and he's a dreamer. I loved seeing him fulfill his dream, and he's still building it. He's got an empire now.

He's also gotten TI a lot of business, because he knows our business model and he's a connector. Dedrick understands that in business—especially in B2B—relationships are the key to long-lasting success, and he loves to connect people who can help each other.

Dedrick introduced me to Darrell Mays, who visited us in Emerald Isle in time to witness our steel-signing ceremony for our new building. Darrell is probably one of the most successful people that I know, and he is the founder of the nsoro Foundation, which supports foster kids who have no support system and nowhere to go when they age out of the system. Nsoro helps them get into a college and get a life plan.

Since then Transportation Impact as a company and a lot of people at TI personally have donated hundreds of thousands of dollars to nsoro because we really believe in it. Their big annual fundraiser is an event in Atlanta called the Starfish Ball, and every time we go it's a cry session. Nsoro is near and dear to our hearts. Contributing generously to this organization that we strongly believe in has repaid us many times over, because Darryl has got us a lot of business through his relationships.

It's like a web that spreads out and certain people are hubs. Darryl is a hub, and Dedrick is a hub. There are a lot of cool people in the circle that he runs in. Through those relationships we've got to meet Steve Smith, a former Michigan State basketball star who went on to play in the pros and is now an NBA analyst. Dikembe Mutombo. Rasheed Wallace. Steve Harvey. Jerome Bettis, "The Bus," who was a great running back with the Pittsburgh Steelers. T.I. (aka Tip), the rapper. One night I had dinner with Tip and I was trying to pitch him to come to the rooftop lounge at Caribsea and do a little just-for-fun rap—because our company was called TI. We'd always laugh and joke about it, but I never could pull it off.

I've met a lot of good people through the relationship with Dedrick, which just goes to show how you never know who you will meet; you never know where it's going to go. Two people starting out at the bottom with dreams and remaining friends to this day, and both businesses a huge success.

Some of the people he's introduced me to, like Steve Smith, have also become good friends. One time I had a potential client that was a big Michigan State fan, and I got Steve to call him on his cell. The guy was over the moon, and we got him signed!

At one nsoro ball, we met four-time NBA All-Star Rasheed Wallace. He had attended The University of North Carolina at Chapel Hill and played for the Tar Heels, so he had ties to our area. We invited him to visit us in Emerald Isle. I was struck by how genuine he was, so I said it would be great if we could share the experience with the kids in our community. From that, we came up with the idea for Rasheed to do a basketball camp for the kids at the Coastal Plains Boys & Girls Club in Morehead City. We were big supporters of that club. It would be a marvelous experience for them, not just the basketball, but also to see the kind of person Rasheed was. I wanted to give the kids a really positive role model. To make it happen, we donated some money to the nsoro Foundation.

Once we'd put together the deal, we came back and pitched the idea to the Boys & Girls club, although we knew it would be a no-brainer. When we told them, they were wild about it. Monica Pantoja at nsoro helped us organize everything, and on November 4, 2016, big Rasheed Wallace showed up at the Sunshine Lady Club in Morehead City, just across the water from little Emerald Isle.

TI employees helped host the camp, and several of us from the leadership team went to watch. Of course it was a huge hit. It was incredibly rewarding to see how excited the kids were and how wonderful Rasheed was with them. It was a very special day.

But I didn't want this to be a one-off event. I hoped that some of the other NBA stars we'd met through Dedrick and Darrell would also come and do camps to help us spread the message to our kids that they are an important part of our community and our world. I wanted more of them to have the chance to meet these guys and to learn first-hand that if you work hard enough and are determined enough, you can reach your dreams.

So the next year, through another donation to nsoro, we got Steve Smith and Dikembe Mutumbo to do a camp at the club in

December. We had pizzas brought in, photographers everywhere—we made a big deal out of it so the kids could get a lot of enjoyment. The guys worked with their own groups, and then they rotated and interacted. Both men have big hearts, and it was an unforgettable experience for the kids to spend a few hours connecting with such wonderful human beings who are also legends.

Dedrick flew in for the weekend too, and I arranged for him, Steve, Dikembe, and John Palmer, Dedrick's mentor, to stay at my sons' beach house. That night we all went out to Caribsea and had a great dinner. There was a lot of good fellowship that day. Everyone got a lot out of it, and we got to help two charitable organizations at the same time. It brought a lot of fun memories to our town.

The day after everybody left, the house cleaners called and said somebody had left their shoes behind. They brought me a pair of huge tennis shoes. They were Steve Smith's. I called him and he told me to keep them. So we made a fun contest at TI and the winner got Steve Smith's sneakers.

*On November 4, 2016, big Rasheed Wallace showed up at the Sunshine Lady Club in Morehead City, just across the water from little Emerald Isle. I wanted the kids at the Coastal Plains Boys & Girls Club to see the kind of person Rasheed was.*

*Dikembe Mutombo, Steve Smith, Ginger, me, and some of the TI leadership and staff at the Coastal Plains Boys & Girls Club, where Steve and Dikembe put on the second wonderful basketball camp sponsored by TI.*

Folks have recognized the role that we play within the community, from a social stewardship perspective and as an employer. They like our philosophies. They recognize that the good people are the ones who are good to their communities. That has brought us into contact with other good people, like Coach Dave Odom and Phil Ford.

Coach Odom I met through our sales contractor Harper Lee. Harper went to school with Dave Odom's son, who now is a big-time basketball coach. Dave lives in Winston Salem, North Carolina, and he has a house here in Emerald Isle. We've become friends, and he loves Caribsea restaurant. His claim to fame was that he helped coach the Olympic team and he recruited one of the best pro basketball players of all time, Tim Duncan, from the Virgin Islands. Not only was he a great coach, he's a great people person, which made him an ideal person to ask to be a motivational speaker at our VIP events.

Years earlier, we came up with the idea to do special off-site events that would allow us to connect in a more personal way with potential customers, while at the same time providing added value. We'd have three a year, sometimes four. It was set up as an educational forum, and we would invite seven potential customers that were on the fence and three existing clients. Everybody would fly in to the Virgin Islands or someplace comparable on Thursday night and we'd have a meet and greet with hors d'oeuvres. Then Friday would be an all-day educational platform, where people in the industry would speak. Saturday was a free day, so everybody ended up in the pool, and by Saturday evening, we'd have all seven people signed up. All of a sudden, we're friends on Facebook and LinkedIn, and Sunday morning we're giving each other high-fives. It was always wonderful how everyone bonded. The key to the success of it was that along with the educational and motivational content, it gave the seven potential customers a chance to hear the three existing clients talk about their experience, without us saying it and without it being a commercial.

At one of these events, I even made a wonderful connection with a person who wasn't one of our guests. Matt Hullander and I met by chance when he asked if I had a phone charger, and as we stayed in touch over the years, a true friendship developed, especially as we both went through the experience of selling our companies at around the same time. Matt is a visionary and entrepreneur, and I have learned a lot from him.

Coach Odom came sometimes to our off-site events as a motivational speaker, and Phil Ford was another one. Phil Ford was like a god at University of North Carolina at Chapel Hill, which is where both my boys went, and I have a lot of respect for him. Many years ago, Travis went to a benefit connected with Richard Petty, and one of the auction items was three tickets to go to a Carolina basketball game with Phil Ford. Travis knew how much I loved Phil and how much I loved basketball, and so did my two sons, so he bought those tickets at the auction for me.

That gift meant the world to me. Brian, Tyler, and I went out to eat with Phil, then we went to a Carolina game. He took us through the museum, but he couldn't really get through it because everybody was attacking him. A couple weeks after the game, I got up my nerves to call and ask if he'd be interested in coming to our VIP event and doing a motivational segment. "Yeah, man," he said. "Anytime." He's done that for years and still does it, just for the relationship, because we've become good friends. He also came to my forty-year high school reunion and gave a motivational speech to my class before the party started. He's a really good Christian man, a great role model who gives back a lot in the community.

Another great motivational speaker we've had is Pat McCrory. Pat has become a wonderful friend—we love getting out for a round of golf—and he has also been a good mentor to me. I like running things by him because he'll bring up aspects I really didn't think about.

Coach Odom, Phil Ford, Pat McCrory—they all recognized our philanthropic endeavors and have truly become friends of the company. The efforts we have made—through IMPACT1, through the nsoro Foundation—have given us connections to folks we never would have been associated with, if it hadn't been for the philanthropic efforts that we believe in. Those beliefs have opened up business opportunities. That's not why we did it. It was truly altruistic. But it has given us lifelong friendships with like-minded people who have also generously given to us.

*Coach Dave Odom, Phil Ford, and former North Carolina governor Pat McCrory have all been great motivational speakers at our off-site events. L-R: Pat McCrory, me, Phil Ford, Dave Odom*

*A promotional flyer for our 2017 business forum, one of our special off-site events that allowed us to connect in a more personal way with potential customers, while at the same time providing added value.*

*Three members of the A Team enjoying the pool at an off-site event. L-R: Berkley Stafford, me, John Howard*

# 25

## PULLING BACK

It was no secret in the company that Berkley was Keith Byrd's "chosen one." From the time I used to see him in the airport when he was working for Envirotainer, I wanted him as the one who would eventually take over from me. The moment he came on board I started grooming him, and in the past months I had been delegating more and more. In 2017 I was still running hard, but now in early 2018 I saw that with the team we had I could start slowing down.

In June, we celebrated our ten-year anniversary with a big pool party at the Dolphin Ridge Club. We went all out on that party. John used to always tell me the stats—fifty percent of new companies don't make it in one year; eighty percent not in five years. We didn't just survive—we had made the Inc. 5000 five consecutive times, and we would make it again this year. And there were all the other awards we had earned: back-to-back NC Fast 40 and North Carolina Top 100 Private Companies, Eastern NC BBB Torch Award for Marketplace Ethics, CAI Ovation Award for Corporate Social Responsibility, Business NC Best Employer in North Carolina and Employer of the Year, back-to-back Inc. Magazine Best Workplace.

When I looked back at those ten years, I saw a lot of sacrifice, a lot of hard work, a lot of dedication. A lot of long hours, a lot of traveling, a lot of being told no. A lot of going back to the whiteboard and regrouping. A lot of learning how to listen to the customer. A lot of growing pains. A lot of learning how to be three steps ahead of everything. A lot of learning how to expect the unexpected. I saw how things went from literally on the back of a napkin when John, Berkley, and I were living in my house, to coming to fruition in a very professional way, in a way that I knew the growth was going to continue.

I was very proud, knowing that work ethic, and wanting something, and having a goal and a plan on how to get there works. That actually works. Especially when you surround yourself with a lot of good people. When you plan the work and work the plan, and everybody's rowing in the same direction, and everybody knows their number, it all comes to fruition.

Every year we had different milestones that we were hitting, different awards. It was very pleasing to be able to lead a group of people to reach those milestones, to make it ten years and have the growth that we experienced—not only revenue, but also with people. To see how we changed lives in the community, the opportunities we gave local people who were employees, to watch their growth over the years was very, very rewarding. That twenty-eight-year-old making big decisions, knowing how to dissect a problem and how to make a plan to fix it.

It wasn't just me—everybody in the company was sticking their chest out. Everybody was proud. It was contagious. We all knew it was a significant milestone, and we had done it as a family company, both in the real sense—Travis's and my children all worked at the company and contributed significant value—and in our culture. It was the TI family. As I told the writer doing our official press release: "We've been offered to be bought out many times, but we've always said no because we want to carry on the legacy of the family.

All four of our kids have stepped up to the plate and learned the industry. That's very important to us." Not to mention, for the past couple of years the company had been making me personally six million a year or more—why would I give that up?

When I read the release, I saw that my son Brian had also told how much it meant to him.

"I watched this business from the outside for five years, and you could see how special it is. I want to continue the legacy for my kids and grandkids. Everybody here is in neck deep, and nobody's going anywhere."

Nineteen days after we officially hit the ten-year mark, we launched a new website that had been almost a year in the making. Our service offerings had expanded over the ten years, so we needed the website to clearly and logically communicate exactly what we offered and how it could benefit the shipper. It was another milestone in our growth. We also wanted to use the website as a recruiting tool, so we created special sections on IMPACT1 and the TI culture: "warm, friendly, and relaxed, while being laser-focused on remaining best in class."

We renewed our partnership with Richard Petty Motorsports, increasing our associate sponsorship and serving as the primary sponsor of the No. 43 Chevrolet Camaro ZL1 driven by Bubba Wallace during the Hollywood Casino 400 at the Kansas Speedway on October 20. It was an honor to be associated with Richard Petty, because he and his operation lived the virtues of character, sincerity, and candor. A few months later, we also renewed our partnership with the fantastic Erica Enders when we signed an agreement as the official sponsor of Erica and the Elite Motorsports team for the 2019 and 2020 seasons.

In between all this we managed to draw up plans for an extension to our building, which would basically be a whole new building constructed beside the existing one with internal connections. Even before we moved in two years ago we had overflowed out of our

new home. The extension would more than double the square footage and available office and conference room space—adding 16,529
square feet to the existing 13,299 square feet, for a total of 29,828
square feet over three floors—and bring all our on-site employees
under one roof. We had grown so fast that some of our employees
were located in offices a mile down the road. It was a great problem
to have, though!

But among all the good feeling, one thing was really starting
to get on my nerves. The web systems engineer that Travis and I
had partnered with to create our audit platform had a management
style that clashed with ours. Over the years we had worked hard
to try to get us all on the same page, but without success. He was
running eAudit like it was his own company—Travis and I were majority owners—and refusing to cooperate with us. I had sent Norm
up to Greenville a few times to learn about the software and offer
his expertise, but he kept hitting a brick wall. I was getting really
frustrated, because I wanted that product to be as good as it could,
but we couldn't get any insight into it or make any changes.

That month of our celebrations, I sent Norm up to Greenville
again, this time with one of our programmers, Wesley Hitson. When
Norm reported back to me about how the meeting went, it was
clear the time had come to get full ownership of eAudit. We started the process of buying out the partner. That took many months
and even more frustration. Finally, in December I declared Norm
CEO of eAudit. He "hired" Wesley and another TI programmer,
Adam Lambert, as new eAudit employees, and they all went up
to Greenville to learn as much as they could before the ownership
transfer completed on December 31. January 2019 was rough for
Norm, Wesley, and Adam as they learned through the school of
hard knocks how to manage various aspects of the systems and keep
the audit running. Then it took them several more months to get the
depth of knowledge they needed to do everything and start to make
improvements. That was a very difficult time on the IT side.

As we entered 2019, though, we were in a good position. We were on target for forty million in revenue. We had full control of our audit, and all the departments in the company were well established, including freight. Freight had become a sustainable revenue generator. We started off rocky. It took fourteen months to start turning a profit. Like any other service, you launch it, and you learn.

This circles back to the challenges that we saw in 2015. We recognized that in business, if you don't evolve, you die. We knew that and it was a slap in the face to us. We knew we needed to pivot. That's when we started focusing more on technology and additional service offerings. That was the pivotal year for us and the future evolution of the company.

As a leadership team there was a conversation we had probably three or four times, every time we were having to make decisions that required more significant investment than we'd previously had to make, but the conversation never really got anywhere. Berkley, John, and I would ask ourselves: "Do we want to be content with being a fifty-million-dollar company? Let's just be the best at what we're doing right now and stop right there." But there's no way on earth any of us could limit ourselves from being better and better and better should the opportunity present itself. We could never tell a client, "No. We don't want your three million more. We're stopping at fifty million. We just don't want to serve you anymore." It's not in our DNA. So we put our foot to the floor and said, "We're going to grow this thing until the wheels spin off."

# 26

## CHA CHING!

"John, I got another one of those damn emails," I said. For the past year or so I had been getting emails from companies wanting to buy TI. I did the same with this one as I'd done with all the rest—put it in a folder in my inbox labelled "Buy."

I was driving with John in Emerald Isle. We were just passing Trading Post restaurant, heading toward Atlantic Beach. Beside me, he said, "You get two or three of them a week, don't you?"

"Yeah."

"Keith," he said. "You need to at least entertain the idea. The way we're growing, there's no telling what this company's worth."

I turned down the radio. John was not like me. Berkley and I were spontaneous, but John would think everything through and look at the pros and the cons, so I really respected when he spoke. It always made sense. And here he was, an employee of TI, telling me that maybe I should sell the company. That got my attention.

I was dead set on not selling. All the time I bragged, "We will never sell," because we were making hand-over-fist money. We'd be stupid to sell. I still kept putting the emails in the folder, but John's remark stuck with me. Maybe one day, if the right buyer offering the right price came along. . . .

In fall 2018, thanks to one of our off-site VIP events (this one was in the Bahamas), we managed to sign GlobalTranz as a partner. In June, GlobalTranz had been sold by its owner, Providence Strategic Growth, to a private equity firm called The Jordan Company for around four hundred million, and since then GlobalTranz had been growing rapidly, mainly through acquisitions. They were a great addition to our partner program. That November we flew up to Minneapolis to train their sales team. As we walked out of a meeting with the CEO, Renee Krug, and chairman of the board, Bob Farrell, Berkley and I looked at each other and said basically the same thing: "Did you hear what I heard? It was like they were planting the seed to talk with us about a future opportunity of acquisition, without saying so."

Things moved quickly after that.

In early February 2019, GlobalTranz began formal conversations with us at a high level. No specifics, just seeing if our cultures and business models would be a good fit and make it worth talking further.

Neither Travis nor I had ever been through anything like this before, so we reached out to our legal team for advice. We learned there was a lot of M&A activity in our industry and we could be picky with the deal we selected. The sale prices of companies in the 3PL space were typically calculated as a multiple of EBITDA (earnings before interest, taxes, depreciation, and amortization), and professionals in the industry told us that the multiples were higher than average right now, up to the mid-teens.

We always knew our EBITDA, so we did the math and got a number in the hundreds of millions. I had no idea our company was worth that much. I remembered what John had said. You just can't walk away from that kind of money. We had never intended to sell at all, but when that number came out, Travis and I knew we would be stupid not to. We told our kids, and all four of them more or less said, "Dad, you're crazy if you don't accept this." So I told the leadership team, and they got excited, too. We were talking about generational wealth.

We set up a meeting for the last day of February with Renee, Bob, and GlobalTranz CFO Lara Stell. They flew down in a private jet to Michael J. Smith Field in Beaufort, North Carolina, where I had a driver waiting for them. I got a room for Bob at the Islander Hotel and put the two women up in the Emerald Isle condo, where wine and fresh flowers greeted them. I made sure everything was perfect. After the meeting with the full TI leadership, we took them to dinner at Caribsea, then they went to their two places and flew out the next morning. Shortly before noon on March 1, I got an email from Bob thanking us for our time and hospitality, praising us on building an exceptional company, and looking forward to "taking the next steps to expand our partnership."

Three days later, I opened my inbox to find an email from someone at Providence, the company that had owned GlobalTranz a year before. It was one of those emails I would have put in the "Buy" folder a month earlier, but the connection with GlobalTranz was so close that I wondered if there was something else behind it. It turned out there wasn't, the guy was just cold prospecting, but I saw an opportunity to use it to my advantage. I replied, thanking him for the interest and saying that we'd been approached, but we were rookies at this. The bankers had told us that the multiples in our industry were in the mid-high teens, or higher. "You know this market better than I do, do you agree with the bankers?"

"The bankers are correct," he replied, and asked to set up a call with me. I wasn't going to break our commitment to wait to hear further from GlobalTranz, so I kept putting him off. Finally I told him I'd be unavailable for the following three weeks, and in the interest of full disclosure, I sent Renee the whole email string. Five days later, on March 26, she sent a formal indication of interest from GlobalTranz.

In anticipation of the due diligence process, we set up an online data room. Meanwhile, discussions continued. The relationship was developing well. I had a lot of respect for Bob, and Renee and I got along great.

The morning of Wednesday, May 1, she and I talked and came to a basic verbal agreement, and then at 6:16 p.m. she emailed me a formal letter of intent. This was a big deal. A letter of intent is basically a promise to buy. There were a few details we weren't aligned on, so we started the process of ironing them out, but that weekend we had an opportunity to celebrate our relationship and the potential joining of our two companies.

Back in March, Renee had accepted an invitation from us to attend the Kentucky Derby (another of our annual relationship-building activities), which this year was held on Saturday, May 4. It ended up having one of the most controversial finishes in the history of the event. Berkley went to represent the company, and it was a great day to enjoy together with Renee.

The following Friday, May 10, we had a draft of the LOI that all sides, including the legal teams, were happy with. I signed and emailed it with a note: "Renee and Bob—please see the attached executed LOI. We remain very excited and committed. Have a great weekend. Renee—Happy Mother's Day!"

The relationship flourished. At the beginning of April, Providence Equity bought GlobalTranz back from TJC, so they were now involved in the sale. When Renee, Bob, and Lara brought the Providence Equity people to Emerald Isle to meet us, Renee made sure I sat next to the decision maker at Providence, and at dinner she asked questions that would help foster that relationship.

John, Berkley, and Norm dove into providing everything GlobalTranz asked for in the due diligence. They put in long hours. John brought in one person from the finance department who he trusted completely, because he had the heaviest load in the due diligence, but we didn't want to involve anyone else from the company because we knew how easily this kind of news leaks.

The letter of intent from GlobalTranz had a "Closing Date" clause stating that an agreement had to be executed on or before sixty days from our acceptance of the LOI. The sixty days would expire on Tuesday, July 9.

On July 2, Ginger and I were driving up to our mountain house in Linville, North Carolina. My phone buzzed—a call was coming in from Bob Farrell. This was the call I had been waiting for. I knew that this was going to be the call to say, "This is a done deal," because everything had been so positive. The relationship was just amazing.

The road to our subdivision winds up through heavily forested mountain ranges to almost five thousand feet above sea level and calls often drop, so I told Ginger to pull over immediately, at the next safe space. I grabbed the pen and piece of paper I'd been carrying with me everywhere since May, waiting on this phone call, so I could make notes. Ginger used to kid me about it, but now the call had come, and I was glad I had that piece of paper and pen right next to me. As I hit the green "accept" button, I was really excited.

Bob's voice was cold. He wasted no time on pleasantries. He stated that Providence Equity answers to a lot of people, and then he told me they were pulling out. He said things were different from what they expected and would be hard to deal with if we "combined." He gave me five reasons.

My heart sank. I didn't interrupt him because I wanted to make sure I wrapped my head around the true root cause of why they were backing out. Every reason he gave, I wrote down on my piece of paper, along with the date and time of the call. I think that of the five, only one was the real reason, and GlobalTranz had only just realized it in the twelfth hour. Bob sounded like he was embarrassed and hated to be the messenger. When he had finished I told him how disappointing it was, especially since some of our leadership team had worked as much as eighty hours a week conducting the due diligence—time they could have used growing the business. We were working off the word and the handshake of doing the deal.

I ended the call and sat for a moment, taking it in. I had no idea this call was coming. My pride was hurt. I felt like somebody had just called my baby ugly.

Ginger pulled back out onto the road and we continued up to the house.

I took a couple of hours to think about what Bob had said and all that had taken place over the past months, and then I wrote an email to the TI leadership. I told them what Bob had said, thanked them for all their efforts, and said that we had learned a lot from this exercise and if we decided to go to market, there were certain things we were going to do to protect ourselves this time. I also stressed that we needed to concentrate on sales, improving our software, and running the business to finish 2019 the best that we could.

After the July Fourth holiday I met with the leadership team in Emerald Isle. GlobalTranz backing out had really got in my gut.

"Come January of 2020," I told them, "we're going down one of two roads. We're either going to go to market and see if our baby's really that pretty. Or we're going to put this behind us and keep growing the business. We've wasted two months of our life going through all this due diligence with them, and then they back out. At the start of 2020, we come out of the gate running. Either the company sold, or it didn't work out, which meant that it wasn't worth the valuation that we thought, and we're going to continue to grow this business like I know we can.

"And this time," I said, "we're going to hire an investment banker to guide us. We need a quarterback that knows the game and has our best interest."

They were dumbfounded and disappointed. But at the same

time, they were ready to pull up their bootstraps and get beyond this. We started discussing which investment banks to approach.

It was July 5, the date that I got out of bed to answer the door on a Saturday morning and was handed a letter from UPS suing me. The day that Transportation Impact almost died before it ever came to life. Who would ever have thought in that moment that eleven years later we would be talking about something worth hundreds of millions of dollars.

Now that we had resolved to go to market, I went back to the folder where I had put all those emails wanting to buy us. There had been some more recent ones that were solid, that I knew had the money, the reputation, and the people—and that I wouldn't mind being aligned with, which was the most important thing. I decided to see if they were serious.

I narrowed it down to three companies and called them. Two came to visit us in Emerald Isle. One was seriously interested but didn't have the money. "You're very well worth it," they told me. "We had no idea it was that kind of EBITDA, those kinds of margins." It was further confirmation that we were the leader in the industry and in our segment. Nobody was doing revenue like we were. Nobody was approaching fifty million a year.

We also interviewed three or four investment banks. Our top pick was Jeff Burkett with Harris Williams, out of Richmond, Virginia. Jeff was a really well-known investment banker in the logistics space. He was the cream of the crop. Jeff and his team came to our office and wined and dined us. They really wanted us, but they kept telling us our company was worth tens of millions less than we had already been offered. However, they were the best, so I called to award them the business. "We've decided not to take you on," Jeff said to me. Again, my pride was hurt. This best-in-class private equity investment banker had just told us no. Jeff told me he had too much going on and couldn't provide the service that we needed. In reality, he didn't think our company was worth the numbers we had been talking about, I think.

So we interviewed another couple of firms. Because of my relationship with Bob Gipp, my wealth advisor, one of them was Royal Bank of Canada. On the first meeting over the phone, we did not like RBC Capital Markets. They were in last place, but we gave them a second chance. Once they come to the office, we fell in love with the guys assigned to us, Matt and Hank—Matthew Thomson and Henry Johnson—and we hired RBCCM to guide us through the process of going to market and selling Transportation Impact. Now we would find out what it was worth.

While we were interviewing investment banks, we got some incredible news. All three of our companies—Transportation Impact, TI's sister company First Flight Solutions, and eAudit—had made the Inc. 5000. For TI it was the seventh consecutive time, the sixth time for FFS, and eAudit actually debuted on the Inc. 500, placing at 450.

I was stunned. It had to be unheard of for one leadership and workforce to have three companies make the Inc. list. I didn't think anybody had ever done that. Our marketing team contacted the Inc. people a few times to try to find out, but we never got a straight answer. The stats that we did have were stunning enough. Companies that make this list even six times represent less than eight-tenths of one percent of all the companies that ever make the list. First Flight had done that, and TI had done it seven times in a row—ultimately TI made the Inc. nine straight years in a row.

We called the whole company out onto the lawn. I thanked everybody for showing up and told them we had an update on the plans for our new building. I actually did give them an update. Then I told them the real news.

"We have a surprise. The real reason you're out here is to make three announcements. The first one is Transportation Impact made the Inc. fastest-growing companies for the seventh time in a row."

Everybody whooped and applauded. I continued, "It's all because we've surrounded ourselves with people like you. You have to remain laser-focused, attention to detail, doing what you say you're going to do, and everyone here has demonstrated that. You display complete passion in everything that you do, and it's incredible. Everybody in this community—everybody in the *industry* tells us this. They ask me, 'How do you recruit those people you have?' So it's a testament to you."

I told them about First Flight making the list for the sixth time, waited while they applauded, and then announced the biggest news of all.

"I don't even think this has ever been done in the world, since 1979, when the Inc. list began. We have a *third* company making the Inc. fastest-growing companies. It's eAudit!" When everybody quieted down, I told them, "You need to be standing here so proud. And we're not just going to tell you how proud we are of you. We're going to compensate you."

That's one of the proudest things I've ever experienced, to have three companies on the Inc. It was very gratifying. During those days when I was lying depressed on the couch, wondering how we were going to do business when UPS was against us and we were banned from working in North and South Carolina, I would say, "How are we ever going to make the Inc.?" And Travis would reply, "Forget the Inc. I just want a bologna sandwich."

In his congratulatory letter, Inc. editor-in-chief James Ledbetter wrote, "What the companies on this list have in common is persistence and seizing opportunities." I would add: *Always listen to the customer. Have the vision to stay three steps ahead of your competitors. Surround yourself with good people. Have a goal. Plan the work and work the plan to get to that goal.* It takes very disciplined traits to make that list.

Not long after that crowning achievement, on September 13,

we signed an engagement agreement with RBCCM, and Hank and Matt started building our go-to-market playbook.

Coming so close to selling the company had made me realize that Travis and I needed to remove ourselves from a leadership role, at least on paper, so that when somebody bought us we were not tied to them. We had been going that direction anyway—this year I was traveling a lot personally, mainly to Florida and our mountain house—but this was the catalyst to actually do it. After getting that payday, Travis and I didn't want to have to be in the day to day of running the company.

On October 1 we made the official announcement: Berkley was now president (later changed to CEO), John was EVP of operations (later, COO), and Norm was EVP of IT (later, CTO). My son Brian was promoted from director to VP of operations. Travis and I remained in an advisory role on the board of directors. We soon changed the top leadership's titles to C-suite because we wanted potential buyers to have a perception of professionalism in our structure and chain of command.

Releasing the reins was gut-wrenching. I was still chairman of the board and Travis was vice chair, but it was no longer our company as far as the day-to-day decision making. But I also felt relief. It was my decision, and I knew it was the right way to go for the future of the company and for my future.

A few weeks later, Matt and Hank told us they were ready to go to market. Now we were really going to find out how pretty our baby was. And it was more than likely going to be public. All our clients would know. All our competitors would know. Everyone in the industry would know. And most difficult of all, every employee of Transportation Impact would know. I was dreading that.

On Wednesday, November 6, 2019, Ginger and I were at Doreen's on Marco Island. Doreen's is famous in southwest Florida for its breakfast. We had just ordered Doreen's famous key lime pancakes when my phone buzzed with an incoming call. It was Bob

Farrell, who was now CEO again of GlobalTranz. *Well, this is odd*, I thought. I was intrigued that he would be calling me, considering how our relationship left off on July 2. I went out into the parking lot to take the call.

Again, he didn't waste time on pleasantries, except to say how sorry he was about how the last call ended.

"I've got a private equity group that is really interested in you. They have asked me to broker a meeting."

I listened.

"When I talked to you last time, Keith, we were owned by Providence. As you know, The Jordan Company owned us for eight months and sold us back to Providence for a price that more than recouped their investment, right at the time we started the due diligence on TI. If Jordan had owned us, the sale would have gone down." He went on to say that Jordan was a big investor in our space, they paid for value, they let operators operate. It was clear he was trying to build me up on how good The Jordan Company was and how smart they were.

"Jordan is interested in you, and they're very serious."

"If they're serious," I said, "y'all need to get on a plane ASAP."

"Let me get with the team and we'll fly down there immediately."

When I got off the phone, I was elated, back on cloud nine. I knew that he wouldn't have had the balls to call me unless this was a serious, serious deal. From his tone, I could tell Bob had been put up to make the call and that they really wanted us. Before I even went back into breakfast I googled The Jordan Company, and then I called the leadership team. They were as excited as I was. We set up a call for three p.m. the next day to discuss next steps and strategy before TJC and Bob flew to Emerald Isle. Thursday morning I followed up with an email listing all the points Bob had made and some questions for our own strategy. We had to work on our narrative because we were going to be really close to making our revenue number for the year. We had lost a couple of months of leadership focus doing the due diligence for GlobalTranz.

On the call with Bob I had managed my information skillfully (another Keithism) and did not tell him that we had engaged with RBCCM. So one of the questions for our team was: Do we tell TJC and Bob before the meeting, or wait until after we've heard what they have to say? We decided on the latter and set up another call to include Matt and Hank so we could get their guidance.

Bob got back to me so quickly with a date for their visit that I had to leave Florida early to return to Emerald Isle for the meeting. He flew down along with two partners at The Jordan Company, Brian Higgins and Peter Suffredini. Brian was a senior partner, and his arena was transportation and logistics. Peter was Brian's right-hand man. I didn't want any of the front office staff to get suspicious, especially my executive assistant, Paula, so I told them that the important visitors were a potential customer. We all hit it off really well, and the meeting was very positive. At the end, Bob turned and looked at me directly.

"Keith, what's your number?"

This was the question I had been waiting for.

"It's ten million higher than when you backed out. Because of what you did, we've hired an investment banker, so now we've got costs. And, by the way, they're getting ready to hit the button to go to market."

When I said that to Bob, I was staying true to a Keithism. "Those who ask for more, get more" was known company-wide, and I like to think that even former employees are still using it to encourage themselves to be bold. It applies to everything, large and small. Ask, or you'll never get it.

I had shared with the team that I was going to throw out the higher number, because I thought Jordan would beat us down. I also told them that we needed to expect an 80/20 type play, where TJC would only want to buy eighty percent.

Less than a month after that meeting, on December 9, The Jordan Company sent us a formal indication of interest. The stated purchase price was exactly what I had asked for, and it was for one hundred percent of the company, with the exception of founder rollover.

It was a huge relief that we didn't have to go to market and announce publicly that we were selling the company, but it also meant that I had done a major part of RBCCM's work for them by bringing the buyer to the table. And on top of that, I had got a price twenty million dollars higher than they had planned to ask for. I negotiated with them that whatever we got over their planned asking price, we would get a discount on their fee. They agreed to split the difference.

Even though I had already established the number, the RBC investment bankers tweaked our expense figures by putting in add-backs to remove expenses that would not be incurred if TJC bought the company, and thereby raise the EBITDA. It's common for investment bankers to do that, and although the add-backs were legitimate, I regret allowing them to do it, because it came back and bit us in the ass post-transaction. Because of this, the revenue and EBITDA plans we agreed to with TJC for 2021 were hard to reach. It was exactly the same problem we had as a sales team at UPS after a really good year.

Once we had the agreement with TJC, we dove into due diligence again. Along with the IOI, TJC sent us a timeline that began immediately and listed eight firms in addition to TJC that we would be dealing with, each responsible for a different area: legal, accounting & tax, environmental, HR, IT, ESG, background checks, financing, and the business itself. They wanted to pick apart everything. That's when we knew that this was going to go. The Jordan Company wouldn't be spending all this money on diligence if they weren't absolutely certain they wanted us.

To kick it off, they wanted to have a couple of in-person meetings, one with our whole leadership team, the other just with Norm on the IT side. Where to hold these meetings was an issue. In the end we arranged with Lee Hodge to hold them at Ward & Smith's New Bern office. For further disguise, we came up with a code name for everything related to the sale: We called it the Outer Banks Project.

They also wanted to get first-hand testimonials from previous and active customers of ours. This was standard practice, but again we had to find a way to conceal the purpose of the interviews. I took care of this myself by reaching out to every customer on the list and telling them they were going to be contacted for a survey. "We're trying to make our company better, and we want you to be honest. We've hired a third party. Whatever questions they ask, no matter how confidential, tell them the good, bad, and certainly the ugly." When the consultant told us that what they learned was all good, I wasn't surprised. We had great relationships with our customers.

For the diligence, we had thought—and hoped—that we would be able to use a lot of what we'd done for GlobalTranz, but whereas GlobalTranz were really doing their due diligence themselves, The Jordan Company was way ahead of them. They hired professionals in each field, and it was a lot more cumbersome and detailed. But we knew it was going to be worth it.

Right after New Year's 2020, The Jordan Company invited our whole leadership to a meeting at their offices in New York City. Travis was comfortable staying in the background, so on January 6, Berkley, John, Norm, and I flew into JFK airport. From there we took a taxi to our hotel, the Omni Berkshire Place. Berkley and I are cut from the same cloth. We never want to be late and we always want to be prepared, so we had chosen a hotel less than five minutes' walk from TJC's offices. After dropping our bags, we walked down the street, around the corner, and a short block and half up Park Ave, then entered the skyscraper at 399 Park Avenue and took the elevator to the thirtieth floor. We were dressed to the nines in Hideoki Bespoke.

The view of Manhattan from the TJC lobby was panoramic, all the way west to the Hudson River and beyond into New Jersey. The lobby was classy, the decor discreet and professional, but we didn't have long to admire it because the receptionist soon led us to a huge conference room and invited us to take a seat.

The first to enter was Peter Suffredini. We rose to greet him, and he said Brian Higgins and the rest of the team would arrive soon. For the next three hours we dove deep into the new services that we had in the hopper, the four or five initiatives we were working on, our three- and five-year plans. The Jordan people sent a clear message that they believed we needed to expedite our technology initiatives, and they were going to be able to help us with that. For TJC, it was paramount from the outset for us to have a SaaS offering.

Before we left, several high-ranking partners came into the conference room to meet with us. It was all very cordial. Berkley, Norm, John, and I kept glancing at each other, smiling without smiling as we politely shook hands and chatted. We knew that Brian wanted everybody to put their eyes on us, because this was a done deal. Under our breath we were saying to each other, "Hell, yeah! This shit is done, dude." We could hardly wait to get out of there.

We controlled ourselves until we got out of sight, and then went nuts. We were shaking and almost crying, we were so excited. We felt so good about what we had just done. We walked straight into the nearest bar and ordered drinks. As we stood there holding our crystal tumblers of liquor, I thought, *Here we are, a bunch of rednecks from North Carolina on Park Avenue, getting ready to sell a company for hundreds of millions of dollars.*

Peter had invited us to join him and Brian for dinner at their favorite restaurant, Bobby Van's, so we finished our drinks and strolled the half-mile to the restaurant, still celebrating our success. That dinner with Brian and Peter was the perfect close to a perfect day.

Nine days later we received a draft purchase agreement, followed on January 28 by an equity commitment letter—essentially a promise that TJC would have the funds to pay us. Now all that remained was to fulfill the last conditions to closing.

The original due diligence timeline TJC sent us projected that it would all be done by the end of January, but as we entered the second week of February, there was still a lot to do. Norm, Berkley, and John had been working their ass off for two months, so I arranged with Travis to give them a bonus to incentivize them and keep them going down the home stretch. I told them that if we closed on time in mid-March and got the full asking price, they would get the bonus. The two things that were important to me were the price tag and the timeline, so it was vital that they not lose focus and attention to detail, because they were working fifteen hours a day. That news gave them the extra boost to keep their head up and keep going. The whole process was excruciating and seemingly endless. But the end was in sight.

Conditions in the outside world, though, were deteriorating. In early March, the World Health Organization declared Covid-19 a pandemic, and two days later President Trump declared a national emergency. Every day, both in the U.S. and globally new restrictions were being placed on travel and even on the movement of people in their daily lives. On March 16, the Dow Jones fell nearly three thousand points, the largest single-day drop in U.S. stock market history. Suddenly, we didn't know if the deal was going to close. I was anxious and nervous. For two days and nights our attorney Lee Hodge and I called back and forth, until finally I told him, "Let's not talk any more until the money's in the bank. Let me know."

On Thursday, March 19, at 1 p.m. precisely, Ginger and I were sitting in our den in Emerald Isle when my phone buzzed with a text message. I looked down. It was from Lee.

I showed Ginger. We cried. We laughed. I quickly called the rest of the leadership team: "We've done it." We all congratulated each other, and I thanked them for putting in those long hours. Then Ginger said, "Let's pray about this right now." She's a very religious

woman, very humble and blessed, and she led us in a prayer.

"Thank you for these blessings and making hard work come to fruition. Please, just guide us in a way to where we help other people with these blessings."

We stayed on our knees for at least three minutes. Then as we tried to take it in, we reminisced about the last twelve years. An hour or so later, I texted Lee back: "Call me back whenever." It took me that long to come to terms with what had just happened.

It's extremely gratifying to know that there was an idea at one time that germinated on thirty-three whiteboards in a beach house, took root in the back of a surf shop, and then grew and flourished in little Emerald Isle, until the idea was recognized as being so valuable that very smart people on Park Avenue in New York were willing—and wanted—to pay a huge sum of money for it. When our transaction closed, with a full equity guarantee from TJC, it was the start of Covid—the week of madness, when the market dropped and global uncertainty shot up. Not many bankers were committing to M&A transactions. RBC told us later that we negotiated a tight contract, and it was a fantastic transaction where all went smoothly. TJC delivered on everything they had promised. It was mind boggling, because instantly, in the moment of receiving that text from Lee Hodge, the lives of ten families were changed forever. It's a hell of a feeling to know that you have just secured wealth for generations to come.

That being said, it ain't all about the money. The money is very nice and it's a lot to do about that, but it's also about the gratification of hard work, paying attention to the details, doing what you say you're going to do, surrounding yourself with good people, working hard and playing hard, planning the work and working the plan, long days, long nights—it's about the gratification of how it all came together with those ingredients. Here in the middle of a pandemic, a financial crisis of the United States, of the world, we were able to sell the company we had created and secure generational wealth for multiple families.

*Travis and I dressed to the nines in Hideoki Bespoke from the waist up—and from the waist down in our usual casual office attire of beach shorts. This photo was taken in the broom closet of South Swell Surf shop, which served as Transportation Impact's first office. The photo ran with a profile of us by Business North Carolina magazine.*

✳

# EPILOGUE

**B**erkley and I faced the video camera on the wall in the conference room. Seated to either side of us around the conference table were the full leadership—the old and the new: Travis; John; Norm; our new CFO David Heath, hired a month earlier with TJC's blessing after working with us on the due diligence; my son Brian; and Jamie Vogel, VP of sales and marketing. On the large screen in front of us we saw the faces of people we had come to know well, people we had worked alongside for years, as well as those who were newer, the ones we didn't yet have relationships with, and who I likely never would get to know.

Berkley had sent out an email the day before inviting the whole company, contractors included, to a mandatory Town Hall meeting, because we had some exciting news to announce. The amazing thing was that during all the developments of the past year, not a single rumor had started. We had done an excellent job of managing that whole process. In planning this moment, we had listed the points we needed to make. We decided to just tell the truth. We knew the best way was to be open and honest, and also upbeat.

Berkley stood up and announced that Transportation Impact was no longer owned by Keith Byrd and Travis Burt.

You could have heard a pin drop. Everybody's shock came through the virtual space.

As I listened to Berkley, one side of me was happy, because I knew that TJC had a lot of money and they were basically going

to hand over the checkbook. The business would grow through acquisitions, and we were going to be able to do a lot of things we
had been wanting to do for a long time. But the other part of me
was thinking, *Hey, that's my baby. I don't own it anymore.* This was the
handoff. Now it was real. A confusion of emotions swirled in me.
Mostly, though, I was happy for the opportunities that this change
would bring for our company and our people.

After Berkley had made the main announcement, I reassured
everyone that I still had a stake in the company, that we had a good
leadership team, and that nothing was going to change. I told them
that The Jordan Company "let operators operate," which is what
Bob Farrell had told me. It was very important to me that our people
should feel comfortable and secure. I wanted them to know nothing
was going to happen to them. They weren't going to move anywhere. Our name wasn't going to change. Our culture wasn't going
to change. An important element of our agreement with TJC was
that our leadership team would stay in place and I would join the
board of directors in an advisory role. Travis was happy to retire.

Less than two years earlier I had stood in front of our assembled people at our ten-year anniversary and told them, "We've been
offered to be bought out many times. But we've always said no, because we want to carry on the legacy of the family for our kids.
That's very important to us." That was a true statement. Those
were my feelings. It makes me look like a hypocrite saying that and
then doing the opposite. But things change. You can't turn away a
number like we got. That's why I made three things clear to The
Jordan Company: 1) Our name wouldn't change. 2) We would not
leave Emerald Isle. 3) Our culture wouldn't change. They promised
me all three. Now, I'm not naive. I know they're a private equity.
But those three things were very important to me, and it was equally
important that my children were fully on board with the decision.
I'm always open and honest with my two boys, and right from the
beginning there was full disclosure. I let them know everything that

was going on, minute by minute, day by day, and their response never differed: "Dad, you're crazy if you don't accept this." Travis's daughter and son were the same.

In the hours after the announcement, several employees emailed or texted me congratulations. Then when the press release hit the news wire the next day, a lot of competitors and people in the industry reached out to say congratulations and job well done, especially in this environment. We started Transportation Impact in June of 2008 when everything crashed. My wife at the time was a Realtor and her business had plummeted. And there I was quitting a job that paid me a hundred thousand a year to start a company. Then, again in the middle of a global crisis, we sold the company. We started at the worst time, and we sold at the worst time—and we did both with great success. Several people put those things together.

For a while my phone and my email were just as overloaded as ever, and then the flood slowed, and then it stopped. Suddenly, I had nothing really important to do. No one was asking my advice. There wasn't a line of people outside my office wanting to talk to me. From fifty emails a day, I was getting almost none. From the high of getting Lee's text and the joy of securing generational wealth and knowing I could do anything I wanted for the rest of my life, suddenly I was empty. About a month after the sale, Ginger and I were sitting on the beach, and I felt like I wasn't needed any more. I didn't know if I had a purpose. Even though I was on the board, I could see things were moving on without me and doing just fine.

Almost daily I was getting overnight letters from people wanting to manage my wealth. Once you sell a company, that's what happens. It's like ambulance-chasing lawyers. One morning, the delivery person handed me a package from yet another financial advisor. But this one was different. He had sent me two books. One was called *Crazy Time: Surviving the First 12 Months after Selling Your Company without Losing Your Fortune or Your Mind*. And the other one was called *The Psychology of Staying Rich: How to Preserve Wealth*, both by J. Ted Oakley. In that first one, *Crazy Time*, he basically says, "You're free. You've sold your business. Everything's been lifted off your shoulders, no more calendar overbooking, no more stressful nights. But with that freedom comes a new uncertainty and anxiety." That was exactly what I was experiencing.

For about six months I went through a state of depression. I think everybody who sells their company goes through that. I kept thinking, *Is this it? Is this really what I want? Yeah, I've got a lot of money, but I don't have anything to do. Nobody counts on me anymore. Nobody's calling me for advice. Nobody's wanting me to help them make decisions.* I was used to being in the office with people wanting to see me all the time, and now I didn't have that.

"It's just the way of the business. It's just the way things evolve; you've got to let it go," Ginger would tell me. "You should feel proud that nobody's reaching out to you." And she was right. I had done such a great job of surrounding myself with good people who were competent. But at the same time, I was hurt they were no longer reaching out to me. Before, wherever I was at, I was talking with Berkley and John, all the time, at least four or five days a week. And now that had stopped. That was probably the biggest hurt, no longer having that interaction with them. It wasn't their fault. They were running the business. But feelings don't follow logic.

During this difficult period of transition and life change, Ginger was my rock and my consolation. She is my true partner. We think the same thing and feed off each other. We love doing stuff together. Ginger says that when she retired from hairdressing her job was to be the wind beneath my wings, and she is. She is my best friend, my biggest fan, my everything. Since Ginger has been in my life, I'm a much better person.

The book the financial advisor sent me recommended not doing anything for a year after the sale, because you're going to have multiple people approaching you asking you to help them with their great idea for a new business, and you need time to clear your head and see your new direction. So I followed that advice, and it was the best thing I could have done. That was a tough year, and it was hard on Ginger, too.

As we adjusted to our new life post-TI, she and I prayed and talked about what was next. At the forefront for both of us was to share our blessing with others, so one of the first things we did was to create the Byrd Family Foundation. We immediately had an opportunity to provide critical support to a cause near and dear to our hearts, the Carolina Museum of the Marine & Al Gray Civic Institute. Located in Jacksonville, North Carolina, the museum and institute honor the legacy of Carolina Marines and Sailors and work to sustain the founding ideals of our nation, but they were facing a funding shortfall of twenty-eight million dollars because the state government was taking years to approve its budget. Ginger and I were proud and happy to be able to step in with a substantial donation to pay salaries and keep the lights on so the museum and institute efforts could continue while waiting for the government to get its act together. They later invited me to join the board, and I accepted. We also support the Macro Patriots, a nonprofit group of heroes who travel anywhere in the Gulf and Southeast Coastlines after hurricanes, wildfires, and tornadoes to provide community service, communications and logistics assistance, rescue, and/or relief services.

By the end of that first year post-sale, a plan had evolved. The landscaping company I'd long used was owned by a dear friend of twenty years or more, Jimmy Farrington, who is a smart businessman. He and I have similar visions. We like to do things right and get creative. We saw an opportunity to get a good deal on two properties about six miles outside Emerald Isle, so we entered into a partnership we called Dirt2Dreams LLC, with me as majority partner, and bought both.

Our vision for the land is taking form in three separate projects that will create a new community.

The first is an eighty-two-acre housing development on the White Oak River that we're calling Hamptons on the White Oak. The site lies near Hampton Bay, so we chose the name to play on the Hamptons in New York. All the streets will be named for the individual Hamptons on Long Island. The development will have a hundred and fifty door fronts, between homes, townhomes, and cottages, with square footage ranging from eight hundred to twenty-eight hundred. Through market research we found out people don't care about having a big house anymore. They want something nice and they want something with a lot of amenities. Taking this as our business model, our development will be a kind of golf cart community offering close to twenty amenities, including a marina. We want everybody to be able to enjoy this unique and special environment, not just the rich guy who owns a lot on the water, so our development will keep the riverfront open for amenities.

Putting in a marina is a big deal, because you're disturbing the water and the cove. I wanted to make sure we did our due diligence, so at considerable expense we hired a consultant to do all the studies. It took months for them to put gadgets in the water to study flows and make sure that we weren't going to do anything harmful to the environment. Now in early 2023 we're getting ready to pitch it to the decision makers, the Corps of Engineers, and we feel good about it, because we've gone about it the right way.

About a mile from our Hamptons, we have planned a hundred-and-sixty-five-acre, five-star RV resort with hundreds of slips. We intend to make it so nice that people don't want to leave and go to Emerald Isle and the beach, but if they do, we'll shuttle them back and forth. Guests will be able to pull up the RV, plug in, and use all the nice amenities. Again, our market research showed us that since Covid-19, having less stuff and spending more time outside is a big thing for the future. The property was a farm owned by a family named Weeks, whose son became the most decorated North Carolinian in World War One. He died when he was nineteen years old in Bellicourt, France, and he's buried on the farm, along with ninety-one other people. In honor of him, we've named our resort Bellicourt, and the family will always have access to the land.

Across the street from Bellicourt, we have sixty-seven acres that we'll use for commercial development.

Together, the three projects will create a community and resort centered around the environment of the White Oak River, which forms the western border of the Croatan National Forest and is an ecological and recreational jewel in our region. The whole basin is full of wildlife, and the river flows through different types of habitats, from hardwood forests to salt marsh flats.

Paula Sutton, the former client who I hired as our first executive assistant in the early days of Transportation Impact, runs Dirt2Dreams behind the scenes. Paula quickly became and remains indispensable to me, as both my business and personal right hand. Our bond and loyalty are unmatched. Sonny Mason capably manages Dirt2Dreams, and Brian Dobler is still my marketing and website guy. Along with creating the Dirt2Dreams website, he did the research to discover the story behind Bellicourt. He was a huge part of our success at TI, and we've had a special friendship for years, spiritually and otherwise. When I need someone to talk to, Brian is my go-to person.

As my life is moving in a different direction, so is the company I created. In July 2021, Berkley oversaw a rebrand of Transportation Impact to TransImpact, with a new logo and a change from TI green to orange. Out of respect, the leadership team called Travis and me in and pitched it to us. The purpose was to differentiate from a competitor with a similar name, and supposedly a rebrand was needed. I think it was the idea of a few people in marketing, and they persuaded the leadership team. I was candid in the meeting. I said I didn't like the colors or the logo, and I wasn't keen on the name change. These days, when I drive by our beautiful building in Emerald Isle, it looks wrong. It's probably just me, because it's so close to me. The average person on the street probably doesn't notice anything strange.

The funny irony, though, is that I am now a sales contractor for TransImpact. I managed to stay away for over two years, but then I couldn't stand it any longer. I missed it! In fact, doing sales for that company is so much a part of me that I named the LLC for my sub-contractor commissions TI Til I Die.

Three years post-sale, Ginger and I are loving our life. We mostly split our time between our place in Marco Island, Florida, and our house in the Blue Ridge Mountains in Linville, North Carolina. In January 2022 we sold our house in Emerald Isle, but we're going to build a house in our Hamptons development. Marco Island is a magical place, where our regular routine includes playing golf at our country club and spending time with some of the best people we've ever met. We often invite some of the close friends we've made here to join us when we get out on the water in our new Tiara. As a personal joke between Ginger and me, we named the Tiara *Cha-Ching*. From early on in our relationship, whenever we saw a FedEx or UPS truck, we'd always say at the same time, "Cha-ching!" All our friends say it now, too! We've also found a wonderful church in Marco Island. In the summers we go up to our mountain house, where we play a lot of golf and enjoy visiting the wineries on the weekends. Our very-loved Frenchie dog Minnie Pearl also requires time and energy, and we spend a lot of time with her.

With the blessings we've been given, we love treating the people we love and care about. We get together when we can with my longtime friends Dennis Rebert, Todd Armstrong, Billy Corn, Kent Cecil, and Lenny Butta, and after more than thirty years since our paths first crossed at UPS, Neal Newhouse is still my closest and best friend.

Family is at the core of our lives, and I've tried to be good to everyone. I've enjoyed being generous to my family and friends. My godson, Lorenzo Carvelli, and goddaughters, Malea and Syan

Hochstein, are important to me. When Ginger moved to Emerald Isle, she made a commitment that she wouldn't go more than about six weeks without visiting her father and our daughter, Kamerin, her only child, who still live in Asheboro, North Carolina. Kamerin and Kadie, my son Brian's wife, are the two daughters I never had, and I love them very much. And of course we adore being with our granddaughters, Arabella and Juliet. How we love those two girls!! Mamaw Wiley lives on in her namesake, Juliet Lucille.

Ginger is my best friend, and we enjoy every minute of our time together. We know every day is a gift, and we treasure it. We've both come a long way.

I started in a little house across the road from a pool hall, where I hustled enough money to buy my first car. Now, I can have the house of my dreams and the car of my dreams. The values I absorbed from my parents and grandparents, the discipline and leadership I gained from the Marines, the encouragement I got from people around me, my determination, my vision, and a whole lot of hard work—those are the paving stones of my journey, and of the journey of Transportation Impact. Looking back, I am proudest to see that I created a company that pioneered an industry, and that continues to grow and provide employment for hundreds of people—without me at its helm.

*

# ADVICE FOR LEADERS AND ENTREPRENEURS

### Execute and Build Relationships

Everyone has an idea. Execution is what separates successful businesses from the ones that fail. Startups require a concerted effort to move the ball down the field every single day. You can't sit back and think, *If I only had this much money, I could do this*, or *If I only had access to this information, I could do that.* You have to get up every day and break down barriers to entry, no matter the market. You also have to understand that business is about relationships, and you must work hard to cultivate, nurture, and maintain all kinds of different relationships, both personal and professional. It's a constant balance between being focused on making your business the best it can be and putting people around you who will help spread the message. Be a risk taker, but always expect the unexpected. Always listen to the customer and employees.

### Surround Yourself with Good People

I believe a great leader is someone who can surround him- or herself with great people. That's what Travis and I maybe take the most pride in at Transportation Impact. We are very fortunate to have assembled a team that is second to none, and most of them we found right here in our backyard. Qualified people are out there; you just need to make the effort to find them.

## Don't Be Afraid to Invest in Your Company

I was never afraid to make an investment in my own company. It was very hard to pull that trigger in the early days when we weren't making a lot of money. When you're a consulting company, your investments are your people. I knew that in order for us to grow, we had to have resources, we had to have headcount. We had to put the people in place, before we could have the revenue. You have to be able to have that vision, that trust in the team and yourself, and find a way to make it happen, because you're spending those dollars before you're able to generate the revenue. That takes a lot of courage. Don't be afraid to spend the money. It requires risk.

## Lead by Example

Always know you have to earn respect. I try to lead by example. I think if you had asked most of the people on our team, they would have told you that there was nothing I would ask them to do that I hadn't done myself. Setting clear expectations up front is also really important. There are definitely people with whom my leadership style doesn't fit, but the majority of people who stick around a while develop a respect and appreciation for knowing where I stand at all times. I think it's important to challenge people to help them get things out of themselves that maybe they didn't know they could. I take a lot of pride in the growth of some of the folks who have worked at TI over the years. Decisiveness, initiative, and loyalty are important leadership traits.

## Utilize Your Team

No one person is bigger than the company. Not even the CEO or the founder. No matter what the team decides, if it's the team's decision, then that's what the company does. That's extremely rare. Most entrepreneurs, if there are three or four people who disagree and a couple who agree, and the entrepreneur or the leader wants to do it the way they want to do it, they're going to do it that way. I always allowed my leadership team the freedom to make a decision that I didn't necessarily agree with. That's a big part of our success. Whenever there was a big decision to make, we'd call or text each other: "Let's be in this office in five minutes. We've got to discuss." We would sit there and pick through everything before we made the decision on what to do. There's no one person bigger than the company. We always said that in front of each other. That keeps everybody grounded.

## Compensate for Your Shortcomings

I am very particular about a lot of things. I like to know what's going on, even at the more granular levels of the business. I think I've gotten better at it over time, but a lot of employees would joke about receiving "Status?" emails from me. Sometimes maybe I get too caught up in the details, but it's just part of who I am. I know that success is a commitment, and I'm only trying to make sure I apply my experience to ensure that subtle but important things aren't missed. The lack of patience is one of my weaknesses. I know that, and I have worked hard over the years to train myself to allow people more leeway.

## Lean on Your Biggest Strengths

I always sought out people who had complementary strengths to mine, so we balanced each other. Perhaps my most important strength is that I care deeply about people. I want our people to feel valued, and I want our customers to know they're appreciated. I have close personal relationships with a lot of employees and customers. I love to have a good time and think it's important to let those around me see that side of me. I'm always willing to help those in need; it gives me a lot of pleasure to be able to put a smile on someone's face or help them out when they're going through a tough situation. It takes a village, as they say. I didn't get here alone, and I never want a friend to feel alone when there's something I could do to help. Also, I can sell the hell out of just about anything!

# ABOUT THE AUTHOR

K eith Byrd began developing his entrepreneurial skills and learning to trust his vision in grade school. Through a term of service as a United States Marine and a stint in the North Carolina State Highway Patrol, he gained early leadership training and experience. Byrd began his 20-year career in the parcel industry with UPS, where he earned numerous accolades and advanced to senior sales manager for North and South Carolina. While with the world's largest parcel carrier, he envisioned starting a company that would leverage his industry experience to help companies reduce their shipping costs. In 2008 he and Travis Burt, a close friend and member of Byrd's sales team, left UPS to found Transportation Impact. Over the next eleven years Byrd's leadership was instrumental in guiding the company from $0 to over $50 MM in annual revenue. In early 2020, Byrd and Burt sold Transportation Impact (now TransImpact) to a private equity firm. A profound understanding of the strength of relationships, the need to lead by example, and the power of vision forms the foundation of Byrd's life and business success. He now directs his entrepreneurial skill toward real estate development. Byrd and his wife, Ginger, enjoy life together in Marco Island, Florida.